Re-constructing the Post-Soviet Industrial Region

The opening of the economies of the communist world to market forces, beginning in the late 1980s, ushered in new opportunities for some through rapid privatisation and flows of foreign investment. However, elsewhere, especially in the former Soviet Union, regions that had once been at the forefront of forced Soviet industrialisation became increasingly marginal to the new economy.

This book examines the complex economic, political, social and cultural transformations of the Soviet Union's 'rustbelt' industrial regions, focusing in particular on the restructuring of the Donbas in eastern Ukraine, once an archetypal Soviet industrial area. It shows how the region's unique history posed not only enormous political and economic challenges, but also provided the resources needed for it to adapt to changing circumstances at different geographical scales. In particular, it appraises the process of restructuring in the coal industry, historically a vital industry for the regional economy. Overall, this book provides detailed analysis of restructuring in a region that continues to shape post-Soviet transition in Ukraine and elsewhere in the former communist world.

Adam Swain is Lecturer in Human Geography at the University of Nottingham, UK. He has been researching regional development, industrial restructuring and labour relations in Hungary, East Germany and Ukraine since the early 1990s. He is co-editor of a special issue of *Regional Studies* (1998) about globalisation and eastern and central Europe and co-editor of *Work, Employment and Transition: Restructuring livelihoods in 'post-communist' Eastern Europe.*

BASEES/Routledge Series on Russian and East European Studies

Series editor:
Richard Sakwa, Department of Politics and International Relations,
    University of Kent

Editorial Committee:
Julian Cooper, Centre for Russian and East European Studies, University of
    Birmingham
Terry Cox, Department of Central and East European Studies, University
    of Glasgow
Rosalind Marsh, Department of European Studies and Modern Languages,
    University of Bath
David Moon, Department of History, University of Durham
Hilary Pilkington, Department of Sociology, University of Warwick
Stephen White, Department of Politics, University of Glasgow

Founding Editorial Committee Member:
George Blazyca, Centre for Contemporary European Studies, University of
    Paisley

This series is published on behalf of BASEES (the British Association for Slavonic and East European Studies). The series comprises original, high-quality, research-level work by both new and established scholars on all aspects of Russian, Soviet, post-Soviet and East European Studies in humanities and social science subjects.

Re-constructing the Post-Soviet Industrial Region

The Donbas in transition

Edited by Adam Swain

LONDON AND NEW YORK

First published 2007
by Routledge
2 Park Square, Milton Park, Abingdon, Oxon OX14 4RN

Simultaneously published in the USA and Canada
by Routledge
270 Madison Ave, New York, NY 10016

Routledge is an imprint of the Taylor & Francis Group, an informa business

Typeset in Times New Roman
by Keystroke, High Street, Tettenhall, Wolverhampton
Printed and bound in Great Britain
by TJI Digital, Padstow, Cornwall

British Library Cataloguing in Publication Data
A catalogue record for this book is available from the British Library

Library of Congress Cataloging in Publication Data
Re-constructing the Post-Soviet industrial region : the Donbas in
transition / edited by Adam Swain.
p. cm. – (Basees/Routledge series on Russian and East European
studies ; 33)
Includes bibliographical references and index.
1. Donets Basin (Ukraine and Russia)–Economic conditions. 2. Donets
Basin (Ukraine and Russia)–Politics and government. 3. Donets Basin
(Ukraine and Russia)–Social conditions. I. Swain, Adam
HC340.19.Z7D667 2007
338.947'74–dc22
2006031338
1 0050056772 T

ISBN10: 0–415–32228–6 (hbk)
ISBN10: 0–203–32826–4 (ebk)

ISBN13: 978–0–415–32228–7 (hbk)
ISBN13: 978–0–203–32826–2 (ebk)

Contents

Figures

Tables

Notes on contributors

Oleg Bogatov is Vice-President of the 'New Conception' Fund in Kyiv. He is a candidate of economic science (2000), researches on the Ukrainian mining and metallurgical industries and is the author of several monographs including *Donbass-100: Who Is Who in the Region* (1999).

Elena Kovaleva is a Political Scientist at the National Institute of Strategic Studies, Kyiv. She was formerly an Associate Professor at Donetsk State Technical University. She was a Fulbright Scholar at the University of Kansas in 2001.

Alexander Lyakh is Associate Professor in the Department of Economics at Donetsk National University. He is also a Director and Head of the Analytical Department of the Regional Development Agency 'Donbass'. He is co-editor of *The Future of Old Industrial Regions in Europe* published by the Foundation for Economic Education (1998).

Vlad Mykhnenko is Research Fellow at the Centre for Public Policy for Regions, University of Glasgow, UK. Previously he was an International Policy Fellow at the Open Society Institute in Budapest. He is the author of several papers on the characteristics of post-soviet capitalism in Ukraine and Poland.

Olena Popova is Deputy Director of Research Methodology at the Kyiv International Institute of Sociology.

Adam Swain is Lecturer in Human Geography at the University of Nottingham, UK. He has been researching regional development, industrial restructuring and labour relations in Hungary, East Germany and Ukraine since the early 1990s. He is co-editor of a special issue of *Regional Studies* (1998) about globalisation and eastern and central Europe and co-editor of *Work, Employment and Transition: Restructuring Livelihoods in 'Post-Communist' Eastern Europe*.

Kerstin Zimmer is a Research Assistant in the Institut für Vergleichende Politikwissenschaft und Internationale Beziehungen (Institute for Comparative Politics and International Relations) at the Johann Wolfgang Goethe Universität, Frankfurt. She completed her Ph.D. thesis entitled 'Transforming an old industrial region: actors and institutions in Donetsk Oblast' in 2003.

Hans van Zon is Professor of Central and East European Studies at the University of Sunderland, UK. Professor van Zon's major publications include *The Political Economy of Independent Ukraine* and *The Future of Industry in Central and Eastern Europe*. He is also co-author of *Social and Economic Change in Eastern Ukraine: The Example of Zaporizhzhya*.

Acknowledgements

This book arises from a conference entitled 'Confronting Change: North East England and East European Coalfields' organised by Hans van Zon, University of Sunderland, and the Institute of Mining and Metallurgy held in Newcastle-upon-Tyne, UK, in November 2001. The conference was funded by the UK government's Department for International Development (DfID) and the EU's TACIS programme. The Nottingham Institute for Russian and East European Studies (NIREES), University of Nottingham, supported the publication of this collection. I would also like to thank our editor at Routledge, Peter Sowden, for his assistance and undue patience.

Introduction

Re-constructing the post-Soviet industrial region

Adam Swain

Industrial and regional restructuring has been a significant feature in central and eastern Europe since the adoption of market reform policies in the late 1980s and early 1990s. Marketisation signalled a new phase of industrial restructuring and uneven development as regional economies across central and eastern Europe followed divergent development pathways. Where privatisation proceeded rapidly and where flows of foreign direct investment were attracted, regional economies were reoriented to new markets and new economic sectors. Elsewhere, especially in the former Soviet Union, regions that had once been at the forefront of forced Soviet industrialisation became increasingly marginal to the new economy. *Re-constructing the Post-Soviet Industrial Region* brings together a series of essays by leading scholars on an archetypal example of such a region, the Donbas in eastern Ukraine. The contributions highlight the complex economic, political, social and cultural transformations that have taken place in what was once a model Soviet region. In particular they show the ways that the region's unique history not only posed enormous challenges but also provided the resources needed for the region to adapt to changing circumstances at different geographical scales.

Most of the essays in this collection have their origins in a conference entitled 'Confronting Change: North East England and East European Coal Fields' organised by the University of Sunderland and the Institute of Mining and Metallurgy in Newcastle-upon-Tyne, UK, in November 2001. The UK government's Department for International Development (DfID) and the EU's TACIS programme financially supported the conference. The conference brought together an international group of leading researchers as well as practitioners and policy makers dealing with coal industry restructuring and coalfield regeneration policies in Europe. In addition to the papers presented at the conference we have been able to commission two further contributions by leading researchers on the Donbas.[1] It should be noted that I have endeavoured to ensure that each chapter consistently uses either Ukrainian or Russian transliteration rules. The only exception is that as it features in the subtitle of the collection we have used the Ukrainian spelling of Donbas throughout.

The collection is divided into two parts and this introduction is designed to outline the core themes running through the book (Chapter 1 provides a more substantive introduction to the collection). The chapters in Part I examine the restructuring of the regional economy of the Donbas since 1991. Chapter 1, by Adam Swain and Vlad Mykhnenko, provides an introduction to the experiences of and theoretical perspectives on industrial and regional restructuring in archetypal Soviet industrial regions. The chapter then uses official statistics to map uneven development in Ukraine and the Donbas in order to highlight the major trends of economic restructuring. The chapter ends with a summary of the way the Donbas in 'transition' has been theorised. Chapter 2 by Hans van Zon provides an analysis of the restructuring of the Ukrainian energy sector and its implications for the Donbas space-economy. He argues that the government's failure to increase financial transparency in the sector and break up monopolies which have emerged since independence means privatisation of energy producers and suppliers might not increase the sector's efficiency but may instead reinforce rent-seeking behaviour. With respect to the coal sector, liberalisation may not significantly reduce output but will result in mass redundancies amongst coal mine workers. Van Zon also points to the way that reform or otherwise of the energy sector is closely connected to the extent to which the Donbas economy is reintegrated with the Russian economy thereby recreating the spatial division of labour that existed in the Soviet Union. Whilst the liberalisation of the energy sector was designed to reduce Ukraine's dependence on energy imports from Russia, the stalling of these reforms after April 2001 raises the prospect of major producers in the Donbas becoming increasingly dependent on Russia not only for energy but also for investment capital and markets.

The contribution by Elena Kovaleva (Chapter 3) explores the evolution of political structures in the Donbas since independence. She argues that independence and economic reform resulted in the emergence of a powerful Donetsk 'clan' comprising individuals spanning the worlds of politics, government, business and official trade unions. Kovaleva suggests that the communist *nomenklatura* retained power after independence by using their privileged political positions to accumulate economic wealth. They established commercial enterprises around state-owned enterprises and imposed themselves, with the connivance of directors of state-owned enterprises and public authorities, as privileged trading partners. As the 1990s proceeded, the violent inter-clan conflict that dominated the mid-1990s was replaced by mutually beneficial co-operation. Gradually the clan captured the media as well as public authorities with the result that they were able to systematically manipulate parliamentary and presidential elections in return for favourable treatment by the central government in Kyiv. Kovaleva concludes that the clan became the strongest opponents to further marketisation.

In Chapter 4 Alexander Lyakh examines the development of the regional economy. In his contribution he uses the available statistical information to chart major changes in the economy. He argues that rather than becoming more diversified the regional economy has become more dependent on energy, metallurgy and other heavy industrial sectors even though investment has fallen dramatically and is confined to particular locations. At the same time, manufacturing of consumer goods has fallen significantly and the impact of new small and medium-sized enterprises remains negligible. He argues that there is little evidence that the privatisation of state-owned enterprises led to significant industrial restructuring.

At the same time the local economic policy produced by the regional authorities either resembled Soviet-style production targets and existed merely on paper or was designed to protect heavy industry through the provision of subsidies and tax exemptions involving for example the establishment of special economic zones.

In the final contribution to Part I, Kerstin Zimmer (Chapter 5) considers the extent to which local cultural resources can be mobilised for the regeneration of the region. She argues that rapid industrialisation of the Donbas especially under Stalin, in which workers were held in high esteem and were well rewarded, and the region's pre-eminent position within the Soviet Union produced a strong regional communist identity based on hard physical labour and the production of 'real' material value. This has bequeathed a distinctive productivist regional identity in which local leaders simultaneously expect external solutions but are suspicious of foreign investors and foreign assistance. She argues that this amounts to 'cognitive lock-in' and is a barrier to future regional development.

Part II focuses on the restructuring of the coal mining industry in the Donbas. Production at the 193 coal mines in the Donbas declined by over 50 per cent between 1990 and 1996 whilst employment fell by over a quarter. Since 1996 the government, supported by multi-lateral institutions such as the World Bank, has sought to implement far-reaching mine closures and commercialisation involving hundreds of thousands of redundancies. However, the largely inefficient and unsafe industry shows that vested local interests may simultaneously frustrate state-sponsored market-orientated reorganisation and engage in self-reorganisation based primarily on 'asset sweating'. Chapter 6 by Oleg Bogatov explores the reorganisation of the coal industry and its relationship to its customers: energy producers and metal-lurgical plants. Developing arguments introduced in Lyakh's contribution, Bogatov suggests that the ownership of the metallurgical sector and increasingly the electricity generating sector has become so concentrated in the hands of what he calls the Donetsk-based Financial Industrial Group (FIG) that the nominally state-owned coal industry is de facto controlled by the FIG. Bogatov argues that the Donetsk FIG is a cohesive group of commercial companies linked to one another through cross-shareholdings and, under the leadership of the Industrial Union of Donbass, has blocked the restructuring of the sectors under its control.

The contribution of Olena Popova (Chapter 7) examines the social effects of the closure of coal mines. She reports quantitative and qualitative research that has been undertaken to monitor the social impacts of the mine closure programme that was introduced in 1996 and supported by two World Bank loans. Coal mines were responsible not only for coal production and related activities but also for the physical and social infrastructure of mining communities. As a result the social and economic life of entire towns has been adversely affected by the closure of coal mines. In Chapter 8 Adam Swain examines the way the mine closure programme involved the transfer of foreign 'models' of industrial restructuring and regional development. He shows how the World Bank encouraged Ukraine to imitate the way that the UK government closed mines and sought to mitigate the social impacts of redundancies in the late 1980s and early 1990s. This involved a series of technical assistance projects funded by the UK government's Department for International

Development (DfID) and the EU TACIS programme that employed British consultants who had been involved in the rationalisation and privatisation of the British coal industry. He concludes that these projects sought to reorganise the armature of the Ukrainian state and to forge a channel of policy transfer from West to East.

The contributions in *Re-constructing the Post-Soviet Industrial Region* seek to shed light on to the post-Soviet restructuring in one of the most important industrial regions in the former USSR. As the events that surrounded the disputed 2004 presidential election and the so-called 'Orange Revolution' showed, the Donbas remains a very important factor in the evolution of the Ukrainian political scene. The Donbas's economic power ensures that whichever political parties secure a political base in the region will be able to play a major role at the national scale. Moreover, the government's treatment of the Donbas and the energy sector will help to shape Ukraine's geo-political position in the future.

Note

1   The chapter by Adam Swain and Vlad Mykhnenko and the contribution by Kerstin Zimmer were not presented at the conference and were independently commissioned. We are grateful to Vlad and Kerstin for agreeing to contribute to the volume.

Part I

The Donbas regional economy in transition

1 The Ukrainian Donbas in 'transition'

Adam Swain and Vlad Mykhnenko

Introduction: a phoenix rises from the ashes?

Until the so-called 'Orange Revolution' in November 2004, Ukraine had been regarded by orthodox transition economists as a failed 'transition country'. According to this view the Western prescription of stabilisation, liberalisation and privatisation had been implemented in Ukraine too late and too haltingly and had been reversed from time to time as the influence of reformers vacillated (Aslund and de Ménil 2000; Aslund 2000; Dubrovskiy and Ivaschenko 2002). It was argued that the prolonged severe economic depression that followed the disintegration of the USSR and the Soviet system was caused by a rent-seeking elite, which spanned the arenas of politics, economics and crime, that served its own interests and frustrated economic reform. Accordingly it was argued that political change was required in order to puncture the increasingly entrenched rent-seeking elite. However, following the financial crisis in Russia in August 1998, the Ukrainian economy began to grow rapidly without any notable political change taking place until the 'Orange Revolution'. (Ironically, following the 'Orange Revolution' economic growth slowed precipitously, from 12.1 per cent in 2004 to 2.6 per cent in 2005.) Whilst some continued to argue that the Ukrainian economy was plagued by a vicious circle of macroeconomic stability and entrenched structural problems, others sought to account for the emergence of economic growth. It was suggested that the structural reforms implemented by Viktor Yushchenko's government in 1999–2001, especially in the energy sector, had finally stimulated economic growth (Aslund 2001). It was also argued that artificially low prices for Russian oil and gas effectively subsidised the growth in industrial production. In addition the devaluation of the hryvnia following the Russian financial crisis also improved Ukraine's competitiveness in international markets.[1]

It is our contention that the economic growth between 1999 and 2004 was in part linked to the revival of the economy in the Ukrainian Donbas. This revival in Ukraine's industrial and financial heartland was due to four key factors. First was the restructuring of the industrial economy in the Donbas. This involved the vertical and horizontal (re)integration of the industrial economy, the accumulation and recycling of capital around the regional economy, the diffusion of financial intermediation, the emergence of new models of organisation and management and the gradual concentration of ownership in the hands of large business groups. Second was the emergence of a political consensus in the region that culminated in the formation of a regional 'party of power', the Party of the Regions, to which nearly all the major regional actors belonged. Third, an accommodation was reached between the leading regional actors in the Donbas and the central authorities in Kyiv. In return for minimising the electoral power base of the hard-line Communist Party of Ukraine and rejecting political regionalism, regional actors secured a favourable legislative regime for large industrial enterprises and industrial areas in the Donbas. Fourth, a benign national political and economic context meant regional actors were prepared to take risks. In particular, macroeconomic stability and a relatively united ruling elite produced a favourable backdrop for collective action.

The revival of the Donbas was symbolised by the appointment, on 21 November 2002, of the governor of Donetsk oblast, Viktor Yanukovych, as the tenth Prime Minister of Ukraine (Kuzio 2002; Kupchinsky 2002a). His nomination under-lined the apparent rebirth of the Donbas in post-Soviet Ukraine. A core heavy industrial region in the Soviet Union's command economy, the 'Communist National Park' (Borisov and Clarke 1994) played a leading role in the construction and destruction of the USSR. The dislocation caused by the disintegration of the Soviet Union and Ukrainian independence led to a dramatic industrial decline that only began to abate in the late 1990s. Increased local autonomy beginning during *perestroika* and accelerating after independence was accompanied by the emer-gence of new actors and institutions for whom the interests of state-owned heavy industry and the region were indistinguishable. The so-called Donetsk 'clan', of which Yanukovych was a leading member, became increasingly influential in industrial and regional governance. Having been general director of several state-owned transportation enterprises in Donetsk, Yanukovych was appointed deputy governor of the oblast in August 1996 by President Kuchma, before rising to first deputy governor a month later and governor in May 1997 (Kupchinsky 2002a). Most of the socio-economic developments in the region discussed in this chapter have occurred under Yanukovych's five-year-long governorship. Hence a major aim of this chapter is to provide an empirically rich and evidence-based assessment of the developmental achievements of the Donbas and its two constituent oblasts at the later stage of the post-communist transformation.

The remainder of the chapter is divided into three parts. In the next section we examine the ways post-Soviet economic development has been theorised. This is then followed by a section that, whilst acknowledging all the caveats that must be attached to them, nonetheless uses official statistics to analyse the Donbas in 'transition'. Here we investigate the position of the region within Ukraine's changing space-economy, the comparative transitions in the two oblasts that make up the Donbas, Donetsk and Luhansk oblasts, and intra-oblast trends. The third section reviews the dominant explanation that has been advocated to explain the rebound in the Donbas economy. In the concluding remarks we challenge the standard analysis and point to ways of rethinking economic development in the Donbas.

Theorising 'transition' in the former Soviet Union

Economic 'transition' in post-Soviet Russia and most of the former USSR resulted in the emergence of two distinctive and related phenomena. Firstly, there was the demonetarisation of the economy and the proliferation of surrogate monies (Woodruff 1999). The liberalisation of prices in the early 1990s resulted in the rapid and inflationary monetarisation of the economy. Subsequent deflationary policies, designed to achieve macroeconomic stabilisation, merely resulted in the demonetarisation of much of the industrial economy, which responded by adopting barter as the primary means of exchange up until the late 1990s. Secondly, demonetarisation and the proliferation of surrogate monies were accompanied by the emergence of new organisational forms, variously called 'financial industrial groups' (Johnson 1997), 'conglomerates' (Burawoy 2001a) or 'holding companies' (Clarke 2004). These business groups – which combined so-called 'red directors', local state officials and alleged Mafia groups – were territorially organised (Pinto *et al.* 2000: 304) and operated their own de facto monies. However, following the Russian financial crisis in August 1998 there was switching of capital from speculative financial activities to investment in the industrial economy. In addition the devaluation of the rouble enhanced the competitiveness of Russian goods and services in both the domestic and the international market, and the increase in oil and gas revenues increased the liquidity of the economy. These trends enhanced the sovereignty of the state, re-monetarised the industrial economy and produced rapid economic growth (Hanson and Teague 2005). Economic change in the former Soviet Union (except for the Baltic states) has been theorised in at least three ways. Firstly, it is argued that an *inauthentic* or 'virtual' capitalism emerged in Russia in the 1990s. Secondly, it is contended that Russia and the other former Soviet states are in a *transitional* phase on a linear path to capitalism. Thirdly, it is theorised that distinctive post-Soviet *varieties* of 'really-existing capitalism' (Hanson and Teague 2006) have emerged. We now consider these three different theories in turn.

'Inauthentic' capitalism: the 'virtual economy' thesis

Gaddy and Ickes (1998a, 1998b, 1999, 2002) argue that, instead of moving towards a market economy, if anything the Russian economy became less like a market economy as the 1990s proceeded. They suggest major industrial enterprises were able to insulate themselves from the market and continue to operate with 'soft budget constraints'.[2] They conclude that a new economic system, which they term a 'virtual economy', emerged that is 'fundamentally not market-based and will ensure continued economic decline and further crises' (Gaddy and Ickes 1998a: 2 (online version)).[3] Gaddy and Ickes suggest that much of the industrial economy, especially manufacturing industry, is value-subtracting and only survives because of artificially low prices for raw materials and energy and the non-payment or non-monetary payment to suppliers, the state and employees. Tompson (1999: 273) defines the virtual economy as:

a non-transparent system of subsidies which, by grossly distorting prices and concealing the true relative costs of various activities, has helped many enterprises that would otherwise have failed to maintain the appearance that they are both larger and more profitable than they are.

He argues that the virtual economy emerged because of the legacy of distorted prices and the dual economy in the USSR and because of the way economic reform in the early 1990s forced industrial enterprises to exaggerate prices. To 'sell' output, enterprises were forced to discount their official prices and engage in non-monetary transactions, creating a de facto parallel currency. Woodruff argues that the emergence of surrogate monies reflects that the Russian state failed to achieve a monopoly of sovereignty over transactions and concludes that the Soviet Union's 'economy of idiosyncrasies' was replaced by what he terms 'shallow marketization' (2000: 452, 439; see also 1999, 2004). Based on his analysis of the role of money and of corporate stock, he suggests that Russia 'created market institutions that function like their international models on the transactional level, but not on the juridical level' (2000: 439). He argues that what might be termed 'economies of practice' (Miller 2002) and the judicial framework are decoupled:

in which ritualistic conformity to the norm of a single means of payments co-exists with the nonmonetary taxation that keeps the government running, and in which tactical conformity to the norms of corporate governance coexist with personalistic power in the factories.

(Woodruff 2000: 471)

There are three important aspects to the virtual economy thesis: first, the role of non-cash payments systems; second, the spatiality of the state and economy; and third, the durability of the economic model. Firstly, it is argued that non-cash payment systems, such as barter or promissory notes, were central to the emergence of the virtual economy. Non-cash payment systems make it difficult to value economic activities and to undertake financial planning – and act as a disincentive to restructure and invest (Lindberg 2002) – and result in distorted prices. Pinto *et al.* (2000: 315–16) argue that non-cash settlements reorganised the industrial economy around alliances between enterprise managers and public officials motivated by personal enrichment. This entailed the formation by enterprise managers and public officials of intermediary companies to organise barter transactions in return for a commission and/or a proportion of the profits. Subsequently cash rich intermediaries became the source of working cash for industrial enterprises and combined to form 'financial industrial groups' (FIGs) (Pinto *et al.* 2000: 316). Pinto *et al.* (2000: 316) argue that production chains became entrenched and non-competitive as chains of barter transactions produced 'vertically integrated conglomerates impeding competition and new entrants. Barter schemes, including multi-stage ones intermediated by unregulated promissory notes, tend to embrace all stages of the production cycle, facilitating informal vertical integration within FIGs.'

Secondly, Pinto *et al.* (2000) argue that tight central government macroeconomic policy was undermined by lax microeconomic policy by the local state. This meant that energy companies subsidised manufacturing enterprises and passed the cost on to the state by not paying taxation, forcing the state to increase borrowing at high interest rates, prompting the 1998 economic crisis. Gaddy and Ickes (2002) argue that the virtual economy first emerged in the large industrial cities in the Urals and along the Volga before later becoming adopted by so-called reformers in Moscow. Oblast governors centralised and informalised economic policy making in their regions and intervened on behalf of local enterprises by providing tax exemptions, state contracts and hidden subsidies. Local governments encouraged barter by accepting non-monetary payments in lieu of tax revenues in order to minimise transfers to the federal government (Tompson 1999: 270–1).

Thirdly, analysts differ as to the durability and rationality of the virtual economy. On the one hand there are those who regard the virtual economy as a rational and potentially stable response to a specific economic and social context (Gaddy and Ickes 2002; Tompson 1999; Woodruff 2000; Lindberg 2002). The financial system and the fiscal and state budgetary regime provide incentives for barter, and the alternative would entail mass bankruptcies and redundancies and a slimmed-down state. On the other hand there are those who argue that the virtual economy is temporary and unstable (Aslund 1999; Pinto *et al.* 2000). Pinto *et al.* (2000) contend that the system depends on unsustainable government borrowing and that the welfare gains used to defend the system are ineffectual as capital is siphoned off into the hands of managers and public officials. Aslund (1999: 101) argues that non-cash payment is only rational for what he terms the 'relational economy'. This comprises large enterprises that preserve their lucrative political influence to evade taxation and to engage in rent seeking and corruption. He maintains that, as manufacturing enterprises engage less in non-monetary exchanges than other parts of the economy, even though they are supposed to have most to benefit, non-cash payment systems are neither rational nor possible for the majority of economic actors.

'Transitional' capitalism

From a variety of theoretical traditions there is a wide literature that argues that post-Soviet capitalism is either incomplete or in a *transitional* phase. Capitalism in Russia has variously been termed 'merchant' (Burawoy 1996), as 'industrial feudalism' (Ericson 2000), as 'extensive' (Clarke 2004), as 'gangster' (Holmstrom and Smith 2000) and as 'chaotic' (Lane 2000).[4] Burawoy (1996: 1109; see also Burawoy 2001a) argues that economic 'involution' has produced a merchant form of capitalism in Russia. Involution, he suggests, 'implies profound economic degeneration in which the economy feeds upon itself. It is the opposite of accumulation.' He argues that a combination of privatisation, persistent soft budget constraints, and re-distributive mechanisms reinforced the Soviet industrial system and led to the transfer of economic resources from the productive economy into trading and financial activities resulting in 'capitalists without capitalism' (Burawoy 2001b: 1112). 'The failure of the Russian state to organize the market economy has led to a coordination and entrepreneurial vacuum into which has stepped conglomerates, banks and mafia, siphoning off surplus from production to exchange' (Burawoy 2001b: 1114). Burawoy argues that economic involution was uneven across sectors and regions, depending on the structure of sectors and the opportunities offered by privatisation compared to lobbying for continued subsidies. A similar argument is made by those who claim that neo-patrimonial forms of political domination have emerged in the former Soviet Union (Erdmann 2002; on Ukraine, see van Zon 2001). Based on Weber's distinction between different forms of political domination, authority and legitimacy (Weber 1968), it is argued that former Soviet states have regressed from a 'legal-rational' bureaucratic state to a 'traditional' patrimonial state involving clientelism, a weak rule of law and a corrupt rent-seeking state bureaucracy. Hellman and his collaborators explain this by suggesting that oligarchic economic forces have been able to force the state to serve their own sectional interests, a process they term 'state capture' (see, for example, Hellman 2000; World Bank 2002).

Ericson (2000; cf. 2001) likens the post-Soviet economic system to 'industrial feudalism'. He argues that the Russian economic system features a 'weak central authority, with strong regional, local and industrial/financial leaderships, each exercising authority over particular, limited domains, although these domains are less territorially, and more functionally, defined' (2000: 15). Whilst Ericson remains uncertain whether 'industrial feudalism' is a durable distinctive form of capitalism or is merely transitional, Simon Clarke (2004: 419) argues that Russian capitalism is in a transitional extensive phase and is not yet intensive capitalism. Adopting an analytical Marxist approach, Clarke argues that whilst labour has been *formally* subsumed under capital this has not yet been achieved in a *real* sense, with the result that production is not subject to the laws of capital (see also Holmstrom and Smith 2000). However, Clarke contends that the economic crisis of 1998 marked a shift away from financial speculation (primitive accumulation) and towards the productive sphere of the economy. Whilst capital has penetrated the industrial economy since 1998 this has been achieved through the emergence of holding companies within which production continues to exhibit features of production under the Soviet system.

Lane (2000: 497–8) argues that a capitalist class has yet to emerge in Russia, resulting in a '"chaotic" social formation', which he defines as a:

> social and economic system which lacks institutional coordination and promotes social fragmentation: goals, law, governing institutions and economic life lack cohesion. Its characteristics are uncertainty about the future, elite disunity, the absence of a dominant and mediating class system, a mixture of media of exchange, criminalization and corruption, rent-seeking entrepreneurs, inadequate political interest articulation and an economy in decline characterized by inflation, unemployment and poverty . . . a chaotic social formation is perverse and system stability is precarious.

A feature of these analyses has been the emergence of new organisational forms, such as the FIGs, that link industrial enterprises and financial institutions and which combine elements of the Soviet system with elements of capitalism. These organisations have been interpreted either as political structures through which the *nomenklatura* used administrative power to socialise costs and rapidly accumulate capital (cf. Staniszkis 1991: 141) or as defensive structures designed to insulate actors from the laws of capital. Burawoy and Krotov's (1995) research on the timber and coal industries in the Republic of Komi suggests how and why these organisations emerged. In the context of a vertically integrated regional timber conglomerate, enterprises that felt exploited in the production chain withdrew from the conglomerate to market their products directly. However, the collapse of the conglomerate led to the disintegration of the sector, which meant individual enterprises lost their traditional suppliers and customers. As a consequence the timber industry became dependent on the local paper factory's ability to win export contracts. In contrast the horizontally organised coal industry conglomerate that had been controlled from Moscow and was used to subsidies from the centre maintained its internal structure as it sought to secure continued subsidies.

Johnson (1997) distinguishes between 'industry-led' and 'bank-led' FIGs in Russia:

> We find that, whereas industry-led FIGs for the most part represent failed efforts by enterprise managers and conservative politicians to salvage uncompetitive industrial ventures without restructuring them, bank-led FIGs have acquired powerful and potentially pivotal positions in the Russian economy today.
>
> (Johnson 1997: 335)

She argues that industry-led FIGs initially emerged spontaneously as a response to the commercialisation of branch ministries, the decentralisation of the planning system and the absence of capital but were subsequently encouraged by local and national public authorities. Johnson suggests industry-led FIGs are transitional structures that will either disintegrate or merge with bank-led FIGs. Similarly, Huber and Wörgötter (1998) identify what they call 'survivalist' business networks primarily engaged in rent seeking. They argue that high sectoral and geographical concentration under the Soviet system encouraged the emergence of vertically organised stable survivalist networks geared towards averting bankruptcy and/or personal enrichment. Industrial enterprises were able first to turn localities' dependence on them for employment, infrastructure and tax revenues into the basis for asserting their influence at the local scale and subsequently to use their local power base to exercise political influence at the national scale. This was achieved through managers at industrial enterprises establishing satellite and/or intermediary companies engaged mostly in trading from whose activities they could personally gain. The legacy of the Soviet economy, in which branch ministries and foreign trade organisations were located in Moscow, means survivalist networks are centred on Moscow with the result that monopoly rents accrued in Moscow where trading in commodities/products produced in the regions took place. Provincial enterprises did not leave the networks because they depended on the network fixers located in

Moscow. Huber and Wörgötter conclude that survivalist networks will only become profit driven entrepreneurial networks 'over a very long time period' (1998: 59).

Varieties of post-Soviet capitalism

In response to the normative orthodox transition literature, critical social scientists highlighted the path-dependency and diversity of post-Soviet transformations (see, for example, Chavance and Magnin 1997; Stark and Bruszt 1998, 2001; Smith and Swain 1998). This work showed that emergent capitalism involved 'self-reorganisation' (Chavance and Magnin 1997: 200) in which already existing social structures and practices in regions and countries inevitably combined with new capitalist practices to produce 'distinctively East European capitalism' (Stark and Bruszt 1998: 3). Stark and Bruszt called this 'recombinant capitalism' but also argued that different national state socialisms together with different paths of reform gave rise to a variety of national post-Soviet capitalisms (for a critique, see Burawoy 2001b). From an evolutionary and network approach, Grabher and Stark (1997) normatively argue that the presence of institutional diversity and friction encourages experimentation and produces regional economies with the capacity to adapt. More recently, drawing on the varieties of capitalism approach developed by Hall and Soskice (2001) and Amable (2003), attempts have been made to compare, contrast and categorise the different institutional forms that post-Soviet capitalism takes in different countries (see Lane and Myant 2006).

This approach highlights the extent to which actors, at the regional scale, acted collectively and strategically in the context of the disintegration of both the Soviet system and the Soviet state. Stoner-Weiss's (1997) research in four Russian oblasts indicates that the characteristics of regional economies, such as the degree of industrial concentration and specialisation, influenced the effectiveness of regional authorities and thereby regional economic performance. Her analysis suggests that: 'the more concentrated the regional economy, the more cooperative were economic and political elites, and the higher was regional government performance as a result' (Stoner-Weiss 1997: 165). She argues that 'the Soviet system's effective establishment of "company towns" appears to have provided a natural impetus for collective action in some regions once the command economy collapsed' (1997: 193–4). Interdependency between regional economic and political elites and dense horizontal professional networks spanning economic and political actors encouraged trust and predictable behaviour. Stoner-Weiss concludes that the acceptance of market principles through enrolment in foreign trade and competitive elections could prevent the emergence of regional oligarchies.

This work also contends that, rather than as barriers to reform, existing informal practices were the resources needed for social actors to self-reorganise, what Stiglitz (1999: 20–2) terms 'restructuring through decentralisation, reconstitution and recombination'. Sabel and Prokop (1996) found that some firms in the Urals actively reorganised and experimented despite both market (demonetarisation and absence of a valuing regime) and governance failure (opaque property relations and insider control). They concluded that corporate restructuring may be less explained by the presence of market signals, the form of property relations or the form of corporate governance than by the spread of economic discourses and particularly discursive quality standards, such as ISO 9000 series. More specifically, barter played an important role in preserving and reorganising the industrial economy. Chang (1999) argues that non-cash payment systems regularised the enterprises' activities in the absence of cash as a means of exchange. Equally, Marin (2002) argues that non-monetary exchange did not mask value-subtracting output but was a response to a lack of trust and liquidity in the economy and concludes that barter prevented an even more marked collapse in industrial output:

> [T]he non-cash economy helps to maintain output which otherwise would collapse due to imperfect input and credit markets. The imperfections of input and credit markets are reflected in the shift in the terms of trade of barter. Through the inflated price for the 'sale' and the price discount on the 'goods payment' the deal is actually saved by guaranteeing both parties a positive profit. The shift in the terms of trade is the mechanism by which the non-cash economy accomplishes the maintenance of output that would otherwise collapse in a cash economy.
>
> (Marin 2002: 198)

Marin (2002) shows that barter transactions increased in Russia after macro-economic stability had been achieved and decreased during the instability of the 1998 economic crisis. Based on an analysis of 165 barter transactions in 1997 in Ukraine, Marin concludes that enterprises resorted to non-monetary exchange because of a lack of liquidity in the economy and that once the rouble depreciated in 1998 increased export earnings permitted more cash transactions to take place (see also Campos and Coricelli 2002).

Similarly the emergence of large business groups may be considered as an innovative vehicle for industrial restructuring in a low-trust society. Even commentators who point to the negative role of business groups recognise that 'bank-led' FIGs (Johnson 1997) and entrepreneurial business networks (Huber and Wörgötter 1998) engaged in reorganisation and restructuring. Moreover, Perotti and Gelfer's (2001) econometric analysis finds that enterprises that formed part of business groups showed evidence of greater financial reallocation than independent enterprises. Following the Yukos affair, Hanson and Teague (2005, 2006) term 'Russia's really-existing capitalism' as Weberian 'political capitalism', verging on state capitalism, involving the allocation of profits according to political administration, a low-trust society and high levels of corruption. Contra the state capture thesis (see page 12), they contend that the legacies of shady privatisation and the size of strategically sensitive energy sectors have produced a form of 'state corporatism' (2005: 658) in which the state informally controls non-state bodies in order to implement government policy.

The Donbas in 'transition'

Post-Soviet restructuring of the Ukrainian space-economy

The disintegration of the Soviet Union and the central planning system plunged Ukraine into a long and severe economic depression.[5] However, the division between the predominantly urban industrial east and south of the country and the mainly rural and agricultural cèntre and west meant post-Soviet 'transition' unevenly affected the Ukrainian space-economy. A notable feature of this new phase of uneven development was that the Donbas, comprising Donetsk and Luhansk oblasts, performed relatively well in the context of the country as a whole. It is not possible to map uneven development from the beginning of transition because the collection of official statistics changed in 1996. The only consistently stable measure for evaluating the long-term impact of transition on different regions is population change. Figure 1.1, which shows population change, by oblast, between 1989 and 2005, reveals that the only territory where population increased is Kyiv city. In all other oblasts, as well as in Sevastopol, population fell, with the greatest fall taking place in Chernihiv oblast at the northern end of central Ukraine. The map also reveals a broad east–west pattern in which population has fallen most in the more populous east of the country and fallen less in the west of the country. Besides Chernihiv, Luhansk and Sumy oblasts, the steepest population decline was suffered by two central Ukrainian provinces, Zhytomyr and Kirovohrad, with Donetsk oblast coming the sixth from the bottom.

To show the impact of 'transition' on uneven development we have used World Bank data to map change in Gross Value Added (GVA) per capita (current prices) by oblast between 1990 and 1995 (Figure 1.2). The World Bank used official statistics to estimate GVA per capita at current prices in 1990 and 1995. In 1996 the Ukrainian government began to publish official GVA per capita data, permitting us to map regional change between 1996 and 2003 (Figure 1.3). It should be noted that until the late 1990s these data did not include estimates for the informal sector which is generally accepted as a significant factor in Ukraine. The two periods broadly correspond to the rapid economic decline in the first half of the 1990s and to the period when economic growth resumed in the late 1990s. Figure 1.2 shows that between 1990 and 1995 the two best performing oblasts were Kharkiv and Odesa and the worst relative to the national average were Kirovohrad and Chernihiv in the centre of the country and a band of oblasts in the west including Chernivtsi, Ternopil, Rivne and Volyn. Although the map shows GVA per capital fell in Kyiv city compared to the national average, the fact that Kyiv oblast performed relatively well suggests that there were spill-over effects from Kyiv city to the surrounding oblast. The map also reveals that GVA per capita fell less in the Donbas (Donetsk and Luhansk oblasts) than the national average. The neighbouring oblasts, Dnipropetrovsk and Kharkiv, also declined less than the national average, whereas the greatest fall was in those predominately agricultural oblasts in the centre and west of the country.

Figure 1.3 reveals that as economic growth in Ukraine resumed the pattern of uneven development became more complicated. Between 1996 and 2003 the cities

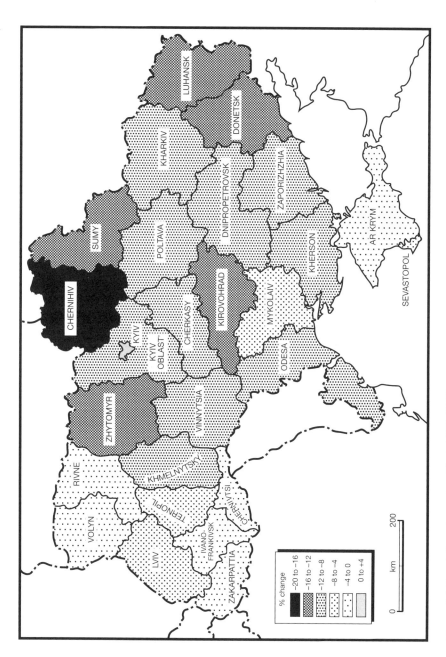

Figure 1.1 Population change by oblast, 1989–2005

Source: Authors' own calculations on the basis of Ukraine State Statistics Committee 2004a, 2005b.

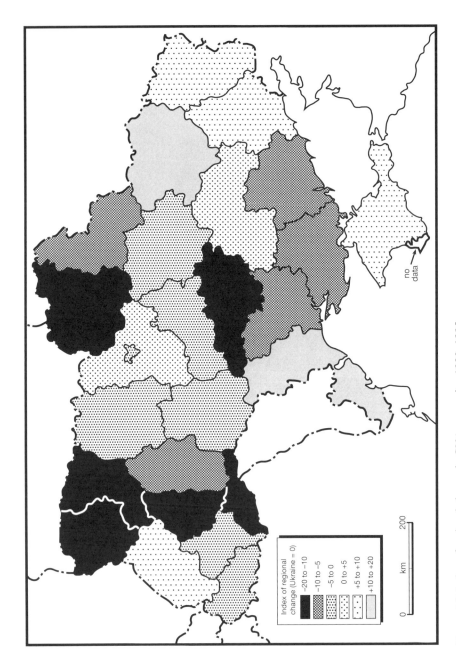

no data

Index of regional
change (Ukraine = 0)
-20 to -10
-10 to -5
-5 to 0
0 to +5
+5 to +10
+10 to +20

0   200
km

Figure 1.2 Index of regional change in GVA per capita, 1990–1995

Source: World Bank 2003a.

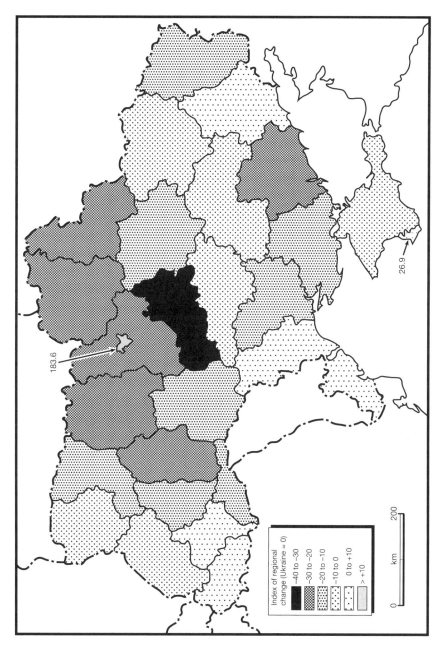

Figure 1.3 Index of regional change in GVA per capita, 1996–2003

Source: Authors' own calculations on the basis of Ukraine State Statistics Committee 2004b: tab. 2.10, 2005a.

of Kyiv and Sevastopol performed best compared to the national average. This can largely be accounted for by Kyiv being the capital city (the location of government and headquarter functions) and the presence of the well-endowed Russian navy in and around Sevastopol. In addition, estimates of per capita GDP or GVA in (any metropolitan centre like) Kyiv do not take into account large numbers of commuters, who reside in an extensive travel-to-work area outside the administrative city boundaries, thus inflating the GDP per resident count. Only four oblasts, Zakarpattia and Ivano-Frankivsk in the west, Odesa in the south and Donetsk in the east, performed better than the national average. Whereas the two oblasts in the west benefited from cross-border trade and the temporary emigration of inhabitants to find work abroad, and Odesa from the growth of trade at the ports, Donetsk's performance reflects expansion of the industrial economy there after 1999. The relatively worst performing oblast was Cherkasy, whilst there was a general pattern of oblasts in the centre of the country performing relatively poorly.

By the end of 2003 the regional pattern of GVA per capita revealed a country with great regional imbalances (Figure 1.4). In broad terms there was a clear south-east/centre-west division as well as a division between key cities and rural areas. GVA per capita in Kyiv was more than three times the national average and more than six times the lowest ranked, Ternopil oblast. Other territories with a GVA per capita above the national average were Donetsk, Dnipropetrovsk, Poltava, Zaporizhzhia and Odesa, mostly in the south-east of the country. In contrast the least developed territories were Chernivtsi, Ternopil, Zhytomyr and Zakarpattia, predominantly in the west of the country. The west and centre of the country were less developed than much of the east and south of the country, with the exception of two noticeable effects. These were the spill-over effects of Kyiv city on Kyiv oblast and the regional effect of Lviv in the west of the country. The regional pattern of unemployment in 2004, calculated according to the standard Labour Force Survey (LFS) methodology developed by the UN International Labour Organization (ILO unemployment), mirrors the GVA data (Figure 1.5). The highest unemployment rates were in four oblasts in the west of the country (Chernivtsi, Ternopil, Khmelnytsky and Rivne) and in Cherkasy and Zhytomyr oblasts in central Ukraine. The lowest unemployment rates were in the cities of Kyiv and Sevastopol, followed by Dnipropetrovsk, Odesa, Crimea, Poltava, Donetsk, Kharkiv and Zaporizhzhia – all regions in the east and south of the country, except for Kyiv and Poltava.

In summary there was a clear division between Kyiv city, with a very high GVA per capita and a very low rate of ILO unemployment, and the rest of the country. There was also a pronounced imbalance between the east of the country plus several southern regions (Odesa and Sevastopol), with high GVA per capita and low rates of ILO unemployment, and the west and centre of the country with lower GVA and higher unemployment. Moreover, whilst the restructuring of the space-economy during transition had been complicated, the data suggest a broad pattern of divergence between the west and the east of the country. However, within the east of the country some oblasts, such as Zaporizhzhia and Luhansk fared less well than other oblasts such as Donetsk and Dnipropetrovsk.

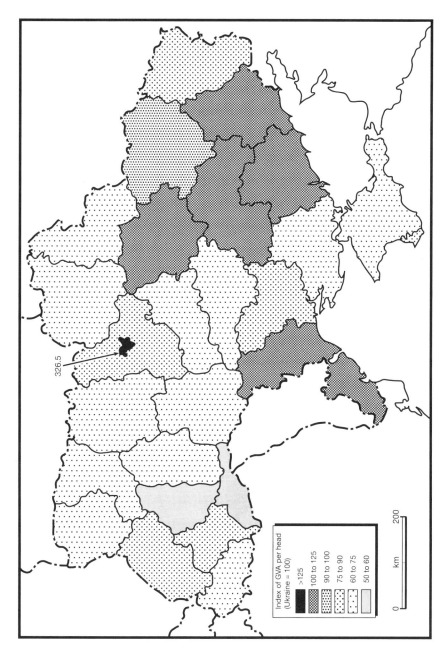

Figure 1.4 Index of GVA per capita by oblast, 2003

Source: Authors' own calculations on the basis of Ukraine State Statistics Committee 2005a.

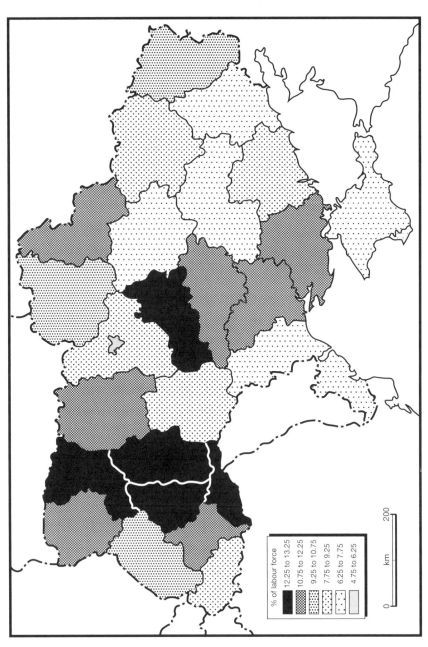

Figure 1.5 Unemployment rate, 2004 (LFS-based methodology)

Source: Ukraine State Statistics Committee 2005c.

% of labour force
- 12.25 to 13.25
- 10.75 to 12.25
- 9.25 to 10.75
- 7.75 to 9.25
- 6.25 to 7.75
- 4.75 to 6.25

0   km   200

Regional development in the Donbas

The Donbas comprises two heavily industrialised and urbanised oblasts, including four large cities with a population of more than 250,000 in Donetsk oblast (Donetsk city, Makiivka, Mariupol and Horlivka) and one in Luhansk oblast (Luhansk city) (Figure 1.6). The strategic role the region played in the USSR meant the region

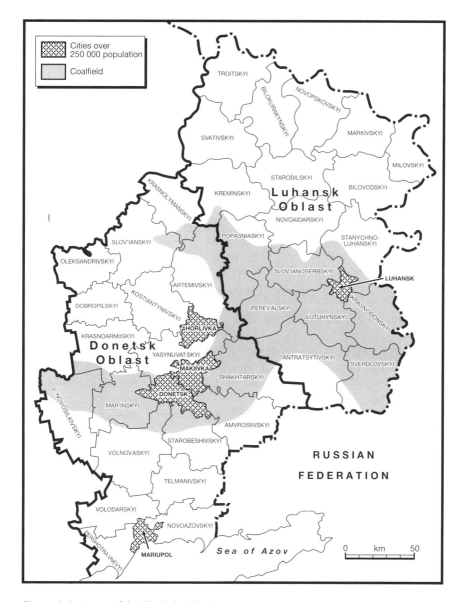

Figure 1.6 A map of the Ukrainian Donbas

possessed a good road and rail infrastructure as well as a large port in Mariupol on the Sea of Azov. In response to a long period of industrial stagnation, an independent miners' movement emerged in the Donbas during *perestroika*. This movement and the region played an important role in the disintegration of the USSR and the Soviet system (see, for example, Friedgut 1994). However, as the region depended on a small number of key sectors, such as coal mining and iron and steel production, controlled by all-union branch ministries and integrated into pan-USSR production networks, the disintegration of the USSR had a particularly pronounced effect on the region (see Mykhnenko 2005).

Statistics on GVA per capita, from 1995 to 2004, provide an insight into the performance of the economy in the region (Table 1.1). (It should be noted that in 2004 Gross Regional Product (GRP) per capita replaced GVA. It was too soon to assess the full impact of the 'Orange Revolution' on the Donbas economy.) GVA per capita shows that the economy in both oblasts bottomed out in 1998 and that the contraction which took place in the 1990s was greater in Luhansk than in Donetsk. Between 1998 and 2000 GVA per capita grew gently in both oblasts before accelerating in Luhansk between 2000 and 2001 and in Donetsk from 2002. In 2004 GRP per capita stood at 146.6 per cent and 149.2 per cent compared to 1995 in Donetsk and Luhansk oblasts respectively. For a region dominated by industrial production, the performance of the regional economy was largely determined by the primary sector (coal and energy) as well as steel, heavy engineering, petrochemicals and other manufacturing branches. Industrial output in both Donetsk and Luhansk oblasts fell steadily from 1990 to 1993 and then rapidly until 1995. At that point industrial output began to level off in Donetsk but continued to decline in Luhansk. Overall, industrial output fell considerably more in Luhansk than in Donetsk oblast. However, once industrial output began to grow in 1999, the upturn was more accelerated in Luhansk than in Donetsk. Whereas industrial output increased significantly in Luhansk between 1999 and 2001, industrial output in Donetsk did not begin to accelerate until 2002. As a result, in 2001 industrial output in Luhansk compared to 1990 overtook Donetsk oblast before the two oblasts converged in 2003. Thus by 2004 industrial output in Donetsk and Luhansk oblasts stood at 78 per cent and 79.3 per cent of the 1990 figure respectively.

As industrial output collapsed so too did fixed capital investment. In 1997 fixed capital investment in Donetsk oblast stood at 22.7 per cent compared to 1990. Thereafter fixed capital investment grew slowly until 2002 before accelerating to reach 55.5 per cent in 2005 compared to 1990. The collapse was even greater in Luhansk oblast where fixed capital investment fell to 16.5 per cent in 1999 compared to 1990. Thereafter fixed capital investment gradually increased until 2002 before accelerating to 47.4 per cent in 2005 compared to 1990. Given that the regional economic accounts data for 2005 will become available only in mid-2007, it is not possible to assess in full the economic impact of the turbulent political events of 2004–2005 on the economy of the Donbas at this stage. However, one does not fail to notice that in 2005, in the aftermath of the Orange Revolution, industrial growth significantly decelerated in Luhansk oblast, whereas Donetsk registered an absolute decline of industrial output for the first time since 1998. This,

Table 1.1 Regional economic change in Donetsk and Luhansk oblasts, 1990–2005

		1990	1991	1992	1993	1994	1995	1996	1997	1998	1999	2000	2001	2002	2003	2004	2005
GVA per capita (1995=100)	Donetsk	100.0					100.0	94.3	92.2	88.5	91.6	97.6	110.3	115.0	130.9	146.6*	...
	Luhansk						100.0	88.5	89.0	84.8	87.8	93.6	113.7	122.8	136.1	149.2*	...
Industrial output (1990=100)	Donetsk	100.0	93.2	86.9	74.4	54.2	49.4	46.4	47.0	43.6	46.6	52.4	55.6	58.1	69.4	78.0	71.9
	Luhansk	100.0	92.5	86.6	71.7	51.0	38.2	34.2	35.5	33.4	36.2	47.1	61.4	64.0	71.6	79.3	80.5
Fixed capital investment (1990=100)	Donetsk	100.0	...	...	...	...	34.6	28.2	22.7	25.5	25.2	27.1	31.8	31.7	38.3	50.0	55.5
	Luhansk	100.0	...	...	...	...	29.1	20.9	21.1	18.8	16.5	17.6	20.5	21.7	28.4	38.6	47.4
Cumulative FDI (US$m)	Donetsk	...	...	...	...	...	52.2	76.3	106.2	166.2	259.4	305.3	334.8	389.4	434.2	501.7	586.0
	Luhansk	...	...	...	...	...	...	...	27.8	28.2	27.6	31.4	39.3	51.6	58.2	146.2	269.5
Cumulative FDI per capita (US$)	Donetsk	...	...	...	...	...	10.0	14.9	21.0	33.2	52.6	62.4	69.2	81.6	92.0	107.4	126.5
	Luhansk	...	...	...	...	...	...	...	...	...	10.5	12.1	15.4	20.6	23.5	59.9	111.4

Sources: Ukraine State Statistics Committee 1996, 2000, 2004b, 2005a, 2005d, 2005e, 2005f, 2006a; Donetsk Oblast Chief Statistical Department 2004a; Luhansk Oblast Chief Statistical Department 2004; and authors' own calculations.

Note: *Gross regional product; ... = no data.

however, did not seem to alter capital investment decisions made by local economic agents, as fixed capital investment continued to grow.

One of the features of the upturn in the regional economy since 1998 has been the attraction of foreign direct investment (FDI). In 1999 the Ukrainian government passed a law that created a special investment regime for domestic and foreign investment located in designated 'depressed' and 'priority development' areas in Donetsk and Luhansk oblasts. Table 1.1 shows that cumulative FDI in Donetsk oblast began to grow rapidly in the late 1990s reaching $586 million by 2005. By comparison, cumulative FDI in Luhansk oblast remained less than $60 million until 2004 when it more than doubled in one year to reach $270 million in 2005. However, these figures need to be treated with a degree of caution for two reasons. First, Ukrainian FDI statistics include foreign loans to local companies and the value of imported capital goods. Second, a significant proportion of FDI was routed through offshore financial centres, such as the British Virgin Islands or Cyprus, and may simply reflect the recycling of money that previously flowed out of the region. Although Donetsk attracted several high-profile foreign investors, including the US-based multinational giant Cargil, which established a 'greenfield' sunflower crushing plant just outside Donetsk city, and ISTIL Group, which acquired a stake in the Donetsk Iron and Steel Works, FDI had a relatively small impact on the regional economy. Cumulative FDI per capita in Donetsk oblast reached $126.50 in 2005 and $111.40 in Luhansk oblast – where the figure had nearly doubled in one year.

The 'transitional' depression and the consequent industrial renaissance of the Donbas economy have had a profound effect on labour. Table 1.2 shows changes in the emergent labour market from 1985 until 2005. The table includes data both on employment, which includes all people in formal work, and on the number of employee jobs, which includes only waged/salaried employees of large industrial and agricultural enterprises and excludes employers, the self-employed, employees of small firms (with less than 50 staff and annual sales of less than EUR500,000), private farmers and seasonal labourers. Employment in the two oblasts fell from 4.09 million in 1985 to 3.18 million in 2005 and most severely in Luhansk. The fall in employment has been caused by enterprise closures and lay-offs in the early and mid-1990s, by people leaving the (formal) world of work, and also through population decline. In both oblasts the number of employees has fallen more sharply than employment as people have moved from the traditional state sector into service activities and self-employment. The data also show that only a small proportion of people leaving formal employment registered as unemployed. Registered unemployment only began to increase in the mid-1990s and peaked at almost 96,000 in Donetsk in 2000 and at almost 58,000 in Luhansk in 2001 before gradually declining. However, registered unemployment did not accurately reflect the real level of joblessness. Since 1999 unemployment as defined by the ILO (using the LFS method) has been collected for both oblasts. These data show that ILO unemployment peaked in Donetsk oblast at around 240,000 (10.3 per cent of the labour force) in both 1999 and 2001 and in Luhansk at around 152,000 (13.3 per cent) in 2001. As the two regional economies rebounded in the early 2000s, ILO

Table 1.2 Labour market change in Donetsk and Luhansk oblasts, 1985–2005

		1985	1990	1995	1996	1997	1998	1999	2000	2001	2002	2003	2004	2005
Present population (000s)	Donetsk		5,339.6	5,266.9	5,198.5	5,125.4	5,064.4	4,987.3	4,932.4	4,893.6	4,834.7	4,774.4	4,720.9	4,671.9
	Luhansk		2,866.9	2,827.1	2,788.5	2,719.0	2,684.4	2,652.7	2,628.6	2,607.4	2,542.5	2,507.3	2,472.6	2,440.3
	Total		8,206.5	8,094.0	7,987.0	7,844.4	7,748.8	7,640.0	7,561.0	7,501.0	7,377.2	7,281.7	7,193.5	7,112.2
Index of present population (1990=100)	Donetsk		100	98.6	97.4	96.0	94.8	93.4	92.4	91.6	90.5	89.4	88.4	87.5
	Luhansk		100	98.6	97.3	94.8	93.6	92.5	91.7	90.9	88.7	87.5	86.2	85.1
	Total		100	98.6	97.3	95.6	94.4	93.1	92.1	91.4	89.9	88.7	87.7	86.7
Employment (000s)	Donetsk	2,652.8	2,589.6	2,480.7	2,427.9	2,314.6	2,310.8	2,197.3	2,125.6	2,078.3	2,033.3	2,074.2	2,086.0	2,124.9
	Luhansk	1,434.9	1,410.4	1,259.5	1,218.1	1,117.7	1,068.8	1,050.9	999.2	950.0	968.8	978.7	1,019.8	1,054.4
	Total	4,087.7	4,000.0	3,740.2	3646.0	3,432.3	3,379.6	3,248.2	3,124.8	3,028.3	3,002.1	3,052.9	3,105.8	3,179.3
Index of total employment (1985=100)	Donetsk	100	97.6	93.5	91.5	87.3	87.1	82.8	80.1	78.3	76.6	78.2	78.6	80.1
	Luhansk	100	98.3	87.8	84.9	77.9	74.5	73.2	69.6	66.2	67.5	68.2	71.1	73.5
	Total	100	97.9	91.5	89.2	84.0	82.7	79.5	76.4	74.1	73.4	74.7	76.0	77.8
Number of employees (000s)	Donetsk	2,568	2,420	1,953.7	1,713.2	1,598.2	1,619.5	1,552.7	1,477.0	1,410.3	1,349.6	1,312.6	...	...
	Luhansk	1,389	1,318	1,008.2	928.0	825.0	787.0	761.0	711.6	669.3	637.4	631.0	...	...
	Total	3,957	3,738	2,961.9	2,641.2	2,423.2	2,406.5	2,313.7	2,188.6	2,079.6	1,987.0	1,943.6	...	...
Index of number of employees (1985=100)	Donetsk	100	94.2	76.1	66.7	62.2	63.1	60.5	57.5	54.9	52.6	51.1	...	...
	Luhansk	100	94.9	72.6	66.8	59.4	56.7	54.8	51.2	48.2	45.9	45.4	...	...
	Total	100	94.5	74.9	66.7	61.2	60.8	58.5	55.3	52.6	50.2	49.1	...	...

continued

Table 1.2 (continued)

		1985	1990	1995	1996	1997	1998	1999	2000	2001	2002	2003	2004	2005
Number of registered unemployed (000s)	Donetsk			4.6	8.5	25.5	50.7	79.6	95.6	95.1	72.1	74.5		
	Luhansk			…	…	…	…	44.9	53.4	57.9	48.4	46.0		
	Total							124.5	149.0	153.0	120.5	120.5		
Registered unemployment (%)*	Donetsk	0.20		0.30	0.90	1.80	2.90	3.50	3.50	2.70	2.80	2.60	2.40	
	Luhansk		0.50	1.70	3.10	3.70	3.90	3.30	3.20	3.10	2.70	2.30		
ILO unemployment (000s)	Donetsk			…	…	…	…	242.6	231.7	241.6	218.3	179.7		
	Luhansk			…	…	…	…	132.8	129.1	152.0	137.0	99.7		
	Total							375.4	360.8	393.6	355.3	279.4		
ILO unemployment (%)**	Donetsk							10.30	9.60	10.30	9.40	8.00	7.30	6.60
	Luhansk							11.40	11.20	13.30	11.90	9.20	9.20	8.20

Sources: Ukraine State Statistics Committee 1996, 2000, 2001, 2002, 2004b, 2004c, 2005g; Donetsk Oblast Chief Statistical Department 2000, 2002, 2004a; Luhansk Oblast Chief Statistical Department 2004; and authors' own calculations.

Notes: * Percentage of population of working age; ** Percentage of population aged 15–70; … = no data.

unemployment fell to 6.6 per cent and 8.2 per cent in Donetsk and Luhansk oblasts respectively, with the Ukraine average in 2005 of 7.8 per cent.

In summary two key points should be highlighted. The first is that the economy in Luhansk was more severely effected that in Donetsk by 'transition'. Its economy contracted more than in Donetsk and, although its rebound was more accelerated, it continued to suffer greater structural problems. This was evidenced by a greater collapse in employment and in the number of employees in Luhansk than in Donetsk as well as higher unemployment and lower levels of FDI. Second, the Donbas regional economy began to recover in 1999; GVA per capita began to increase again, as did fixed capital investment and FDI, whilst unemployment began to level off and then fall. The only trend that continued even after economic growth began was the decline in the number of employee jobs. This indicates that economic growth was driven, at least in part, by greater productivity as well as by considerable structural changes involving the expansion of small and medium business and the consequent growth of self-employment.

Sub-regional inequalities

Central planning resulted in the creation of labour settlements orientated to one sector and often to one enormous enterprise. These 'company towns' depended almost entirely on the economic situation of the local enterprise, which in turn depended on its age, size, ability to access labour and so on, and on the relevant industrial branch, such as the capacity to find markets, access to investment capital and so on. Consequently in addition to the general pattern of deindustrialisation, which was more severe in Luhansk than in Donetsk, there was a very uneven micro-geography within the region. One of the most important factors affecting sub-regional inequalities has been the restructuring of the coal industry (see Chapter 7; Chapter 8; Swain 2006). The coalfield, which covers the central and eastern half of Donetsk oblast and the southern half of Luhansk oblast (Figure 1.6), has been affected by the closure of more than 50 coal mines since 1996. In contrast, the southern part of Donetsk oblast, with the exception of the city of Mariupol, and the northern half of Luhansk are more rural and agricultural. Figure 1.7 shows that there was an enormous variation in the change in industrial output between 1990 and 2003 by towns and districts in the two oblasts. The figure shows that this variety was greater in Donetsk oblast's urban areas than in Luhansk, and that the variation was especially pronounced in rural areas compared to urban areas, especially in Luhansk oblast. This indicates that rural areas were more likely to be dependent on the performance of one or two industrial enterprises whereas urban areas were more diversified.

The complex map of administrative boundaries within the two oblasts means it is difficult to map sub-regional data. We have overcome this by combining official statistics for rayons with data for towns located within those rayons and by mapping data for the large five cities.[6] To examine the impact of 'transition' at the sub-regional scale it is possible to map present population change from 1989 to 2004 (Figure 1.8). With the exception of Pershotravnevyi, adjacent to Mariupol on the

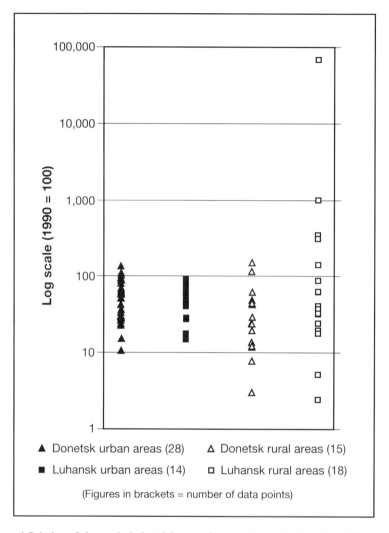

Figure 1.7 Index of change in industrial output by town/rayon in Donetsk and Luhansk
    oblasts, 1990–2003

Source: Authors' own calculations on the basis of Donetsk Oblast Chief Statistical Department
2004a: tab. 5.6; Luhansk Oblast Chief Statistical Department 2004: tab. 5.1.

coast, all territories saw a decline in population. However, the greatest declines
were seen in the more industrial areas and especially in those rayons, such as
Shakhtarskyi in Donetsk, and Antratsytskyi and Sverdlovskyi in Luhansk, where
coal mines have been closed. Figure 1.9 shows the change in the number of salaried
employees, which indicates the extent to which the traditional state-owned industrial
and agricultural economy has declined, between 1995 and 2003. This map reveals
that the number of employees decreased most in large cities, such as in Makiivka

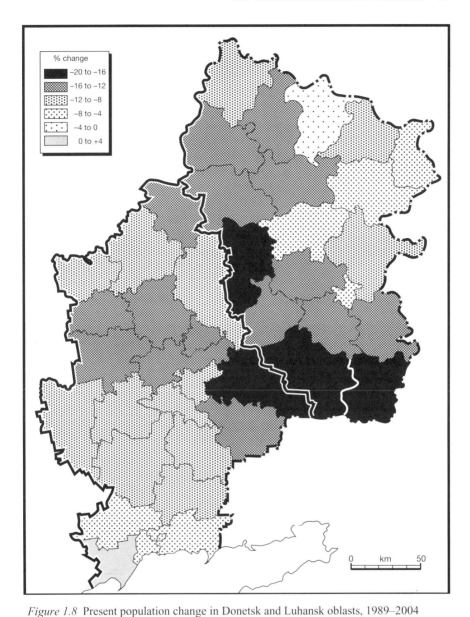

Figure 1.8 Present population change in Donetsk and Luhansk oblasts, 1989–2004

Sources: Authors' own calculations on the basis of Ukraine State Statistics Committee 2004a; Donetsk Oblast Chief Statistical Department 2004a: tab. 15.4; Luhansk Oblast Chief Statistical Department 2004: tab. 15.2.

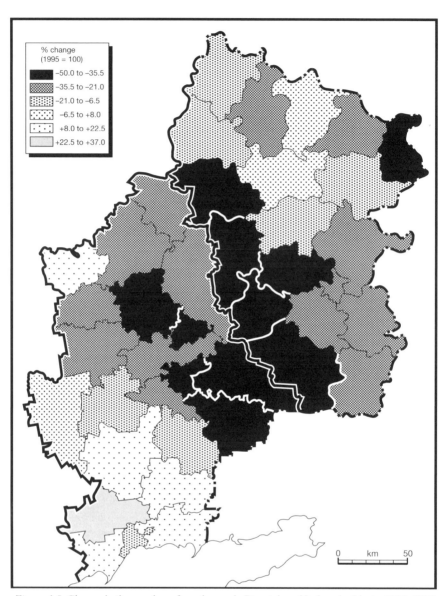

Figure 1.9 Change in the number of employees in Donetsk and Luhansk oblasts, 1995–2003

Sources: Donetsk Oblast Chief Statistical Department 2004a: tab. 16.9, 2004b; Luhansk Oblast Chief Statistical Department 2004: tab. 16.7.

and Horlivka, which depended on steel and coal and machine building and chemicals respectively, and/or individual plants that did not benefit very much from the rebound in the industrial economy after 1998. The number of employees also fell most precipitously in territories where coal mines had been closed. Elsewhere in the more rural and agricultural area to the south of Donetsk oblast and the north of Luhansk oblast, the number of jobs fell least and in some cases even increased, especially in the coastal areas.

Figure 1.10 shows that industrial output in 2003 was geographically concentrated in the larger cities and in territories that lie on the coalfield. The map shows that industrial output in Donetsk oblast was highest in Mariupol because of the presence of two huge steel works, Azovstal and Illich, as well as a very large machine build-ing factory and the port. The next highest concentration of industrial output was in Donetsk city itself, followed by Yasynuvatskyi rayon which includes one of the largest coke coal factories in Europe in the town of Avdiivka and a large steel works in Yenakieve. Industrial output in Luhansk oblast is concentrated in Popasnianskyi, with its large number of coal mines and petrochemical enterprises in and around the cities of Kirovske, Stakhanov, Severodonetsk, Lysychansk and Pervomaisk, in Perevalskyi (the location of a huge steel works in Alchevsk city and coal mines in and around the town of Brianka) and in Luhansk city.

Another means of mapping sub-regional inequalities is provided by mapping employment in small firms (those with fewer than 50 employees and annual sales of less that EUR50,000) as a percentage of total average employment (Figure 1.11). The map reveals that large employers remain very important to the regional economy and shows that employment in small firms is highest in cities, such as Donetsk city and Luhansk city, and lowest in coal mining areas. There also seem to be two further factors. First, areas like Pershotravnevyi appear to benefit from spill-over effects from Mariupol and the impact of tourism along the Sea of Azov coast. Second, areas such as Milovskyi and Bilokurakynskyi along Luhansk's northern border with Russia appear to be benefiting from cross-border trade activities.

In summary this section highlights that there are important geographical imbalances within the region. Industrial output in the Donbas is geographically concentrated in Mariupol and Donetsk city where many of the region's most impor-tant companies are located or where their head offices are situated. Donetsk city in particular plays an important role as the location of not only headquarters but also government functions and financial institutions. For these reasons the city is a hub with spokes radiating outwards to large industrial enterprises around the region, especially in Mariupol and in industrial areas of Luhansk oblast (e.g. Alchevsk). This entails the transfer of value from the enterprises to Donetsk city and has produced a high level of inequality at the sub-regional scale, with localities where small and old coal mines were located being most severely affected by deindustrialisation.

Explaining regional development in the Donbas: transitional neo-patrimonial capitalism?

In the first part of this chapter we outlined three broad theories of post-Soviet economic development. The Donbas has been analysed as exhibiting the

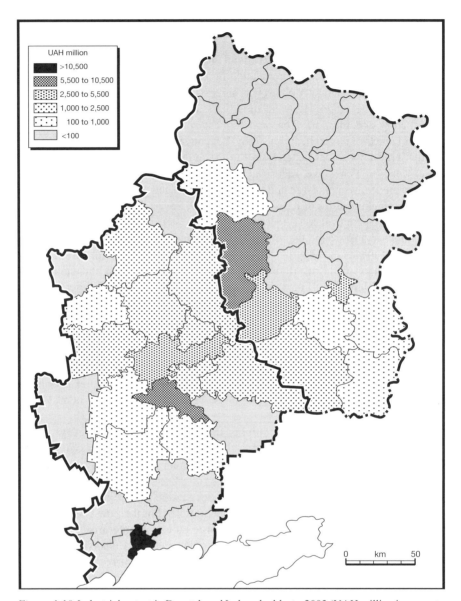

Figure 1.10 Industrial output in Donetsk and Luhansk oblasts, 2003 (UAH million in current
            prices)

Source: Authors' own calculations on the basis of Donetsk Oblast Chief Statistical Department 2004b;
Luhansk Oblast Chief Statistical Department 2004: tab. 5.4.

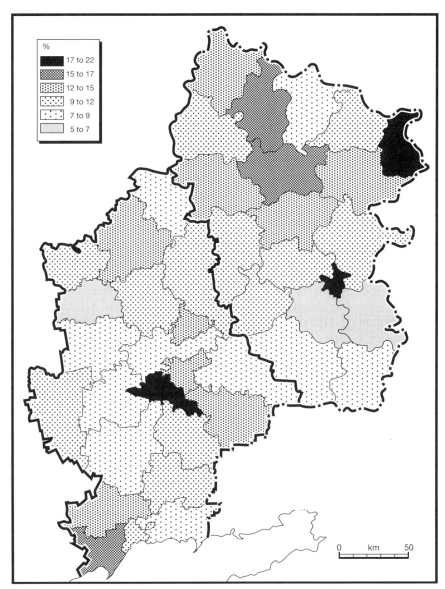

Figure 1.11 Employment in small firms as a percentage of total average paid employment in Donetsk and Luhansk oblasts, 2003

Sources: Donetsk Oblast Chief Statistical Department 2004a: tab. 13.5; Luhansk Oblast Chief Statistical Department 2004: tab. 13.4.

characteristics of an inauthentic/virtual economy, such as less-than-transparent price formation initially through barter transactions and subsequently through opaque cash transactions within FIGs, but fundamentally as a *transitional* capitalism, namely neo-patrimonial, in structural decline (van Zon 2005; Zimmer 2004; see also Zimmer 2005a and 2005b). Contra this analysis it has recently been argued that the Donbas has undergone a process of 'informal marketisation' which has resulted in the emergence of an indigenous and distinctive regional capitalism with the potential to adapt to international competition (see Swain 2006). Hans van Zon (2005) argues that the Donbas possesses a virtual capitalist institutional landscape but is in reality embedded in an informal neo-patrimonial institutional environment that is a legacy of the tsarist and Soviet eras. He argues that political and economic power is centralised (with dissent not tolerated) and that economic practices are reminiscent of the USSR. However, he contends that as Western models of democracy spread across the region the emergence of a civil society will demand new forms of political authority and result in the end of neo-patrimonialism. Kerstin Zimmer (2004: 343) argues that neo-patrimonialism in the Donbas has resulted in what she terms a 'captured region'. Her contention is based on Joel Hellman's argument that oligarchic business interests have captured and corrupted post-Soviet states (see page 12). However, she extends the argument to examine the connection between the local state and regional development and also by arguing that the local elite used its control over the region to lobby central government for a policy regime suited to its business interests.

Zimmer argues that the Donbas is an exaggerated example of a so-called 'old industrial region' (OIR) found in western Europe, such as the Ruhr or north-east England. OIRs are regions 'locked in' to a path of structural economic decline owing to their dependence on traditional industrial sectors, such as the coal and steel industry, that are no longer at the forefront of capitalist economic development. She suggests that the Soviet system, together with 'transition', has produced an exaggerated OIR (Zimmer 2004: 233–4). She argues that the Soviet planning system, in which industrial enterprises responded to the central planners located in Moscow, resulted in a form of functional lock-in even more profound than that found in market economies. She maintains that the role of the Donbas as a core industrial region, first in the USSR and subsequently in independent Ukraine, produced clientelist relations not only between the region and Moscow and then Kyiv, but also within the region. Moreover, she suggests that post-independence privatisation – which she terms '*nomenklatura* privatisation' – reinforced rather than transformed inherited social relations. Privatisation encouraged a neo-patrimonial regime in which the boundaries between different functional arenas of social action, such as the economic and the political, and between different institutions, for example legislative, executive and judiciary, were not clearly drawn. Thus, she maintains that relations amongst economic and political actors in the Donbas and between them and the weak central state in Kyiv reinforced patrimonialism at both the national and the regional scale. Accordingly, Zimmer concludes that the Donbas is functionally, politically and cognitively 'locked in' to an exhausted model of economic development (see also Chapter 5).

Van Zon and Zimmer agree that neo-patrimonialism in the Donbas is based on five economic and political practices: clan behaviour, rent seeking, orientation towards traditional economic sectors, collusion between economic and political actors, and the projection of power beyond the region.[7] We will now examine each of these five practices in turn. First, a regional economy emerged that was dominated by informal 'clans' that sought to rig the nascent market economy by preventing competition, in part by preventing external business interests from establishing a presence in the region. It is suggested these 'clans' emerged prior to independence and articulated legal and illegal economic practices. Gradually, the informal 'clans' evolved to take on a more permanent organisational form resembling the FIGs found in Russia (see page 9). The first FIG to emerge was the Industrial Union of the Donbas (IUD) in late 1995. Formally established by several research institutes, the regional Chamber of Commerce and a number of private companies, IUD was widely associated with figures allegedly linked to the criminal underworld (Kupchinsky 2002a). Following a series of assassinations in the mid-1990s, IUD came under the influence of a young 'oligarch', Rinat Akhmetov, and a local 'red director' and former deputy governor, Vitaliy Hayduk (Kupchinsky 2002b). IUD monopolised the supply of gas to industrial consumers in the Donbas and used the accumulated profits to acquire industrial assets once they were privatised by the state. In 2000, IUD was estimated to have sales revenues of over UAH6 billion (*Kiev Post*, 11 October 2001) and by late 2002 it owned 600 enterprises in Donetsk and Luhansk oblasts and was beginning to acquire assets in other regions (Kupchinsky 2002b). Around the same time IUD was reorganised, which culminated in the emergence of a new FIG, System Capital Management (SCM), owned almost entirely by Akhmetov. It is argued that these industry-led FIGs (see page 13) played a role analogous to that of Soviet branch ministries but combined a territorial focus and control over commodity chains rather than single industrial sectors.

Second, it is argued that the informal 'clans' and later the FIGs predominantly engaged in monopolising economic sectors and recycled monopoly rents by acquiring, first, attractive commercial and property assets and, subsequently, industrial assets. Monopolistic behaviour meant the 'clans' could 'fix' prices initially as part of barter transactions and subsequently through cash transactions. Initially the 'clans' sought to horizontally integrate the supply of key upstream commodities, such as gas, coke coal, and power generation. Once a degree of horizontal integration had been achieved the 'clans' sought to extend their control downstream as part of a process of vertical integration. The rigging of prices meant the informal 'clans' could extend their formal ownership of an enterprise or particular sector in the region to include informal influence on upstream and downstream companies and sectors. In this way the 'clans' could form prices which meant that individual enterprises and sectors cross-subsidised other enterprises and sectors. In short, van Zon argues that prices in the Donbas did not necessarily reflect two independent parties engaging in an economically regulated transaction. Rather prices reflected the control that 'clans' had over a sector and vertical commodity chain. Consequently 'clans' were able to coordinate prices, akin to internal transfer prices within large companies, and allocate profits and losses to different enterprises and sectors irrespective of their fundamental economic performance.

Third, the 'clans' were orientated to a small number of industrial sectors, such as the coal, iron and steel, and heavy engineering associated with 'old industrial regions' (Zimmer 2004). Industrial restructuring in the Donbas since independence increased the regional economy's dependence on these traditional sectors (see Chapter 4). Recent industrial growth has largely been driven by the steel industry and in particular a handful of individual large steel mills, such as Azovstal located in Mariupol and Alchevsk Iron and Steel Works in Luhansk oblast. It is argued that the success of these producers in penetrating export markets is due to a particular set of unsustainable circumstances in which traditional industries have appeared profitable when they may have been in fact value-subtracting. Ukraine's close geo-political relationship to Russia helped to ensure the supply of gas to large industrial consumers at prices much lower than for competitors in, for example, western Europe. In addition the steel industry benefited from the supply of coking coal at prices often considered to be below the cost of production – in part because the state continued to subsidise loss-making coal mines (World Bank 2003b). Equally, producers benefited from the way deindustrialisation generated a plentiful supply of cheap scrap metal that could be used instead of more expensive iron ore. The depreciation of the hryvnia following the Russian financial crisis in 1998 also helped to increase the competitiveness of Ukrainian producers in international markets. The success of Ukrainian producers in winning market share in overseas markets was reflected in the introduction of anti-dumping measures by several countries. Moreover, recent industrial growth in the Donbas may be explained more by the global boom in the demand for steel – fuelled by economic growth in China – than by the modernisation of the industry's energy-intensive obsolete technologies (Mykhnenko 2004). Most steel producers increasingly export low-value-added semi-finished steel products, such as billets, which are re-rolled overseas. In this way Ukraine may be regarded as a major producer of steel as a commodity rather than of steel products. Thus it is argued that the buoyancy of the regional economy is highly dependent upon factors that are politically sensitive and on the fluctuations in global demand for certain types of steel.

Fourth, control over enterprises and sectors depended on the connections of the 'clans' to political authorities in the region. Both van Zon and Zimmer argue that the emergence of the 'clans' is largely explained by their capacity to 'capture' the local state. The local state comprises, first, the regional offices of central state executive bodies based in Kyiv and, second, directly elected mayors and city and regional assemblies. Up until the 'Orange Revolution' the Ukrainian central state executive was effectively territorially organised, with regional offices relatively autonomous from their central offices located in Kyiv. This meant that the offices of, for example, the National Property Fund, the Ukraine Security Service (SBU) (successor to the KGB) or the tax administration often had a stronger allegiance to other regional actors than to their formally higher authorities in central government. The most influential manifestation of the state executive in Donetsk is the oblast governor, appointed directly by the president, and his or her oblast administration, which has wide-ranging responsibility for economic development, the so-called budget sector and the operation of political processes, such as elections. The appointment of successive governors in the 1990s reflected the relative balance of power between regional and central government actors. Towards the end of the 1990s regional actors effectively exchanged their allegiance to President Kuchma and the independent Ukrainian state in return for relative autonomy in the field of economic and political management of the Donbas (Chapter 3). The most significant governor appointment was of Viktor Yanukovych in 1997, who went on to create a political context in which the 'clans', and specifically IUD and SCM, could expand their operations without fearing punitive and arbitrary interference from the political authorities in Kyiv. The re-election of President Kuchma in 1999 was widely considered to have been in part due to the adept way that Yanukovych aligned pro-presidential forces in Donetsk oblast. This involved an emergent managed democracy in which so-called 'administrative resources' and control over mass media were used to support favoured candidates.

The 'clans' also established a political presence in local and regional assemblies and directly elected positions, such as city mayors. This was in large part by building on and transforming the role that the independent coal miners' movement played in the final years of the USSR and the first years of independence. In the early 1990s the miners' movement became an increasingly regionalist movement demanding political autonomy from the new Ukrainian state. This culminated in a strike in the Donbas in 1993 that was initiated by miners but which spread to most sectors of the economy and resulted in the fall of the government, early elections and the brief appointment of a Donetsk industrialist as prime minister (Borisov and Clarke 1994). Inside the region, the traditional regional elite, the so-called 'red directors', used the strike to re-establish their influence over the workers' movement which it had lost during *perestroika*. By the late 1990s political regionalism had been sacrificed for a narrower form of economic regionalism that was palatable to Kyiv (Swain 2006). Economic regionalism combined with a productivist ideology effaced the Communist Party, which had had widespread support in the region. This transformation culminated in the formation of a regional 'party of power' in early 2001, the Party of the Regions, to which all significant regional actors swore allegiance (Mykhnenko 2003).

The establishment of the Party of the Regions was a significant example of the fifth factor that was central to the recent growth in the Donbas, namely the capacity of the 'clans' to create mechanisms to project their power beyond the region and specifically to Kyiv. Van Zon argues that the Donetsk 'clan' unfairly pressurised the central authorities to establish a favourable legislative regime as a price for securing their political loyalty. Perhaps the clearest example surrounds the formation of special economic zones and territories of priority development in Donetsk and Luhansk oblasts in 1999. The establishment of the zones and territories was linked to securing local consent for the closure of coal mines as part of a World Bank-supported restructuring programme (see Chapter 7; Chapter 8; Swain 2006). Thus, whilst the zones and territories covered a large swathe of the region, they were concentrated in towns most affected by the closure of mines. However, central government's support for the zones and territories was also linked to securing the Donetsk elite's support in Kuchma's re-election campaign. Investment in the designated areas, whether by a domestic or a foreign company, was subject to a preferential tax regime for a specific period of time. Despite a stated aim to encourage diversification and high-technology sectors, it was argued that the zones and territories were simply used to evade taxation and provide cover for illegal economic activities.

Conclusion: an ambiguous transition?

Economic growth in the Donbas since 1999 poses an empirical challenge to the orthodox transition literature. Even though privatisation and macroeconomic stability had been achieved, how can economic growth be explained given the (alleged) absence of structural economic reform or despite the (alleged) presence of rampant rent-seeking 'clans'? Given the comparative inter-oblast analysis undertaken in this chapter, why has the socio-economic record of the Donbas, and Donetsk oblast in particular, been far better than that of other Ukrainian regions, where local economies presumably are not 'locked in' to the excessive 'neo-patrimonialism'? In response it has been argued that growth has in some sense or other been inauthentic, transitory and/or fraudulent. Liberal economists and political scientists have argued that capital accumulation in regions such as the Donbas has resulted from asset sweating, asset stripping and rent seeking in a context of fictitious economic signs. From a leftist Marxist position it would be argued that the region has not been subsumed to the law of capital in a *real* sense and that a form of primitive accumulation is taking place in the region. One has to add the conservative nationalist Ukrainian position which portrays the entire region as pathogenic per se, and its inhabitants and their experiences as deviant, 'Russianised' and untruly Ukrainian in nature. Curiously the diagnosis and prescribed medicine of both the liberals and the leftists are essentially the same: namely that the region requires a dose of technocratic economic rationalism involving the emulation of advanced capitalist countries. Suggestions emanating from the nationalist camp are often of a more harsh nature (Lubkivskyi 2006).

However, drawing on the theorisation of the emergence of varieties of post-Soviet capitalism, there is an alternative way of answering the question. This entails questioning the extent to which structural economic reform really has been absent and highlighting the self-reorganisation that has taken place in the region. We want to conclude this chapter by suggesting that critiques of regions such as the Donbas from both the liberal and the Marxist tradition are at least in part the product of a colonial Western-centric view that renders invisible the actually occurring transformations. Could it be the case that an emergent indigenous capitalism that is not a satellite client of the Euro-Atlantic geo-economic bloc has provoked a process of de-legitimisation or 'othering'? Equally, could it not be the case that the dominant discourses of political and economic 'reform', which conform to the prevailing orthodoxy amongst transnational policy elites, aim to reconstitute 'an economy' as an object which is defined by Western categories precisely so that it becomes a malleable object to the instruments of Western power? (See also Swain 2006; Chapter 8.)

It is our contention that many of the economic and political practices associated with economic development in the Donbas are ambiguous and may be 'read' in different ways. Put more prosaically, is it so bad that steel plants in the Donbas have been able to compete on international markets and earn significant export revenues which have been recycled around the region? Would it have been better if crude economic logic had resulted in the closure of more mines and some steel works with the resultant increases in poverty, energy insecurity and reduced competition for foreign steel companies? Instead of emphasising the strong tradition of paternalist social solidarity that exists in the Donbas, we read of 'authoritarianism' and 'cognitive lock-in'. Instead of highlighting the rise of successful capitalist entrepreneurs we read of 'oligarchs' with questionable backgrounds and supposedly dubious motives. Instead of focusing on the emergence of increasingly diversified international companies out of the ruins of the state-planned industrial economy, we read of opaque 'financial industrial groups' that solely engage in allegedly corrupt practices. Instead of celebrating the way regional corporatism has stimulated economic growth we read of collusion between nefarious private interests and renegade public officials solely motivated by personal enrichment. Instead of revealing the self-reorganisation, we read of asset stripping, asset sweating and rent seeking. Instead of a critical engagement with an indigenous capitalism, involving local capital accumulation and local expanded reproduction, and which has its faults, we read of neo-patrimonialism and regional 'lock-ins'. Local capital accumulation cements the region's position in the embryonic national economy and in the global economy. By not relying on foreign investment, the region limits its exposure to rapidly switching international capital. That the Donbas's family silver has been reserved for locals may be a source of annoyance to predatory Western companies supported by their sponsors in Western governments and international financial institutions, but it is hardly a crime and might even be a cause for celebration.

Notes

1 In an assessment of Ukrainian output developments in 2000–2001, the International Monetary Fund (Berengaut *et al.* 2002) has noticed no major changes in the structural policy environment in Ukraine precipitating the return to economic growth. Instead, the IMF stressed 'an eclectic explanation involving a confluence of factors specific to Ukraine', which were 'at least not inimical to output growth'. In addition to the favourable role of external factors (e.g. export performance, export market growth and real exchange rate), restructuring through 'learning by doing', and reduced real wages, the Ukrainian mix of pro-growth variables according to the IMF also included 'changes in the Oligarchs' Objective Function' from the re-distribution of assets to the engagement in productive activity.

2 'Soft budget constraint' is a termed coined by János Kornai – a dissident Hungarian economist inspired by the libertarian writings of von Mises and von Hayek – to describe the ill-natured 'paternalistic' role of the state towards economic organisation, private firms, non-profit institutions and households (1980, 1992, 1998).

3   Recently Wilson (2005) has extended the virtual economy thesis to include the way non-representative parties in the FSU simply act in ways to support the commercial interests of party benefactors.
4   For similar arguments in central Europe see Staniszkis (1991) on 'political capitalism' and Eyal *et al.* (1997, 1998) on 'managerial capitalism'.
5   We would like to thank the following people for their assistance in compiling the official statistics: Mike Chambers (and his colleagues at Actiondonbass), Alexey Danilin, Svitlana Dem'yanova and Illya Khadzhynov. We would also like to thank Chris Lewis, Cartographic Unit, School of Geography, University of Nottingham, for drawing the maps.
6   References in the text to a specific rayon also include all the cities located within its mapped territory. For example, in Donetsk oblast, we have included the cities of Yasynuvata, Avdiivka, Yenakieve and Yasynuvatskyi rayon itself into the mapped territory of Yasynuvatskyi. Similarly, in Luhansk oblast, Popasnianskyi rayon's data amalgamate both the rayon itself and the cities of Kirovske, Stakhanov, Severodonetsk, Lysychansk and Pervomaisk.
7   As none of the authors of the (neo-)patrimonial approach provides a definition of 'clan', it is rather perplexing to understand whether they refer to a group of people tracing descent from a common ancestor or to a group united by a common interest or common characteristics, or both.

References

Amable, B. (2003) *The Diversity of Modern Capitalism*, Oxford: Oxford University Press.
Aslund, A. (1999) 'Russia's virtual economy: a comment', *Post-Soviet Geography and Economics*, **40**(2): 98–102.
Aslund, A. (2000) 'Why has Ukraine failed to achieve economic growth?', in A. Aslund and G. de Ménil (eds), *Economic Reform in Ukraine: The Unfinished Agenda*, New York: M. E. Sharpe, pp. 255–77.
Aslund, A. (2001) 'Ukraine's return to economic growth', *Post-Soviet Geography and Economics*, **42**(5): 313–28.
Aslund, A. and G. de Ménil (2000) 'The dilemmas of Ukrainian economic reforms', in A. Aslund and G. de Ménil (eds), *Economic Reform in Ukraine: The Unfinished Agenda*, New York: M. E. Sharpe, pp. 3–26.
Berengaut, J., E. de Vrijer, K. Elborgh-Woytek, M. Lewis and B. Lissovolik (2002) 'An interim assessment of Ukrainian output developments, 2000–01', International Monetary Fund Working Paper, WP/02/97 (May).
Borisov, V. and S. Clarke (1994) 'Reform and revolution in the communist national park', *Capital and Class*, **53**: 9–13.
Burawoy, M. (1996) 'The state and economic involution: Russia through a China lens', *World Development*, **24**(6): 1105–17.
Burawoy, M. (2001a) 'Transition without transformation: Russia's involutionary road to capitalism', *East European Politics and Societies*, **15**(2): 269–90.
Burawoy, M. (2001b) 'Neoclassical sociology: from the end of communism to the end of classes', *American Journal of Sociology*, **106**(4): 1099–120.
Burawoy, M. and P. Krotov (1995) 'Russian miners bow to the angel of history', *Antipode*, **27**(2): 115–36.
Campos, N. F. and F. Coricelli (2002) 'Growth in transition: what we know, what we don't, and what we should', *William Davidson Working Paper Series*, 470 (February).
Chang, G. H. (1999) 'Observations on the nature of Russia's virtual economy', *Post-Soviet Geography and Economics*, **40**(2): 114–20.

Chavance, B. and E. Magnin (1997) 'Emergence of path-dependent mixed economies in central Europe', in A. Amin and J. Hausner (eds), *Beyond Market and Hierarchy: Interactive Governance and Social Complexity*, Cheltenham: Edward Elgar, pp. 196–232.

Clarke, S. (2004) 'A very Soviet form of capitalism? The management of holding companies in Russia', *Post-Communist Economies*, **16**(4): 405–22.

Donetsk Oblast Chief Statistical Department (2000) *Donetskaia oblast' v tsifrakh v 1999 godu*, Donetsk: Chief Statistical Department.

Donetsk Oblast Chief Statistical Department (2002) *Statystychnyi shchorichnyk Donetskoi oblasti za 2001 rik*, Donetsk: Chief Statistical Department.

Donetsk Oblast Chief Statistical Department (2004a) *Statystychnyi shchorichnyk Donetskoi oblasti za 2003 rik*, Donetsk: Chief Statistical Department.

Donetsk Oblast Chief Statistical Department (2004b) *Statystychnyi shchorichnyk Donetskoi oblasti za 2003 rik: Dodatok (tablychnyi material)*, Donetsk: Chief Statistical Department.

Dubrovskiy, V. and O. Ivaschenko (eds) (2002) *Ukraine: The Lost Decade... and Coming Boom?*, Kyiv: CASE – Ukraine.

Erdmann, G. (2002) 'Neo-patrimonial rule: transition to democracy has not succeeded', *Development and Cooperation*, **1**: 8–11.

Ericson, R. E. (2000) 'The post-Soviet Russian economic system: an industrial feudalism?', *BOFIT Online*, **8**: 1–25.

Ericson, R. E. (2001) 'Does Russia have a "market economy"?', *East European Politics and Societies*, **15**(2): 291–319.

Eyal, G., I. Szelényi and E. Townsley (1997) 'The theory of post-communist managerialism', *New Left Review*, **222**: 60–92.

Eyal, G., I. Szelényi and E. Townsley (1998) *Making Capitalism without Capitalists: Class Formation and Elite Struggles in Post-Communist Central Europe*, London: Verso.

Friedgut, T. H. (1994) 'Perestroika in the provinces: the politics of transition in Donetsk', in T. H. Friedgut and J. W. Hahn (eds), *Local Power and Post-Soviet Politics*, New York: M. E. Sharpe, pp. 162–83.

Gaddy, C. G. and B. W. Ickes (1998a) 'Russia's virtual economy', *Foreign Affairs*, **77**(5): 53–67.

Gaddy, C. G. and B. W. Ickes (1998b) 'Underneath the formal economy: why are Russian enterprises not restructuring?', *Transition*, **9**(4): 1–5.

Gaddy, C. and B. W. Ickes (1999) 'An accounting model of the virtual economy in Russia', *Post-Soviet Geography and Economics*, **40**(2): 79–97.

Gaddy, C. and B. W. Ickes (2002) *Russia's Virtual Economy*, Washington, DC: Brookings Institution.

Grabher, G. and D. Stark (eds) (1997) *Restructuring Networks in Post-Socialism: Legacies, Linkages and Localities*, Oxford: Oxford University Press.

Hall, P. A. and D. Soskice (eds) (2001) *Varieties of Capitalism: The Institutional Foundations of Comparative Advantage*, Oxford: Oxford University Press.

Hanson, P. and E. Teague (2005) 'Big business and the state in Russia', *Europe–Asia Studies*, **57**(5): 657–80.

Hanson, P. and E. Teague (2006) 'Russian political capitalism and its environment', in D. Lane and M. Myant (eds), *Varieties of Capitalism in Post-Communist Countries*, Basingstoke: Palgrave Macmillan.

Hellman, J. (2000) *Seize the State, Seize the Day: State Capture, Corruption, and Influence in Transition*, Washington, DC: World Bank and European Bank for Reconstruction and Development.

Holmstrom, N. and R. Smith (2000) 'The necessity of gangster capitalism: primitive accumulation in Russia and China', *Monthly Review*, **51**(9): 1–15.

Huber, P. and A. Wörgötter (1998) 'Political survival or entrepreneurial development? Observations on Russian business networks', in S. S. Cohen, A. Schwartz and J. Zysman (eds), *The Tunnel at the End of the Light: Privatization, Business Networks, and Economic Transformation in Russia*, University of California International and Area Studies Digital Collection, Research Series 100, pp. 51–65.

Johnson, J. (1997) 'Russia's emerging financial-industrial groups', *Post-Soviet Affairs*, **13**(4): 333–65.

Kornai, J. (1980) *Economics of Shortage*, Amsterdam: North Holland.

Kornai, J. (1992) *The Socialist System: The Political Economy of Communism*, Oxford: Clarendon Press.

Kornai, J. (1998) 'The place of the soft budget constraint syndrome in economic theory', *Journal of Comparative Economics*, 26: 11–17.

Kupchinsky, R. (2002a) 'The clan from Donetsk (Part 1)', *RFE/RL Poland, Belarus and Ukraine Report*, **4**(45).

Kupchinsky, R. (2002b) 'The clan from Donetsk (Part 2)', *RFE/RL Poland, Belarus and Ukraine Report*, **4**(47).

Kuzio, T. (2002) 'Kuchma replaces prime minister and appoints a possible successor', *RFE/RL Poland, Belarus and Ukraine Report*, **4**(45),

Lane, D. (2000) 'What kind of capitalism for Russia? A comparative analysis', *Communist and Post-Communist Studies*, **33**: 485–504.

Lane, D. and M. Myant (eds) (2006) *Varieties of Capitalism in Post-Communist Countries*, Basingstoke: Palgrave Macmillan.

Lindberg, D. L. (2002) 'The use of barter hampers implementation of International Accounting Standards and contributes to financial woes in the Russian Federation', *Russian and East European Finance and Trade*, **38**(3): 5–17.

Lubkivskyi, I. (2006) 'Ukrainskyi natsional'nyi kharakter', *Sila Naroda: narodnaya gazeta*, 27 February.

Luhansk Oblast Chief Statistical Department (2004) *Statystychnyi shchorichnyk Luhans'koi oblasti za 2003 rik*, Luhansk: Chief Statistical Department.

Marin, D. (2002) 'Trust versus illusion: what is driving demonetization in the former Soviet Union?', *Economics of Transition*, **10**(1): 173–99.

Miller, D. (2002) 'Turning Callon the right way up', *Economy and Society*, **31**(2): 218–33.

Mykhnenko, V. (2003) 'State, society and protest under post-communism: Ukrainian miners and their defeat', in C. Mudde and P. Kopecky (eds), *Uncivil Society? Contentious Politics in Eastern Europe*, Routledge: London, pp. 93–113.

Mykhnenko, V. (2004) *Rusting Away? The Ukrainian Iron and Steel Industry in Transition*, Budapest: Open Society Institute (http://www.policy.hu/mykhnenko/Final_Research_ Paper.pdf, accessed 7 September 2004).

Mykhnenko, V. (2005) 'The political economy of post-communism: a comparison of Upper Silesia (Poland) and the Donbas (Ukraine)', Ph.D. dissertation, Department of Social and Political Sciences, University of Cambridge (http://www.policy.hu/mykhnenko/ Political_Economy_of_Post-Communism.html).

Perotti, E. C. and S. Gelfer (2001) 'Red barons or robber barons? Governance and investment in Russian financial-industrial groups', *European Economic Review*, **45**(9): 1601–17.

Pinto, B., V. Drebentsov and A. Morozov (2000) 'Give macroeconomic stability and growth in Russia a chance: harden budgets by eliminating non-payments', *Economics of Transition*, **8**(2): 297–324.

Sabel, C. and J. Prokop (1996) 'Stabilization through reorganization: some preliminary implications of Russia's entry into world markets in the age of discursive quality standards', in R. Frydman, C. W. Gray and A. Rapaczynski (eds), *Corporate Governance in Central Europe and Russia: Insiders and the State*, Vol. 2, Budapest: Central European University Press, pp. 151–91.

Smith, A. and A. Swain (1998) 'Regulating and institutionalising capitalisms: the micro-foundations of transformation in Eastern and Central Europe', in J. Pickles and A. Smith (eds), *Theorizing Transition: The Political Economy of Change in Central and Eastern Europe*, London: Routledge, pp. 25–53.

Staniszkis, J. (1991) '"Political capitalism" in Poland', *East European Politics and Societies*, **5**: 127–41.

Stark, D. and L. Bruszt (1998) *Postsocialist Pathways: Transforming Politics and Property in East Central Europe*, Cambridge: Cambridge University Press.

Stark, D. and L. Bruszt (2001) 'One way or multiple paths? For a comparative sociology of East European capitalism', *American Journal of Sociology*, **106**(4): 1129–37.

Stiglitz, J. E. (1999) *Whither Reform? Ten Years of the Transition*, Washington, DC: World Bank.

Stoner-Weiss, K. (1997) *Local Heroes: The Political Economy of Russian Regional Governance*, Princeton, NJ: Princeton University Press.

Swain, A. (2006) 'Soft capitalism and a hard industry: virtualism, the "transition industry" and the restructuring of the Ukrainian coal industry', *Transactions and Papers of the Institute of British Geographers*, **31**: 208–33.

Tompson, W. (1999) 'The price of everything and the value of nothing? Unravelling the workings of Russia's "virtual economy"', *Economy and Society*, **28**(2): 256–80.

Ukraine State Statistics Committee (1996) *Statystychnyi shchorichnyk Ukrainy za 1995 rik*, Kyiv: Tekhnika.

Ukraine State Statistics Committee (2000) *Statystychnyi shchorichnyk Ukrainy za 1999 rik*, Kyiv: Tekhnika.

Ukraine State Statistics Committee (2001) *Statystychnyi shchorichnyk Ukrainy za 2000 rik*, Kyiv: Tekhnika.

Ukraine State Statistics Committee (2002) *Statystychnyi shchorichnyk Ukrainy za 2001 rik*, Kyiv: Tekhnika.

Ukraine State Statistics Committee (2004a) *Vseukrainskii perepys naselennia '2001. Rezul'taty: Pro kil'kist' ta sklad nasellennia Ukrainy za pidsumkamy Vseukrains'koho perepysu naselennia 2001 roku*, Kyiv: Ukraine State Statistics Committee (available at http://www.ukrcensus.gov.ua/results/general).

Ukraine State Statistics Committee (2004b) *Statystychnyi shchorichnyk Ukrainy za 2003 rik*, Kyiv: Tekhnika.

Ukraine State Statistics Committee (2004c) *Rynok pratsi Ukrainy za 2003 rik: Dopovid' 8 kvitnia 2004 r.*, Kyiv: Ukraine State Statistics Committee (available at http://www.ukrstat. gov.ua/).

Ukraine State Statistics Committee (2005a) *Ekspres-informatsiya Derzhkomstatu Ukrainy. Valova dodana vartist' za regionamy Ukrainy za 2003 rik*, Kyiv: Ukraine State Statistics Committee.

Ukraine State Statistics Committee (2005b) *Statystychna informatsiia. Demografichna sytuatsiia: Chusel'nist' naselennia na 1 travnia 2005 roku*, Kyiv: Ukraine State Statistics Committee (available at http://www.ukrstat.gov.ua/).

Ukraine State Statistics Committee (2005c) *Rynok pratsi Ukrainy za 2004 rik: Dopovid' 15 chervnia 2005 r.*, Kyiv: Ukraine State Statistics Committee (available at http://www. ukrstat.gov.ua/).

Ukraine State Statistics Committee (2005d) *Ekspres-informatsiya Derzhkomstatu Ukrainy. Kapital'ni investytsii v Ukraini za 2004 rik*, Kyiv: Ukraine State Statistics Committee.

Ukraine State Statistics Committee (2005e) *Ekspres-dopovid' Derzhkomstatu Ukrainy. Investytsii zovnishnioekonomichnoi diial'nosti u 2005 rotsi*, Kyiv: Ukraine State Statistics Committee.

Ukraine State Statistics Committee (2005f) *Ekspres-informatsiya Derzhkomstatu Ukrainy. Indeksy fizychnoho obsiahu vypusku tovariv ta posluh I valovoho regional'noho produktu Ukrainy za 2004 rik*, Kyiv: Ukraine State Statistics Committee.

Ukraine State Statistics Committee (2005g) *Statystychno-analitychnyi ohliad stanu rynku pratsi u 2005 rotsi*, Kyiv: Ukraine State Statistics Committee (available at http://www.ukrstat.gov.ua/operativ/operativ2005/rp/pres-reliz/pres_2005/pres_2005.htm).

Ukraine State Statistics Committee (2006a) *Ekspres-informatsiia Derzhkomstatu Ukrainy. Valovyi regional'nyi product za 2004 rik*, Kyiv: Ukraine State Statistics Committee.

Weber, M. (1968) *Economy and Society: An Outline of Interpretive Sociology*, New York: Bedminster.

Wilson, A. (2005) *Virtual Politics: Faking Democracy in the Post-Soviet World*, New Haven, CT: Yale University Press.

Woodruff, D. M. (1999) *Money Unmade: Barter and the Fate of Russian Capitalism*, Ithaca, NY: Cornell University Press.

Woodruff, D. M. (2000) 'Rules for followers: institutional theory and the new politics of economic backwardness in Russia', *Politics and Society*, **28**(4): 437–82.

Woodruff, D. M. (2004) 'Property rights in context: privatization's legacy for corporate legality in Poland and Russia', *Studies in Comparative International Development*, **38**(4): 82–108.

World Bank (2002) *Transition – The First Ten Years: Analysis and Lessons for Eastern Europe and the Former Soviet Union*, Washington, DC, World Bank.

World Bank (2003a) *Regional Development Study*, Kyiv: World Bank (copy available from the authors).

World Bank (2003b) *The Major Problems of Development of the Coal Sector and Donbass Region*, Kyiv: World Bank (copy available from the authors).

Zimmer, K. (2004) 'The captured region: actors and institutions in the Ukrainian Donbass', in M. Tatur (ed.), *The Making of Regions in Post-Socialist Europe: The Impact of Culture, Economic Structure and Institutions*, Vol. 2, Wiesbaden: VS Verlag, pp. 231–348.

Zimmer, K. (2005a) 'Die Kohle, der Clan und die Macht. Zur politischen Anatomie des Gebiets Donec'k', *Osteuropa*, **55**(1): 34–49.

Zimmer, K. (2005b) 'Klientelismus im neopatrimonialen Staat. Regionale Machtsicherung in der Ukraine', *Osteuropa*, **55**(10): 59–74.

Zon, H. van (2001) 'Neo-patrimonialism as an impediment to economic development: the case of Ukraine', *Journal of Communist Studies and Transition Politics*, **17**: 71–95.

Zon, H. van (2005) 'The regional economy of Donetsk', *Geographia Polonica*, **78**(2): 77–91.

2 The reform of Ukraine's energy complex and its consequences for Donetsk

Hans van Zon

Introduction

The energy sector is a key factor in the economic development of Ukraine and more in particular of Donetsk oblast. A little over 40 per cent of Ukraine's energy consumption is imported, mainly from Russia (World Bank 2004: 14). In 2003, 37 per cent of Ukraine's imports consisted of energy, while exports consisted 37 per cent of low-quality and energy-intensive steel and 15 per cent of energy. Power and energy production together with steel production accounted in 2001 for 63.5 per cent of the country's industrial production. From an international perspective this is an extraordinary situation and means that the modalities of change in the energy sector determine to a large extent the development of other sectors. In this chapter I analyse reforms in the energy sector and their possible consequences for Donetsk oblast. The chapter is organised in the following way. The problems of energy consumption and domestic trade in energy are analysed first. This is then followed by an examination of domestic energy production, energy imports and Ukraine's energy dependence on Russia. Finally the chapter considers the consequences of market-oriented reforms for the energy economy in Donetsk oblast. This is then followed by some concluding remarks.

Waste of energy

In Soviet times, enterprises and households did not have any incentive to economise on energy consumption. Enterprises consumed huge amounts of energy that was delivered at a very low price because the Soviet Union possessed enormous energy reserves. Moreover, all enterprises operated with soft budget constraints that meant that the state automatically covered any losses. This resulted in the Soviet Union becoming one of the most energy-intensive economies in the world. The situation changed after Ukraine became independent in 1991. Ukraine imported almost half of its energy needs and soon had to pay commercial prices for oil and gas that was mainly supplied by Russia. Although not all delivered energy was paid for and Russia regularly cut supplies, the increase in energy prices had an enormous impact upon the economic situation in Ukraine. Higher energy prices contributed to an economic collapse (production declined 65 per cent between 1991 and 1996) and partly explains why Ukraine's economy performed so much worse than Russia's. Various estimates show that this supply shock reduced GDP by more than 10 per cent (von Hirschhausen and Vincentz 2000: 63).

Although Ukraine paid much more for its energy, the wasteful attitude of households and enterprises towards energy usage hardly changed. Enterprises paid more for energy but the budget constraints of big state-owned enterprises and many privatised enterprises remained rather soft, and the non-payment of energy bills often did not result in the curtailment of energy supplies. On the other hand, newly founded private enterprises usually had to pay for energy and had incentives to minimise energy consumption. Although households had to pay more for their energy, they were not provided with the means to diminish energy consumption. Even in early 2006 only one-third of households had individual heating and/or gas meters.[1] Household energy bills did not relate to actual energy consumption but rather to the size of the house and the number of occupants. The local energy providers responded to the lack of energy supplies by switching district heating systems on later in autumn and switching them off earlier in springtime.

The change in the industrial structure of the economy contributed to the energy crisis (see Chapter 4). The share of energy-intensive industries, such as heavy metallurgy and the chemical industry, increased from the early 1990s. Heavy metallurgy as a share of total industrial production increased from 14.4 per cent in 1990 to 22.1 per cent in 2003, mainly as a result of increased exports of steel. The energy intensity of heavy metallurgy was such that, had the cost of energy been correctly reflected in the price of the steel, much of it would not have been internationally competitive. In the mid-1990s energy accounted for 60 per cent of the production costs of cast iron in Ukraine compared to 18 to 25 per cent in OECD countries (*Zerkalo Nedeli*, 5 January 2002). In 2003, 46 per cent of steel was produced in open-hearth furnaces (Martin ovens) that had been replaced by Western companies decades earlier. No other country in the world had such a high share of steel production by Martin ovens.[2] However, the steel enterprises depended on artificially low energy prices and were consequently faced with anti-dumping procedures in export markets.

Primary energy consumption in relation to GDP in purchasing power terms (PPP) in 1999 was five times higher in Ukraine than in western Europe and higher than in all the other countries of the former Soviet Union (Russia consumed 3.2 times the west European level). Energy use per capita in Ukraine was higher than in Poland in 2002 (2,694 kilograms of oil equivalent per capita against 2,332 kilograms) whilst Poland's GDP per capita was much higher ($5,280 against $970 in PPP). In the late 1990s the share of energy in the cost structure of goods was 25 per cent in Ukraine, 8.3 times more than in France, and four times more than in the USA (Balmaceda 2004a). Only in Uzbekistan, Nigeria, Tanzania and Zambia was GDP per unit of energy use lower than in Ukraine in 2001 (World Bank 2004: 144). Energy losses through the energy grid system were enormous; electricity transmission losses in the early 2000s increased from 8 to 10 per cent compared to 3 per cent in the USA (EIA 2005).

Little has been done to reduce the energy intensity of production. According to the Energy Research Institute of the Ukrainian Academy of Sciences the electricity bill could be reduced by 40 per cent through more efficient use of electricity (von Hirschhausen *et al.* 1997: 159). However, as the decline of power consumption has been less than the general decline in industrial production, energy intensity of industrial production has increased since the early 1990s; between 1991 and 1999 the energy intensity of production increased by 50 per cent (Balmaceda 2004a). There was little awareness of the problem of energy waste. There was also the misconception that energy saving technologies were expensive. Some energy conservation projects clearly showed the problem. With the help of a US agency, a school in Lviv insulated its windows and installed a new heating control system which reduced energy use by 43 per cent. This required an investment of $29,000 but resulted in savings of $5,000 per year (*Kyiv Post*, 18 May 2000). Unfortunately, very few institutions followed this example. For example, hospitals continued to spend on average 20 to 30 per cent of their budget on heating, whilst conserving energy would have permitted the transfer of funds to cover salaries and equipment (IMF 1999: 19). Lack of incentives and ignorance prevented energy saving. Also, institutions often did not possess the funds required, and were unable to secure credit, to invest in energy saving programmes.

Energy payments crisis

The wastage of energy was related to the malfunctioning economic system and in particular the malfunctioning energy sector. The role played by energy traders, which 'squeezed' the sector by depriving it of much needed investment, was especially significant. Since independence, energy trading has been one of the most profitable forms of business. The situation was further complicated by the fact that energy traders often won the exclusive right to supply energy to enterprises. This enabled traders to 'squeeze' enterprises, whose managers were often offered a share of the profits. For an example of such an arrangement we may consider the supply of gas to steel works that was common until the privatisation of steel works at the end of the 1990s. A steel enterprise might be told by local public authorities to purchase gas from a specific energy trader. This trader then delivered the gas at a high price and received in exchange a small cash payment and a larger barter payment in the form of undervalued steel. On paper the steel enterprise had only paid for a small proportion of the gas that was supplied. The energy trader would then sell the undervalued steel at a price below the world market price to an offshore steel trader that would be owned by the energy trader. Subsequently this offshore company would sell the undervalued steel at a world market price in an export market. Consequently the energy trader that owned the offshore company accrued a considerable profit. However, on paper both the steel enterprise and the energy trader had made a loss. In many cases steel enterprises were loss making and received direct or indirect subsidies from the state. Energy traders were also on paper loss making and did not pay for all of the energy delivered by energy producers.

Often the state made good the paper losses by subsidising both the energy producers and the energy traders. Until the early 2000s energy traders often bought energy from energy producers using loans guaranteed by the state. When the energy trader failed to pay, the state paid back the loan. Energy traders and producers were the country's largest tax debtors; United Energy Systems, for example, owed the state budget $1.44 billion, a figure that represented more than 17 per cent of the country's budget revenues in 2001 (*Kyiv Post*, 19 September 2001). Fortunes were made through shadowy deals that surrounded the importation of gas. For example, Itera, the Florida-based energy trader that was controlled by the Russian gas company Gazprom, sold gas to Ukraine for a price that was considerably higher than the gas producers' price. The difference between the price charged to customers in Ukraine and the producers' price was accumulated by Itera and Ukrainian energy tycoons. Using their privileged access to Russian gas, Ukrainian energy tycoons made a net profit of about $2 billion per year in the late 1990s whilst their Russian counterparts made an approximately similar amount (Aslund 2001: 318). The organisation of the energy sector favoured the energy traders at the expense of energy producers. As President Kuchma commented in early 2000, '[b]y getting hold of and monopolising the [energy] market, countless intermediaries are making super-profits, looting energy facilities and enterprises' (*The Day*, 22 February 2000). However, the president personally oversaw all developments in the energy sector himself and helped to create this situation. The energy producers were, until recently, all state owned, with the result that the state directly and indirectly sub-sidised the producers. Even though the energy traders accumulated significant profits, they did not invest in the energy transportation infrastructure because off-budget profits were laundered abroad. The deteriorating state of the electricity grid resulted in more power outages each year. Gas leakage also increased each year owing to the poor maintenance of the pipeline system. Most Ukrainian pipelines were designed for a 25-year service life. However, by the early 2000s 54 per cent were at least 21 years old and in a poor state of repair (Balmaceda 2004b: 43). Pumping units were in a particularly poor condition and in 2001 almost 10 per cent of Ukraine's annual gas consumption was used to pump gas through the pipelines (Balmaceda 2004b: 43). Governments under President Kuchma pro-duced a list of enterprises and institutions that could not be disconnected from the energy grid for non-payment. This further aggravated the payments crisis in the energy sector as many of these entities accumulated the highest payment arrears. Successive governments perceived energy as an instrument of government policy rather than as a commodity that had to be paid for.

Reform of the energy sector

Pressure from the IMF, the World Bank and other international financial institutions and donors led the government under Prime Minister Viktor Yushchenko (December 1999–May 2001) to embark on reforming the energy sector in early 2000. The government outlawed barter trade and made it compulsory to settle energy transactions through special government-controlled bank accounts to increase cash payments to energy producers. To eliminate private trading in gas, the state-owned company, Naftohaz Ukraine, was awarded a monopoly to import gas. In addition, a state-owned electricity wholesaler, Enerhorynok, was established to oversee the electricity market. These reforms increased payments to energy producers as well as to the state-owned wholesalers. The banning of barter transactions circumscribed the energy traders that relied on such forms of payment. As many members of the Verkhovna Rada (supreme parliament) were associated with the energy sector and because energy traders had financed the re-election campaign of President Kuchma in 1999, the reforms were continuously criticised and undermined by the state bureaucracy, the presidential administration and the Verkhovna Rada. Moreover, the judiciary also failed to tackle the endemic corruption in the energy sector.[3] Another component of the energy sector reforms was the privatisation of some of the 27 Oblenergos, the regional electricity distributors. In early 2000 six Oblenergos were privatised, often involving opaque methods that involved selling shares cheaply to offshore companies. In early 2001, three more Oblenergos were sold to foreign companies, one of which was a Slovak company backed by Ukrainian investors.

In 2000 the mispricing of energy (i.e. fixing energy prices below the world market level) amounted to 4.7 per cent of GDP, whilst payment arrears for energy deliveries accounted for 1.8 per cent of GDP. According to the IMF, this constituted 'quasi-fiscal activities' because ultimately the government bore the cost (Petri *et al.* 2002). Although collection rates improved, tax and supplier arrears increased following the reforms. In 2000 the estimated stock of debt of state-owned energy monopolies amounted to at least 13 per cent of GDP (IMF 2003). In 2002 Naftohaz accumulated a $1.06 billion debt to the government owing to the non-payment of taxes and the mispricing of gas (World Bank 2003a: 9). This also meant that the company did not have resources for investment. It was unclear whether privatisation of the energy distributors would improve their performance in a socio-economic context that encouraged asset stripping rather than long-term investment. The privatisation of Donbassenergo for a very small sum and its subsequent fragmentation led the government to cease the privatisation of the Oblenergos in 2001 (see Chapter 6).

Despite the reforms, insufficient liquidity and political interference meant that the state of the energy sector continued to deteriorate. Monopolistic suppliers of energy remained and were protected by President Kuchma and his entourage. Monopolisation of energy supply constituted a bigger problem than had barter trade. Moreover, energy traders devised new methods to 'squeeze' the energy sector. This was clearly the case in Donetsk oblast where transactions between mines, steel enterprises, cokes factories and electricity power generators, which were all controlled by local clans, involved new ways by which the clans could siphon off large amounts of money (see Chapters 4 and 6). Indeed the partial implementation of reforms meant increased opportunities for accumulating profits. In 2004 cash payments for electricity reached 95 per cent, and Enerhorynok paid between 92.5 and 93.5 per cent to the power generating companies (*The Day*, 22 June 2004). In 2002 the gas collection rate as a percentage of billings was 90.4

per cent compared to 33.8 per cent in 1999. Cash collections increased during this period from 15.8 to 88.9 per cent (World Bank 2003a: 15).

In January 2001 Yulia Tymoshenko, vice-prime minister responsible for the energy sector, was sacked by President Kuchma and in April 2001 Prime Minister Yushchenko was also removed. Most observers interpreted their removal as a victory for the oligarchs linked to the energy trade and as an indication of just how deeply rooted were the vested interests that profited from a non-reformed energy sector. Energy sector reforms slowed down and almost stalled under Prime Minister Anatoliy Kinakh and his successor Viktor Yanukovych. This meant that the most important problem of the energy sector, rent seeking, had not been resolved. However, greater payments transparency and the decline of barter transactions meant that there were fewer opportunities to steal energy and extract excess profits. Although government subsidies to the energy sector decreased they remained substantial. The indebtedness of the Oblenergos increased to UAH1.3 billion or by 8.7 per cent in 2003 compared to an increase of 13.3 per cent in 2002 (*Zerkalo Nedeli*, 16 April 2004). By early 2004 the total debt for electric energy was UAH16.2 billion.

Although payment collection rates increased, tariffs were still far below the cost recovery level. According to a World Bank analysis, the 2002 tariffs would have to have been 70 per cent higher to achieve full economic value recovery (household tariffs would have to have been 195 per cent higher) (World Bank 2003a: 23). This analysis was based on a number of assumptions including the importation of gas for $50 per 1,000 cubic metres. However, the price of imported gas increased in the early 2000s. The 2003 contract with Turkmenistan priced gas imports at $44 per 1,000 cubic metres with half of the payment in cash. The average price of gas for domestic consumers was $33.68 per 1,000 cubic metres in 2002 while the payment level was around 85 per cent (World Bank 2003a: 46). For political reasons the government could not raise tariffs to achieve full cost recovery levels as the overwhelming majority of the population would not have been able to pay their full bills. Consequently measures designed to conserve energy were considered to be more politically palatable.

Energy production

In 1999, 42 per cent of Ukraine's energy consumption was produced domestically (see Table 2.1). In 2003, 96 per cent of coal, 25.5 per cent of gas and 17.5 per cent of oil were produced domestically. In addition, nuclear power stations produced 45 per cent of the electricity consumed in Ukraine. Ukraine's energy consumption comprised 26 per cent oil, 35 per cent gas, 34 per cent coal and 4 per cent from nuclear and hydroelectric power.

The country's estimated coal reserves, mostly located in the south-east of the country, amount to 45 billion tons, sufficient for between 350 and 400 years. However, mining conditions are difficult and many seams are very deep. After the mid-1970s investment in the mines was reduced as the USSR developed new coalfields farther east. Coal output in Ukraine fell from 216 million tons in 1975

Table 2.1 Energy production in Ukraine

	1990	1995	1999	2001	2003
Coal (million tons)	165.0	83.8	81.8	83.9	80.3
Electric energy (kWh)	298.0	194.0	172.0	173.0	180.4
Gas (m³)	28.1	18.2	18.1	18.3	19.6
Oil (million tonnes)	5.3	4.1	3.8	3.7	3.7

Source: State Statistics Committee 2004.

to 165 million tons in 1990 and since independence production has declined by more than a half. In the middle of 2004, 185 mines were operating compared to 220 in 1996 when a programme of closures began. The quality of coal was poor and the technology obsolete; 75 per cent of all jobs in coal mines were manual. One-third of the mines are more than 50 years old, and some date from the nineteenth century. Since the mid-1970s miners have found themselves in a vicious circle of declining productivity and falling investment leading to greater health and safety problems. In 1998 four miners' lives were lost for every thousand tons of coal extracted (BBC/SWB, FSU, 5 January 1999). Most of the mines remained state owned but were controlled by private financial-industrial groupings (see Chapter 6). Only seven mines operated without a state subsidy (*Kyiv Post*, 4 November 2002). In 2003 the mines were reorganised to form 21 joint stock companies that were to be privatised. However, cross-subsidisation continued to take place. The most profitable mines were privatised and in early 2005 accounted for more than 35 per cent of coal extraction (*ICPS Newsletter*, 25 April 2005). In some instances in order to demonstrate their political commitment to restructuring the sector, public authorities closed mines. However, many of these were the most profitable mines and were bought cheaply by private investors who reopened them.

The United Kingdom produced 57.9 per cent of the output of Ukraine but with only 3.8 per cent of the employees. This does not take into account that on average Ukrainian coal contained 4,000–5,000 kilocalories per kilogram, compared to the international standard of 7,000 kilocalories per kilogram (von Hirschhausen *et al.* 1997: 155). Coal mines that produced coal at twice the world market price continued to be subsidised whilst conditions for coal mining deteriorated and costs increased. In mid-2002, the mines owed $2 billion to suppliers (*Kyiv Post*, 4 November 2002) and in March 2003 owed $244 million in wages (Radio Free Europe, 4 March 2003). Lack of investment further contributed to low labour productivity and high production costs. This meant that currently unprofitable seams would be profitable if more modern technology was utilised. Some experts have argued that a healthy mining sector could easily produce 150 million tons per year (*Zerkalo Nedeli*, 24 March 2001). The government's 'Ukrainian Coal Programme' envisaged increasing production from 81 million tons in 2001 to 110 million tons by 2010, consisting of 63 million tons of energy coal and 47.1 million tons of coke coal. After 2000, investment in the coal sector increased but this did not result in significant modernisation. This was because of the perverse incentives that existed in the sector; profit from viable mines was extracted by shady business interests whilst unviable mines continued to receive state subsidies. The 60 to 70 most loss-making mines received two-thirds of all subsidies to the sector but produced only 3 to 4 per cent of the coal (*Zerkalo Nedeli*, 24 March 2001; Interfax News Agency, 12 September 2001). Mines that produced coke coal sold to solvent iron and steel works were more financially secure than those that depended on selling energy coal to electric power stations which had large receivable payment arrears (see Chapter 6).

Transparent accounting methods would have shown that large amounts of money disappeared to coal traders' offshore bank accounts. The absence of open competition hindered the performance of coal mines. Other factors, such as direct and indirect state subsidies, meant that an assessment of the performance of coal mines was difficult. However, the elimination of cross-subsidisation and corruption could transform the industry into a viable and profitable sector that would not require state subsidies. Even the World Bank changed its opinion and acknowledged in 2003 that:

> Ukraine possesses a coal resource base of significant value that is capable, under the condition of an effective completion of the sector restructuring program, of providing a considerable share of the coal required by the Ukrainian economy and contributing to the country's energy security.
>
> (World Bank 2003b: 2)

It went on to say that a 'large part of Ukrainian coal could be cost effective in comparison with alternative energy resources, even if the mines had to cover additional expenses for environmental protection and improved mine safety' (World Bank 2003b: 15). The Bank identified the sector's major problem as an 'inappropriate mixture of commercial and public interests' (World Bank 2003b: 17). The prospects of the coal sector also had to be seen in the context of a rapid escalation of coal prices on the world market in the early 2000s (International Energy Agency 2004). However, the clans that controlled the coal trade resisted reform of the sector. These clans profited from state ownership and the opaque management of the sector (output and prices were centrally administered), which provided opportunities for asset stripping. The lack of investment capital in the coal industry prevented the development of methane gas extraction from existing coal mines. Estimates of methane reserves varied from 1 trillion to 20 trillion cubic metres depending on the depth of occurrence. Even though local researchers developed detailed proposals to begin methane extraction, foreign investors were unwilling to invest owing to the poor investment climate in the country (*Zerkalo Nedeli*, 12 June 2000). Moreover, the government and the energy bosses also showed little willingness to invest in methane extraction (*Zerkalo Nedeli*, 15 September 2001).

Ukrainian gas consumption was 66 billion cubic metres in 2001, only 30 per cent below the level of 1990 (for comparison GDP in 2001 was 48 per cent of the 1990 level), whilst domestic production was 18 billion cubic metres. Within Ukraine the state-owned company Naftohaz, founded in 1998 to unite all state oil and gas enterprises, was responsible for most gas and oil extraction and transportation. In April 1996, the national gas distribution system was commercialised, and by mid-2000 the gas market was divided among Naftohaz and ten private firms that together accounted for 80 per cent of the gas supply. By early 2003, Naftohaz had become a monopolist in the wholesale market for gas. As a result of poor payment discipline on the part of its customers, Naftohaz accumulated large debts to the government. Lack of investment led to a deterioration in the condition of the transportation systems; almost one-third of all gas pipelines were poorly coated, resulting in the corrosion of the pipes. Reserves of around 100 trillion cubic metres lie under the Black Sea which if they were developed would meet gas consumption for 25 years (*Zerkalo Nedeli*, 15 September 2001).[4] In order to increase gas production, between $1.5 billion and $2 billion of investment would be required (World Bank 2003a: 10). However, foreign investors were reluctant to invest, especially after a dispute between the British and Ukrainian partners in the Poltava Gas and Oil Company over commitments made by the State Property Agency that were not honoured.

Ukraine produced only 20 to 25 per cent of the oil it consumed. The remainder was imported mainly from Russia. According to the *Oil and Gas Journal*, Ukraine had 395 million barrels of proven oil reserves, mainly located in the Dnipr–Don basin (EIA 2005). With modern technologies, oil production could easily be increased but in their absence production declined. Ukraine had six oil refineries, four of which were owned by Russian companies. Only half of the crude oil was refined into benzene (petrol), diesel and other clean fuels; the other half was supplied as fuel to thermal power stations. Utilisation of modern refining methods would allow between 80 and 90 per cent of crude oil to be refined into high-quality fuels.

In 2000, nuclear power stations generated 45 per cent of Ukraine's electricity. As with all power stations, customers often failed to pay their energy bills. This resulted in the nuclear power stations accumulating wage arrears, lacking funds for investment and maintenance and even the non-payment of nuclear fuels supplied by Russia. The government sought to remedy the situation by designating the most liquid industrial enterprises as privileged customers of Enerhoatom, the umbrella organisation for all nuclear power stations in Ukraine. It was argued that this arrangement would mean Enerhoatom received sufficient cash payments to purchase fuel from Russia. However, Enerhoatom remained in a financially difficult position (at the end of 2001 it had only one-third of the money needed to buy fuel (*Zerkalo Nedeli*, 29 December 2001)), and the measure affected the financial situation of the thermal power stations. A government inquiry found that 40 per cent of Enerhoatom's costs were not directly related to energy production (*Kyiv Post*, 17 February 2000). It was revealed that the intermediary companies that supplied the nuclear fuel received a 30 per cent commission. In addition they received a 23 per cent commission for sending spent fuel back to Russia. According to President Kuchma, in 1999 Enerhoatom provided intermediaries with approximately $300 million worth of electricity at a one-third discount (*The Day*, 22 February 2000). The then minister for energy, Yulia Tymoshenko, accused the

Ukrainian Credit Bank of 'squeezing' Enerhoatom by levying an interest rate of 1 per cent per day on loans (*Kyiv Post*, 22 June 2000). Nuclear power stations did not have sufficient money to maintain safety standards, and poor maintenance meant that all nuclear power stations faced frequent shutdowns. Safety was also undermined by unqualified or poorly qualified personnel. Many qualified nuclear power engineers emigrated to Russia where they were much better paid. In August 2002 it was revealed that several top engineers working at the nuclear power station in Rivne had falsified their educational background (*Kyiv Post*, 10 October 2002). In the same year, payment arrears for water meant supplies to several nuclear power plants were stopped, with supplies only recommencing after protests (Radio Free Europe, 22 October 2002).

The financial situation in thermal power stations was even worse. They were mostly built in the 1960s and 1970s and had already exceeded their anticipated service life, meaning that operating expenses were very high.[5] The electricity sector not only managed to avoid shedding labour but had even increased its labour force by 50 per cent since 1991 (von Hirschhausen and Vincentz 2000: 55). Increasingly, thermal power stations were overloaded (owing to a lack of fuel supplies), which resulted in the automatic shutdown of atomic power stations because of the low frequency in the grid. This in turn meant that thermal power stations became even more overloaded and were forced to cut off energy supplies to customers, especially those in the countryside. Owing to the lack of maintenance, distribution losses soared during the 1990s from 13 per cent of total electricity sales in 1996 to 18 per cent in 2002 (in comparison, losses in Hungary were 12 per cent in 1998, and the world standard is 5 to 6 per cent) (Reuters, 19 February 2003).

A major problem for all energy producers was their dependence on Russia and other former Soviet Union countries for equipment such as electricity transforming and transmission equipment, units of refinery equipment, pumping stations and nuclear reactor parts. The break-up of the Soviet Union significantly affected the Ukrainian energy complex. For example, uranium was extracted in Ukraine before being processed into nuclear fuel in Russia and exported to Ukraine. Used fuel was then returned to Russia for reprocessing. Energy producers were 'squeezed' by intermediaries and had little incentive to invest. Investment in the energy complex in 2000 was between 25 and 60 per cent of the level in 1990.[6] In 2002 the operational deficit in the energy sector was approximately 2 to 3 per cent of GDP (IMF 2003). Domestic energy production could be increased significantly by reforming the sector to reduce subsidies and encourage investment. It can be concluded that energy production was 'squeezed' by energy traders that found willing accomplices amongst the senior management of the energy producing companies. Rent-seeking parasitic structures rather than barter transactions constituted the major obstacle to the creation of a better-functioning energy sector. After the Orange Revolution little changed in the energy sector.

Energy imports

During the 1990s on average half of domestically consumed energy was imported, and between 35 and 50 per cent of these imports were from Russia. Between 1991 and 1994 Ukraine had great difficulties paying for Russian oil and gas and consequently accumulated debts to Russia even though Russia continued to charge prices well below the world market price. Russia tried to use this as leverage by linking energy supplies to political demands, especially during 1993–1994 when interruptions of energy supplies led to the closure of enterprises and schools. Consequently in the early 1990s the Ukrainian government prioritised coal mining and nuclear power in order to reduce its dependence on Russian energy. Ukraine withstood Russia's demands by, for example, refusing to sell a majority stake in a gas pipeline that transits the country. From mid-1994, Western lending helped Ukraine pay its energy bill; the USA realised that Ukrainian independence was at stake. Meanwhile Russia steadily increased oil and gas prices. Russian and Ukrainian energy traders colluded in shadowy transactions in which both sides profited. For example, if Russian traders sold gas to Ukraine for $28 per 1,000 cubic metres, they still made a profit as gas was sold to end consumers in the Russian market for $24 per 1,000 cubic metres (BKC Broker Service, 15 March 2005). Also the Ukrainian party to the transaction could make a profit by selling the gas for approximately $35 per 1,000 cubic metres in the domestic market or by re-exporting the gas to Europe (in 2004 west European gas import prices were about $120 per 1,000 cubic metres).

Ukraine did not respond to its energy dependence by reforming the sector and even with Western financial and diplomatic assistance it continued to have difficulties securing energy supplies from Russia. However, at times Russia was willing to agree to barter transactions that were not always favourable and even accepted payment arrears. For example, in 1994 and 1995 Gazprom accepted settlement of a part of the gas debt with the delivery of paper (*Kyiv Post*, 17 November 2000). Later, gas was also delivered in exchange for 11 strategic bomber aircraft and food. The 1997 agreement relating to the Black Sea Fleet cleared $3.07 billion of Ukraine's debt to Russia in exchange for Ukraine granting permission for Russia to use military equipment and rent a naval base in Sevastopol. During the late 1990s Ukraine illegally siphoned off gas destined for central Europe, western Europe and Turkey. Following the election of Vladimir Putin as president in 2000, Russia began to demand prompt cash payments and began to levy value added tax. Ukraine responded by trying to diversify its gas and oil suppliers, but its poor payments record ensured this was difficult. It was foreseen that between 2002 and 2006 approximately 60 per cent of Ukraine's gas imports would be supplied by Turkmenistan (this compared to 45 per cent in 2002) (*Zerkalo Nedeli*, 29 March–4 April 2003). However, this gas would have to flow through pipelines that were controlled by Russia's Gazprom.

A number of other problems relating to gas imports emerged. In mid-2001 the Ukrainian gas importer Itera changed its practice and began to mix gas supplies from Russia and Turkmenistan. After Ukrainian power stations failed to pay for the delivery of Russian gas, Itera delayed payments to the pipeline company that transported Turkmen gas to Ukraine. As a result the non-payment by Ukraine of Russian gas was turned into a problem for Turkmenistan with the result that the latter reduced its gas supplies to Ukraine. Intermediaries, first Itera and subsequently Eural Trans Gas, charged Ukraine 41 per cent and 38 per cent respectively as a transit fee for gas from Turkmenistan (*Kyiv Post*, 6 March 2003). The transit fees from Russian gas flowing to Europe were an important source of revenue for Ukraine. In the early 2000s annual revenues from gas transit totalled approximately $1.5 billion. In 2002 Ukraine received $141 million in cash and 26 billion cubic metres of gas in kind. These receipts were primarily used to subsidise domestic energy consumption rather than to fund investment in the decrepit gas transport infrastructure. As Russian gas was purchased below the world market price, Ukraine re-exported 7.5 billion cubic metres (World Bank 2003a: 63). It was alleged that many re-export contracts were fraudulent but Ukraine claimed only to export domestically produced gas. Russia responded to the continuous stealing and re-exporting of its gas by proposing a new gas pipeline to Europe via Belarus. Re-routeing gas supplied to western Europe through Belarus would deprive Ukraine of transit fees worth one-third of the domestic consumption of natural gas. In February 2005 Russia agreed with Germany to construct a gas pipeline from Russia to Germany under the Baltic Sea.

Russian leverage over energy supplies to Ukraine appeared to have played a role in the reorientation of foreign policy towards Russia after 2001. In 2002 Russia and Ukraine established a consortium, in which Russia had a 50 per cent share, to manage the pipeline that transported Russian gas through Ukraine to Europe. According to the former American ambassador to Ukraine, Carlos Pascual, 'Gazprom has a veto over Ukraine's management of its own gas transit system. Gazprom cannot be happier: this has been one of the things that they have been seeking since 1992' (www.csis.org, 9 January 2003). Moreover, in early 2003 the ambassadors of Germany, Poland and the USA urged Ukraine to retain control over the Odesa–Brody oil pipeline and connect it to a pan-European energy transport scheme through which oil from the Caspian basin would flow from Brody to Odesa rather than the other way around. However, it appeared few Western companies were prepared to invest in the scheme.

Russia had always supported President Kuchma, especially after a scandal in which tapes secretly recorded in the presidential offices implicated him in the murder of a critical journalist and resulted in his international isolation. Consistently Russia shunned Ukrainian politicians who were either critical of Kuchma or perceived to be too close to the West. Russia appeared to have a strategic interest in an unreformed Ukrainian energy sector as it provided Russia with ample opportunities to exert pressure on Ukrainian politicians who were implicated in shadowy and corrupt energy transactions. Consequently a non-reformed energy sector helped to keep Ukraine dependent on Russian energy and provided Russia with the leverage needed to influence Ukrainian policies. Whilst reliance on Russian energy resulted in cheap energy for Ukraine, it came at the price of larger Russian influence over Ukrainian affairs. Following the Orange Revolution, when Ukraine reoriented its foreign policy and made preparations for NATO entry, Russia changed its policy. In January 2006 Gazprom signed a contract with Naftohaz in which the gas price for the first half of 2006 was fixed at $95 per 1,000 cubic metres compared to the $60 per 1,000 cubic metres Ukraine paid in 2005. This consisted of a mixture of Turkmen gas for $60 and Russian gas for $230 and was still well below world market levels (customers in western Europe pay more than $200 per 1,000 cubic metres). It was agreed that the company Rosukrenergo (a Russian–Ukrainian joint venture) would deliver the gas coming from or through Russia and would also deliver gas to the lucrative market of Ukrainian industrial enterprises. The gas deal, which was signed after Russia interrupted gas supplies for several days, created a political storm in Ukraine. President Yushchenko had already said in April 2005 that '[t]he main task . . . is to make Ukraine energy independent in the full sense of that phrase, from gas and oil supplies to electricity' (Interfax, 27 April 2005). However, a new consistent energy policy had not been formulated and gas trade with Russia continued to be conducted on a non-transparent basis.

The reform of the energy sector and the consequences for Donetsk

Compared to other Ukrainian oblasts, the economic structure of Donetsk was dominated by energy-intensive heavy industry with unfavourable future prospects (see Chapter 4). In 2002 ferrous metals accounted for 38.9 per cent of industrial production in Donetsk while coal mining accounted for 16.9 per cent and electric power generation 12.9 per cent. Moreover, non-payment for energy was more common in Donetsk than in Ukraine as a whole. In 2004 only 78 per cent of energy deliveries were paid for and in January 2005 only 66 per cent, the lowest percentages for Ukraine (*Ukrayinska Pravda*, 10 February 2005). Market-oriented reform of the energy sector would result in redundancy for many miners in Donetsk, although output would not necessarily decline. Energy inputs for the steel industry, which was so important for the Donetsk economy, would become more expensive. However, the competitiveness of the steel industry also depended on other factors such as the use of energy saving technologies and the quality of the steel. Reform of the energy sector could be expected to increase demand for companies producing equipment for the sector. For example, the production of pipes for the oil and gas industry was concentrated in Donetsk oblast. Higher energy prices and a better investment climate could also mean that methane, gas and oil fields in and near Donetsk could be exploited, providing an impetus for regional development.

Market-oriented reform would also entail breaking up the monopolies created by the Donetsk clans (see Chapter 6). Greater transparency would expose the rent-seeking behaviour of the Donetsk conglomerates. However, further privatisation of the energy sector might strengthen the grip of the clans on the energy sector in Donetsk. Consequently, market-oriented reforms need to be accompanied by a new power configuration in the region, involving a reduction in the power of the Donetsk clan and a lessening of its grip on the regional authorities. Currently, energy dependence upon Russia is one of the main arguments for subsidising the coal industry (along with a fear of the social consequences if subsidies were cut). Only radical economic reform leading to energy conservation and an increase in domestic energy production would diminish dependence on Russian energy imports.

Conclusion

During 15 years of continual shortfalls of energy supplies, especially during winter-time, Ukraine has done very little to promote energy conservation measures and little to reform the energy sector. Reform could save billions of hryvnia per year that could be invested to increase domestic production of coal, gas, nuclear energy and methane. The reform of the energy sector that took place in 2000 was half-hearted. Although collection rates improved, mispricing, payment arrears and rent seeking continued to constitute a significant drain on the energy sector. Attempted reform highlighted the bottlenecks in the energy sector and the deeply rooted vested interests that block energy reform. Under President Putin, Russia's attitude to Ukraine's payment arrears and unauthorised siphoning off of gas became stricter. Diversification of energy sources was made difficult because of Ukraine's poor payments record and because the shipment of non-Russian energy has to pass through Russian territory. Lack of reform in the energy sector will further undermine Ukrainian sovereignty while giving Russia greater economic leverage. Donetsk is even more dependent on the energy sector than Ukraine as a whole and consequently the relationship with Russia is more important there. A reform scenario might mean less employment for miners but new development potential in other sectors.

Notes

1   Official website of the President of Ukraine, 11 February 2006 (http://www.president. gov.ua/).
2   In 2003 Russia was second on the list with 23.7 per cent of steel production in Martin ovens. China had no steel production in Martin ovens (International Iron and Steel Institute 2004). In the mid-1990s, 60 per cent of Ukrainian steel was produced in Martin ovens and this figure was decreasing only slowly.
3   Yulia Tymoshenko, vice-prime minister responsible for fuel and energy in the government of Yushchenko, complained that the general prosecutor failed to instigate criminal proceedings against embezzlement in the energy sector (Radio Free Europe, 11 October 2000).
4   According to the *Oil and Gas Journal*, Ukraine had gas reserves of 40 trillion cubic feet. According to *World Pipelines* journal, proven gas reserves in Ukraine totalled 560.7 billion cubic metres in 2005.
5   The majority of equipment at thermal power stations was installed in the 1960s and 1970s. Eighty per cent of equipment had been in use for more than 30 years. Ninety-eight out of 104 energy generating units had exceeded their design lifetime, and 66 of them had exceeded their lifetime limit (Gesellschaft für Anlagen- und Reaktorsicherheit 2000: 15).
6   Investment in 2000 as a percentage of 1990 was 25.5 per cent in the coal industry, 53 per cent in electric energy generation, 62 per cent in the oil industry and 59 per cent in the gas industry. For industry as a whole the figure was 29.7 per cent (State Statistics Committee 2002: 219).

References

Aslund, A. (2001) 'Ukraine's return to economic growth', *Post-Soviet Geography and Economics*, **42**(5): 313–28.

Balmaceda, M. M. (2004a) 'Ukraine's energy policy and US strategic interests in Eurasia', *Kennan Institute Occasional Papers Series*, 291, Washington, DC: Kennan Institute.

Balmaceda, M. M. (2004b) 'Ukraine's persistent energy crisis', *Problems of Post-Communism*, July/August: 40–50.

Energy Information Association (EIA) (2005) *Ukraine Country Analysis Brief*, Washington, DC: EIA.

Gesellschaft für Anlagen- und Reaktorsicherheit (2000) *Primary Energy: Report 2 within the Project 'Tschernobyl Aktionsprogramm 1999', Review and Analysis of Basic Data and Development of a Future Concept for the Modernisation of the Ukrainian Power Sector*, Darmstadt: Gesellschaft für Anlagen- und Reaktorsicherheit.

Hirschhausen, C. von and V. Vincentz (2000) 'Energy policy and structural reform', *Eastern European Economics*, **38**(1): 51–70.

Hirschhausen, C. von, I. Lunina and T. Vachnenko (1997) 'Die Energiewirtschaft der Ukraine: Bestandsaufnahme und Reformbedarf zur Unternehmisierung', in L. Hoffman and A. Siedenberg (eds), *Aufbruch in die Marktwirtschaft: Reformen in die Ukraine von innen betrachtet*, Frankfurt/New York: Campus Verlag, pp. 144–62.

International Energy Agency (2004) *World Energy Outlook 2004*, Paris: International Energy Agency.

International Iron and Steel Institute (2004) *World Steel in Figures – 2003*, Brussels: International Iron and Steel Institute.

International Monetary Fund (IMF) (1999) *Ukraine: Recent Economic Trends*, Washington, DC: IMF.

International Monetary Fund (IMF) (2003) *Concluding Statement of the 2003 IMF Article IV Consultation Mission*, Washington, DC: IMF.

Petri, M., G. Taube and A. Tsyvinski (2002) 'Energy sector quasi-fiscal activities in the countries of the former Soviet Union', *IMF Working Paper*, March, WP/02/60, Washington, DC: International Monetary Fund.

State Statistics Committee (2002) *Statistisjnii Tsbornik Ukraini 2001*, Kyiv: State Statistics Committee.

State Statistics Committee (2004) *Statistisjnii Tsbornik Ukraini 2003*, Kyiv: State Statistics Committee.

World Bank (2003a) *Ukraine: Challenges Facing the Gas Sector*, Washington, DC: World Bank.

World Bank (2003b) *The Coal Sector and Mining Communities of Ukraine: Advancing Restructuring to the Benefit of All*, Washington, DC: World Bank.

World Bank (2004) *World Development Indicators 2004*, Washington, DC: World Bank.

3 Regional politics in Ukraine's transition

The Donetsk elite

Elena Kovaleva

Introduction

Following independence Ukraine experienced a failed democratic transition. Until the Orange Revolution there had not been an irreversible manifestation of democratisation and the consolidation of Ukrainian society. Rather the legacies of the Soviet period had been transformed into a pseudo-democratic regime balancing on the edge of authoritarianism. The most important cause of this development was the role played by Ukrainian elites in the transition process. As with all transitions imposed from above, Ukraine's path of development crucially depended on the elites' visions of transformation and was defined by intra-elite interaction (Sorensen 1998: 55–6). While the accumulation of economic might and political power is a common aim of elite behaviour during unstable periods, the formation of oligarchic clans is a specific post-communist factor in the former Soviet Union. The patrimonial communism[1] of the past has produced a copy of itself adjusted to new economic and political conditions.

Owing to the way clans reproduce themselves, the clan has become a fundamental characteristic of political behaviour with particular traits. Reciprocal exchange of benefits and loyalty, together with patronage, corruption and clientelistic networks that involve hierarchical patterns of subordination, has created the rules of the game, and has become obligatory for any actors seeking to join the game. Whilst these forms of organisation have remained constant, the criteria used to define who is included in and excluded from particular clans have in part altered. Whilst economic wealth has replaced ideology as the prime factor in determining clan membership, position in the state administrative system, which provides immediate access to material gains, has became even more significant than it was during the Soviet era.

The orthodox view that leftist political parties have been the main obstacles to economic and political reforms has not been the case in Ukraine. Here elite groups that benefited significantly from reforms made during earlier transformation stages have sought to oppose further reform in case it undermines their power. According to Hellman's partial reform concept, the major impediments to reform have come not from the left but from:

enterprise insiders who have become new owners only to strip their firms' assets; from commercial bankers who have opposed macroeconomic stabilization to preserve their enormously profitable arbitrage opportunities in distorted financial markets; from local officials who have prevented market entry into their regions to protect their share of local monopoly rents; and from so called mafiosi who have undermined the creation of a stable legal foundation for the market economy.

(Hellman 1998: 203)

These industrial, financial, administrative and criminal groups, whom Hellman identifies as 'short-term winners', have become central to the regional and central clientelistic networks that monopolise the country's power and resources. Those who have been critical of the existence of these networks have been silenced by a variety of different means – from no-confidence votes and direct administrative interference to assassinations. The logic of Ukraine's transition has been determined by both rivalry between different regional and central clans over political power and economic resources, and the way rival groups have co-operated to modify economic reforms which could have ended the clans' monopolistic control over parts of the economy.

This chapter analyses the way the Donetsk elite achieved not only local political power but also subsequently political power at the national scale. It considers the political evolution of the Donetsk clan, one of the most powerful in the country, and discusses its role in Ukraine's transition. Clan political behaviour, which may be defined as the preoccupation by the elite with rent seeking and the influence of political office for their own interests, has become a commonplace characteristic of Ukraine's entire political elite. The instituted political regime reproduces such a type of political behaviour at all spatial scales – from the local and regional to the national scale. In this context, the Donetsk elite is not unique; it simply follows the commonly accepted rules. What appears to be unique, however, is the degree to which power is abused and the cohesion amongst clan members who are loyal to the group's interests.

When big business becomes big politics

Donetsk oblast, one of the most inhabited and industrially developed regions in Ukraine, possesses substantial resources to influence the country's development. Donetsk oblast produces nearly a quarter of gross industrial production and along with two other oblasts – Dnipropetrovsk and Kharkiv – is a net contributor to the state budget. The total production of the region's economy consists 62 per cent of industrial production, 14 per cent of construction, 7 per cent of transport and communication, 5 per cent of agriculture, 5 per cent of services and 7 per cent of food industry and others. Of the 62 per cent of industrial production, the production of ferrous and non-ferrous metals accounts for 46 per cent, the production of fuel and energy for 31 per cent and the production of heavy machinery for 9 per cent (Donetsk Oblast Administration 2000: 10). The structure of the oblast's economy reflects the main problem of Ukraine: the absence of structural reforms and the predominance of obsolete heavy industries, especially the metallurgical and coal sectors.

Paradoxically, these unreformed heavy industrial sectors play a crucial role in the national economy. In total, 20 per cent of Ukraine's manufacturing is concentrated in Donetsk oblast. Moreover, plants in Donetsk oblast produce 95.8 per cent of all rolling equipment, 54.3 per cent of coke, 50.5 per cent of all finished rolling products, 49.8 per cent of steel and 47.5 per cent of pig iron (Donetsk Oblast Administration 2000: 10). Ferrous and non-ferrous metals account for almost 40 per cent of Ukraine's exports (IMF 1999: 124). Three out of the five largest metallurgical plants in the country are located in Donetsk oblast and in addition another 80 plants export metal products to 59 countries. The largest metallurgical plants, such as Azovstal and Illich steel works, have often been the subject of international anti-dumping investigations. The cut-throat competition between rival elites for control over metallurgical enterprises has been a feature of the domestic political and economic scene for the last ten years. The coal industry, the most important economic symbol of the region, produces 54.4 per cent of all Ukraine's coal and is undergoing a difficult reform process. Owing to the high cost of coal, output has been decreasing during the last few years. According to Mykola Volynets, the leader of the Independent Trade Union Centre (NPH), the coal industry in Donetsk oblast, which he describes as 'the most corrupt of all', requested approximately 5 billion hryvnia of budget funding but only received 2 billion (BBC Monitoring Service, 19 July 2001). Simultaneously the coking coal sector, which supplies the metallurgical industry, accumulates huge profits owing to the existence of several mediating companies that monopolise the market. Companies such as the Industrial Union of the Donbass (IUD), ARS, Danko and Embrol-Ukraine have gradually replaced almost a thousand small mediating companies since 1996 to control the coke trade (*Dzerkalo tyzhnya*, 2000, No. 26). As one observer points out:

> It is widely believed that a group of well-connected businessmen is not interested in fast and transparent reform of the coal industry. They are Donetsk businessmen – or 'the Dons' – who have made fortunes by exporting steel cast in the region's numerous steelworks, which burn Donetsk coal bought from local state-subsidized mines at low prices. In short, cheap, state-subsidized coal has made many private fortunes, and public coal mines have become private gold mines.
>
> (Varfolomeyev 2002)

The Donetsk elite has significantly influenced Kyiv's policies and has challenged the further development of market reforms. When the governor of Donetsk oblast, Viktor Yanukovych, was appointed prime minister of Ukraine in November 2002, it was the first example of a regional governor moving to a senior position in the executive power without having previously occupied an intermediate position in the central state administration. In addition, his new Cabinet of Ministers included several other members of the Donetsk elite. Mykola Azarov, formerly the head of the state tax administration, was appointed first deputy prime minister and finance minister; Vitaliy Hayduk, a former director of IUD, became the deputy prime minister for the fuel and energy complex. Other prominent members of the Donetsk elite who moved to Kyiv included Serhiy Tulub, who was appointed minister for energy and later became the director of Enerhoatom, the country's nuclear power company. Former finance minister Ihor Yushko, and Serhiy Lyovochkin, a senior aide to President Kuchma's top aide, were also nominees of the Donetsk elite. The Donetsk group also exercises influence over two parliamentary factions in the Verkhovna Rada (supreme parliament) that was elected in March 2002. Andriy Kliuyev, a member of the Regions of Ukraine Party who was previously the deputy head of the Board on Special Economic Zones in Donetsk oblast, became head of the Committee of the Verkhovna Rada on the fuel and energy complex, nuclear policy and nuclear safety.

Donetsk oblast is the only region of Ukraine that enjoys relative autonomy from the authorities in Kyiv. This is only possible because of the co-operation amongst the local elite to defend their extra-profits. The economy of the region is characterised by the domination of heavy industries that are difficult and costly to modernise. This has meant that the state budget has not been able to finance structural reform over an extended period of time, with the result that public oversight of the reform process has been undermined. Currently these industries generate super-profits that in turn create the material preconditions for the elite groups to gradually penetrate the state administration. Whilst the region is de facto economically autonomous, there is no pressure for increased political autonomy but rather a concentration on business expansion beyond the region's borders. Having nominees of the Donetsk elite in key political positions in Kyiv can help to provide opportunities for such expansion.

The failed attempt at political autonomy, 1991–1994

In the first stage of transition the Donetsk elite managed to overcome two different but equally important obstacles on their way to establishing a cohesive network. The elite were able to implement minimal reforms, to resist both workers' and competitor clans' pressure, and to negotiate the central authorities' vision of nation and state building. During the period of the Soviet Union the geographical concentration of the coal industry in Donetsk oblast meant it was a site of both economic and political power. In neighbouring Dnipropetrovsk oblast the presence of plants that specialised in missile manufacturing meant Dnipropetrovsk city was a closed city that produced secrecy, nepotism and a totally controlled workforce. In contrast the labour-intensive industries in Donetsk oblast produced a powerful workers' movement, opposed equally to both Moscow and Kyiv. In 1989 spontaneous mine workers' strikes took place which were organised not by the existing official trade union structures but by ad hoc strike committees. The ordinary workers who led these strikes made broad complaints about, on the one hand, low salaries and inhuman working conditions and, on the other, the lack of consumer goods and the view that Moscow was exploiting them. However, the strikers' appeals did not include any demands for radical economic reforms and nor were they anti-communist. Even though the Ukrainian leadership at the local and Ukrainian scale condemned the strikes, Volodymyr Shcherbytskyi, the secretary of the Communist Party of Ukraine, was dismissed.

In 1990–1991 the miners' movement entered a new stage characterised by a higher level of political mobilisation with demands being directed at the appa-ratchiks, the Communist Party and the official trade unions. The all-Soviet Union congresses of coal miners that were organised in June and October of 1990 resulted in the establishment of the Independent Trade Union of Coal Miners (NPH) (*Stenogramma II s'yezda shakhtyerov SSSR*, 23 October 1990: 18, 35, 41; 24 October 1990: 14–15; 25 October 1990: 29). However, the NPH never represented the majority of coal miners in the region because of the miners' diverse interests and the continuing existence of the official trade unions. The NPH was only one of several new trade unions of coal miners and there have never been any reliable statistics on the size of its membership. In addition to the NPH, there was the Strike Committee, which had been created in 1989 and which continued to operate and is now, as a semi-trade union, the Trade Union of Coal Workers organised by O. Miller, and a number of other coal workers' organisations. These unions were often based at particular coal mines, and the positions they took often reflected the ambitions of their leaders. The official trade unions, the Trade Union of Coal Industry Employees and the Trade Union of Underground Workers, which were both members of the Federation of Ukrainian Trade Unions, possessed a wide range of economic levers that could be used to substantially influence the workers' movement (Kubicek 1996: 32–3). Furthermore, as Oosterbaan comments, 'since the eastern coal miners have not linked their demands with any other worker's or social movements, labour has not been an inclusive political or social movement nor has it catalyzed the development of civil society' (1997: 2). This period was the only moment when the local elite lost control over the use of strikes to further their own interests. Later, after the declaration of independence, the Donetsk elite skilfully channelled coal miners' strikes to support their own interests.

After the declaration of independence, the Donetsk elite made the transition to the new conditions relatively easily. The 'old' *nomenklatura* who heavily dominated the region did not formulate any affirmative commitment to either market reforms or democratisation. They were not primarily concerned with the ideological, political and cultural aspect of independence nor with the idea of historical justice. Instead they were critical of the way the central authorities in Moscow had in the past extracted industrial surpluses from the region, and they sought ways to ensure such surpluses would lead to the accumulation of private wealth in the region. At this time Kyiv was not regarded as likely to be a serious obstacle to this scenario. The central authorities in Kyiv were preoccupied with the formal attributes of independence and dwelt upon national romanticism, while the local population dominated by Russian-speaking people and Russophiles remained indifferent to the national idea. After independence, local state executive power was automatically transferred to the Donetsk Oblast Executive Committee (Oblvykonkom) and local legislative power to the Donetsk Oblast Council of People's Deputies (Oblrada). However, prior to independence both institutions had never played an independent role and had been totally dominated by the Donetsk Oblast Committee of the Communist Party of Ukraine (Obkom). Leonid Kravchuk, the newly elected president of Ukraine, who had previously been party secretary, simply re-appointed all the heads of all of the Oblradas as representatives of the president of Ukraine in the regions without any system changes.

Yuriy Smirnov, the head of the Donetsk Oblrada, was re-appointed by Presidential Edict 164 of 20 March 1992. He had held office since August 1989, when the Donetsk Oblrada elected him to the position of the head of the Donetsk Oblvykonkom. (He had previously been the second secretary of Donetsk Obkom.) From 11 April to 7 December 1990, Smirnov also performed the function of the head of the Donetsk Oblrada, while his protégé Shcheludchenko occupied the post of the head of the Donetsk Oblvykonkom. Following the acceptance by the Supreme Council of the Ukrainian Soviet Socialist Republic in December 1990 of the 'Law on Local Councils of People's Deputies and Local Self-Governance', Smirnov concentrated both executive and legislative power in his hands. The way Smirnov secured such a powerful position in the region was significant in two ways. First, it was an example of the way Communist Party officials tried to circumvent Gorbachev's policy to prevent first secretaries of Obkoms from also holding the office of the head of the Oblrada. Smirnov was not the first secretary of the Obkom when he took the office of head of the Oblrada as he was a non-party official who was elected because he was an informal nominee of the first secretary. (All of the other candidates were not connected to the party apparatus.) Second, the rise of Smirnov also helps to explain the programmed partiality of reforms because it shows how the administrative system was used to establish clans and, equally, how party apparatchiks formed new elite groups. Following the presidential edict, Smirnov was replaced by his deputy head, Oleksandr Petrenko, as head of the Donetsk Oblrada. In August 1992 Petrenko was in turn replaced by Vadym Chuprun, another former secretary of the Donetsk Obkom, who held the office until June 1994.

During this period Donetsk's 'old' *nomenklatura* attempted to gain political autonomy for the region from Kyiv. Political mobilisation remained high in the region owing to hyperinflation, the scarcity of goods and energy supplies and the proximity of the oblast to Russia where living standards were higher. In 1993 numerous protest movements were organised under the slogan of autonomy for the Donbas within the territory of Ukraine, and for a new union with the Russian Federation.[2] However, it would be misleading not to point out that these protests were at least in part provoked by the oblast authorities. Beginning in 1992, Chuprun repeatedly stated that the 'primary task is independence in the decision of economic questions' and that 'regions of Ukraine should have domestic and external independence' (*Socialistichesky Donbass*, 16 October 1992; *Donetsky Kryazh*, 19 February 1993). According to the version of local officials, in response to the protest movements the oblast legislators made several decisions that undermined the very existence of Ukraine as a unitary state and even questioned the independence of Ukraine.[3] Among these decisions was the expression of no confidence in President Kravchuk relating to policies on federal arrangements and the 'consultative' referendum on the status of the Russian language.

These decisions coincided with miners' strikes, although the miners' demands were more radical than those of the Oblrada. The miners sought regional autonomy, the resignation of the president and government and the bringing forward of the date of the elections. The outcome of these strikes was significantly better than anticipated. The new parliamentary and presidential elections were rescheduled for the following year, and a 'Donbas' government comprising members of the regional elite was formed in Kyiv. Yukhym Zviahylskyi, the director of the Zasyadko coal mine, was appointed as the acting prime minister. Oosterbaan comments that:

> [t]he Donetsk elites painted the unrest not as separatism, but as resistance to the early economic reforms of then-prime minister Kuchma. While the strikes did force early parliamentary and presidential elections and have helped delay coal-sector reforms, the elites benefited the most. In return for their loyalty, Donetsk elites were allowed to continue dealing directly with Russia and to continue reaping the benefits.
>
> (Oosterbaan 1997: 2)

However, it was a short-term success as, thereafter, the Donetsk elite was gradually excluded from government in favour of the regional elite from Dnipropetrovsk, where President Leonid Kuchma originates from.

The referendum on Russian as a state language also included questions about the federal arrangement of Ukraine and its relationship to the CIS and Russia. It was conducted in the oblast simultaneously with the parliamentary elections in March 1994 and the support obtained was indeed impressive. Eighty per cent of Donetsk oblast's voters supported the principle of a federal Ukraine; 87 per cent agreed that Russian should be made a second state language; 89 per cent agreed that Russian should be the language of education, science and administration in Donetsk oblast; and 89 per cent agreed that Ukraine should become a full member of the CIS Economic Union and Parliamentary Assembly (*Aktsent, Donetsk*, 1 April 1994). None of these demands have ever been supported by the state authorities in Kyiv but the issues played an important role in the 1994 presidential election, when eastern Ukraine voted for Kuchma on the basis of his pledges to make Russian the second state language and to ensure close relationships with Russia and the CIS. However, oblast leaders subsequently frequently referred to the results of the referendum when dealing with officials in Kyiv as a means to influence government policy. In summary, during the first stage of its development, the Donetsk elite managed to secure control over the worker movement and impose its vision of the Donetsk oblast–Kyiv relationship. The elite groups abandoned the goal of political autonomy in order to retain economic control and to secure economic autonomy from the centre.

Rivalry over economic autonomy, 1994–1997

In July 1994 Volodymyr Shcherban was elected as the head of the Oblrada. He did not belong to the former party *nomenklatura* and represented new commercial structures within the oblast. Under conditions of total scarcity, which were typical during the late 1980s and the early 1990s, the representatives of commercial structures accumulated significant wealth and social prestige. The rise of V. Shcherban was the first visible sign of changes in the nature of the regional elite and the beginning of a new era in Donetsk oblast–Kyiv relations in the context of de facto regional economic autonomy. It was also the outcome of the first stage of the privatisation of small and medium-size businesses such as shops, restaurants and cafés. The former directors of these state-owned firms seized property by semi-criminal means, which in turn provided them with financial resources that could be used to secure the support of administrative, business and criminal structures.

V. Shcherban was able to count upon the support of the mass media in the region, which had always been closely controlled by the local elite. In numerous interviews, in order to win popular support he skilfully played the trump card of being critical of the local and central authorities. When Kuchma began his presidential campaign against the former acting Prime Minister Zviahylskyi,[4] one of the Donetsk newspapers wrote:

> the Donetsk 'stars' with their anti-*nomenklatura* economy pose threats to the Cabinet of Ministers. The Dnipropetrovsk clan also does not depend on them . . . That is why the Cabinet of Ministers will try to undermine the Donetsk 'stars' . . . A month after the [1994 presidential] elections the domestic 'Waterloo' began . . . Shcherban and co. have not yet come under attack, but they soon will.
>
> (*Donetchyna*, 13 October 1994)

In order to try to strengthen central state power, Kuchma created a hierarchical administrative chain, in which V. Shcherban was appointed as head of the Donetsk State Oblast Administration (re-named Oblvykonkom) in July 1995 by Edict 597/95. Kyiv tolerated V. Shcherban's local business interests as long as they did not extend beyond commerce.[5] However, once he became involved in the energy sector and proposed in July 1996 that the management of the coal industry should be transferred to the oblast administration he was removed from office. In addition, it is widely believed, although officially never confirmed, that V. Shcherban lost his position for trying and failing to use the 1996 miners' strike to become prime minister.

The deterioration in the relationship between the Donetsk elite and Kyiv also meant that the relationship with the Dnipropetrovsk clan deteriorated, since almost all of them moved to Kyiv after the 1994 presidential election. Both President Kuchma and Prime Minister Lazarenko attributed Ukraine's slow transition to a market economy to President Kravchuk's inability to enforce reforming decrees and legislation at the regional scale. Consequently the new president and his prime minister sought to limit regional autonomy. The BBC's comments on those relationships were as follows:

> When Prime Minister Pavlo Lazarenko was appointed last June, he was quick to summon regional leaders to Kiev for a meeting focusing on the economy. Mr Lazarenko is telling his audience that the key to success in solving Ukraine's economic difficulties lies in co-operation between leaders in Kiev and those in power in the regions. Increasingly internal stability seems to hinge on how those relations evolve. Last summer a bomb exploded near the prime minister's car as he was driving from Kiev to the national airport. This month a rich and prominent MP was gunned down at his local airport in the East Ukrainian city Donetsk. Press reports have suggested that the attacks are linked to a battle between clans of powerful politicians and businesses in rival regions of the country.
>
> (BBC World Service, November 1996)

The rivalry between the Donetsk and Dnipropetrovsk clans became a real battle involving assassinations of businessmen connected to commercial structures in the energy sector. In October 1995 Akhmet Brahin, widely known as Alec the Greek, who was the owner of football club Shakhtar Donetsk, was blown up with six of his bodyguards during a football match at the local stadium. Brahin had been the 'childhood mentor' of the current local tycoon Rinat Akhmetov, who is linked to such companies as IUD, ARS, Kiev-Konty, Keramet, Embrol-Ukraine Limited and Ukrpodshipnik amongst others (*Financial Times*, 11 July 2001; *Korrespondent*, 10 January 2002). In November 1996, a deputy in the Verkhovna Rada, Yevgen Shcherban, was gunned down together with his wife. His firm, Aton, was directly related to Igor Markulov, a close associate of Zviahylskyi, who used a $70 million credit guaranteed by the state to purchase fuel and who left the country to go to the UK in 1994. Markulov was also a co-founder of the Liberal Party of Ukraine, which was headed first by Y. Shcherban and subsequently by V. Shcherban. In the spring of 1996 a further two businessmen were assassinated. Oleksandr Momot, the head of the firm Danko, which is currently an important operator in the coke coal market, was attacked in Donetsk. Oleksandr Shvedchenko, who was the head of the gas trading company Itera, was killed in Kyiv. All these events provide an insight into the formation of the Ukrainian state. As Marko Bojcun has said:

> You have this patron–client type of relationship where business interests and people in state power work together to further their own interests but this patron–client type of relationship denies and is not interested in the development of a civic society, where more people are involved in the decision-making process. This is what is really dangerous in the long run for Ukraine, that a civil society will not emerge and that the economy and the whole society in

fact will be run by some kind of a corporate cum clientist arrangement between powerful oligarchies.

(BBC World Service, November 1996)

The major changes of the second period of elite development included: the beginning of the unification of fragmented elite groups under the idea of economic autonomy; the involvement of previously underground criminal groups in legal business; the clash between Donetsk and Dnipropetrovsk clans over economic resources and access to the energy sector; the criminalisation of political relationships; and the establishment of fake mechanisms for people's participation in decision-making. Serhiy Polyakov, a former Communist Party apparatchik, was appointed governor of Donetsk Oblast Administration in July 1996. He was perceived by the local elite as Prime Minister Lazarenko's protégé and was never popular. In May 1997 Viktor Yanukovych, the deputy head of the Donetsk Oblast Administration, was appointed governor by Presidential Edict 435/97. His appointment was a compromise between Kyiv and the oblast. He was deeply involved in local business and simultaneously had a reputation as a supporter of President Kuchma.

Summing up the results of the second period of elite development, it is necessary to emphasise that the main outcomes were not connected to the anti-Kyiv démarche nor were they related to the obligation to meet public needs or reduce the social cost of the first stage of transformations. The major developments were associated with the beginning of the process of economic reform that led to the accumulation of significant private capital, the development of the unofficial or shadow economy,[6] and internal changes to the make-up of the elite. The new elite included: (1) the old *nomenklatura* that consisted of former senior Communist Party apparatchiks and directors of industrial enterprises who secured administrative positions or became entrepreneurs and industrialists; (2) representatives of service businesses, such as commerce, transport and communications who used privatisation for their own purposes; (3) senior regional and local administrative officials; (4) big business; and (5) criminal groups.

Although the opportunities for rent seeking varied, they were broadly similar to those found in other post-communist countries. The most common of them, as defined by Hellman (1998: 205–6), were as follows:

1   Rapid liberalisation of foreign trade without complete price liberalisation permitted the directors of large state enterprises to sell highly subsidised natural resource inputs, for instance non-finished steel products, to foreign buyers at much higher world market prices.
2   Rapid price liberalisation without breaking up monopolies created opportunities for some producers to earn monopoly rents. Privatisation prior to reform of the banking and credit system allowed enterprise managers to divert subsidised state credits, designed to ensure production continued, into the short-term high-interest money market.
3   Unregulated access to foreign direct and indirect investment allowed investors to circumvent structural reform in key industrial sectors.

4   The absence of a market-determined exchange rate meant that state bank managers could manipulate the exchange rate to influence private banks and postpone demand for currency.

One can add a further method of rent seeking. The regional elite, which benefited from the first stage of economic reform through lobbying and taking advantage of the absence of transparent government decisions by which profits were chan-nelled to those who were deemed loyal, had a financial incentive to resist further political or economic reform. This resulted in partial economic reform in which short-term winners accumulated wealth, partly or wholly determined by rents generated from distortions in the developing market economy. Furthermore, these rents were concentrated in the hands of a few people who were in a position to benefit from arbitrage between the reformed and unreformed sectors of the economy.

From economic autonomy to the political top: manipulation with reforms, 1998–2002

Currently one can observe two key elements in the political behaviour of the Donetsk elite: conditional political assistance to the centre and the further devel-opment of cohesion amongst the elite inside the region. Since 1998 the Donetsk elite has gradually strengthened its position in Ukraine by granting political concessions to the centre in exchange for the centre not interfering in regional business structures, resulting in greater economic autonomy. The Donetsk elite provided electoral support to President Kuchma in the 1999 presidential election and assisted him during the political crisis connected to the assassination of the journalist Heorhiy Gongadze and the so-called 'tape-gate' affair. In addition the Donetsk elite opposed the reformist programme of the Yushchenko government and supported pro-presidential forces during the 2002 parliamentary election.

By the beginning of 1999 the formation of the Donetsk elite as a united group had been almost completed. In December 1998 the Verkhovna Rada passed the 'Law on Special Economic Zones and the Special Investment Regime in Donetsk Oblast'. That demonstrated that the Donetsk elite could play a role as a united actor at the national state level. Indeed the Donetsk elite successfully lobbied the centre to pass an ambiguous law that was incompatible with the principles that the IMF had set for Ukraine. According to the law, the special eco-nomic zones and so-called territories of priority development were exempted from import duties and taxes for five years. The full exemption from income taxes was for three years followed by a 50 per cent reduction for a further two years. The law also reduced the rate of tax on dividends by 10 per cent for residents and 20 per cent for non-residents. The law therefore maintained unequal conditions for business, a major problem during the whole period of economic transformation in Ukraine. The passing of the law also indicated that the central authorities in Kyiv were willing to grant concessions to the Donetsk elite in exchange for their support in the 1999 presidential election.

According to Article 5 of the law, the Council of Special Economic Zones and Special Investment Regime of Donetsk Oblast (hereafter Council) was formed as a management body for two special economic zones: Donetsk and Azov (located in Mariupol). Since the Donetsk Oblrada appointed the Council members it can determine which companies benefit from the preferential investment regime. Resolution 23/2-18 in March 1999 outlined the functions of the Council. According to the resolution, the Council acts as an intermediary between investors, local authorities and central legislative and executive authorities and supervises the proper utilisation of investment. In addition, the Council is responsible for the development of appropriate measures to attract investment. The Council comprises 86 members, including representatives of the oblast administration, the city council and official trade unions as well as the directors of leading plants and companies. The Council also includes the deputies in the Verkhovna Rada elected in single-member constituencies in the oblast. The Council is authorised to control both regional businesses and investment flows into the region. In addition the Council has a mediating function between the regional and central government interests. This means that whoever controls the membership of the Council can play a crucial role in the regional economy.

To control the process the head of the oblast administration needed to be elected as the head of the Oblrada but this was incompatible with Ukrainian law. However, in May 1999 representatives of the different elite groups, such as the former acting Prime Minister Zviahylskyi, the mayor of Donetsk city and a former prosecutor of Donetsk oblast, supported the election of the head of the oblast administration, Yanukovych, as the head of the Oblrada. Yanukovych held both positions until May 2001 when he was replaced as head of the Oblrada by the president of the private company Kiev-Konty, who was also one of the vice-presidents of Shakhtar Donetsk football club. Despite the election of Yanukovych as head of the Oblrada being contrary to Ukrainian law, it was accepted by Kyiv. One commentator speculated that this might have been connected to the influence of the Oblrada on the formation of electoral commissions in what was the period leading up to the 1999 presidential election (*Donetsky Kryazh*, 18–24 June 1999). It should be noted that the social movement 'For Unity, Accord and Rebirth', which was led by Yanukovych, subsequently became part of the pro-President Kuchma movement Zlagoda (see Chapter 5).

In the first round of the presidential election, Kuchma received 31.96 per cent of the vote in Donetsk oblast, and his opponent Petro Symonenko, the head of the Communist Party of Ukraine, won 39.40 per cent. The other popular candidates were the leaders of leftist parties; the leader of the Progressive Socialist Party of Ukraine, Vitrenko, won 11.51 per cent of the vote, and Moroz, the leader of the Socialist Party of Ukraine won 6.30 per cent. The turnout in the first round of the election was 65.61 per cent (Tsentrvyborchkom (Central Electoral Committee), 30 October 1999). The results of the first round were predictable and reasonable for a region in which the communists and other left parties has been traditionally strong. However, in the second round Kuchma achieved a sensational victory in the oblast, winning 52.98 per cent of the vote while Symonenko received 41.22

per cent (*Donbass*, 25 November 1999). The turnout in the second round was 77.46 per cent. This outcome was due to the support of the oblast administration, so-called '*adminresource*', for Kuchma. This involved illegal activities by the administration to support Kuchma in the election in exchange for his support for local business groups, such as IUD and ARS. OCSE election observers reported that extreme electoral infringements took place in Donetsk oblast (Office for Democratic Institutions and Human Rights 2000). This claim is likely to be accurate, since the 21.02 per cent increase in Kuchma's vote between the first and the second round cannot reasonably be explained, with the results of the first round showing that almost 50 per cent of voters supported left parties. Increased voter turnout could not explain such incredible growth either. A similar pattern also took place in Kharkiv and Sumy oblasts. In Kharkiv, where the vote for leftist political parties was 51.20 per cent in the first round, Kuchma's vote increased from 28.07 to 46.64 per cent. In Sumy, Kuchma's vote increased from 26.68 to 48.56 per cent even though the vote for the leftist parties was 59.67 per cent in the first round (Tsentrvyborchkom (Central Electoral Committee), 14 December 1999). In all other regions where Symonenko led in the first round, such as in Crimea, Zaporizhzhia, Kirovohrad, Luhansk, Kherson and elsewhere, he went on to win the second round. By coincidence Kuchma's election campaign was directed by Y. Kushnarev, the former head of the Kharkiv State Administration, and V. Shcherban, the former head of the Donetsk Oblast Administration, who was appointed as governor of Sumy oblast in March 1999.

During the political crisis over the Gongadze case, the Donetsk Oblast Administration prevented any protests from taking place. The tactic adopted in the region was either to ignore the case altogether or to channel information to the mass media so it supported the president, administrative structures and security ministries (*Zerkalo Nedeli*, 2001, No. 9). In comparison, when Yushchenko's government came under criticism, all local mass media published and broadcast anti-Yushchenko and anti-government opinions, in both the Ukrainian and the Russian language.

During the period when Yushchenko was prime minister, from December 1999 to April 2001, all attempts by his government to reform the energy sector and to break the monopoly in the coke coal market were sabotaged or openly opposed by the Donetsk elite. On the initiative of the oblast administration, the commodity chain 'coking coal–coke–metal' was implemented in which a limited number of mediating companies were established without whose agreement transactions between producers could not take place (*Zerkalo Nedeli*, 2000, No. 26). In order to try to make transactions transparent, the government tried in July 2000 to introduce auctions for coking coal. However, not one consumer bought a single ton of coking coal at these auctions. The fact that not one single director of a metallurgical plant took advantage of the commercial benefits of the auction is an indication of the kinds of shadow relationships that exist between participants in the commodity chain. The interests of the Donetsk Oblast Administration spread even wider. There were plans to extend control over the energy market by establishing another commodity chain, 'steam coal–Donbassenergo–power stations', in order to capture more of the value added in the region (*Zerkalo Nedeli*, 2000, No. 17; see also Chapter 6). There was also evidence that Donetsk capital was gradually penetrating the economies in the neighbouring oblasts of Luhansk and Zaporizhzhia.

In March 2001, shortly before the Verkhovna Rada passed a motion of no confidence in Yushchenko's government, President Kuchma visited Donetsk. During a meeting devoted to discussion of the outcomes of the socio-economic development of the region between 1998 and 2000, Kuchma concluded that Yushchenko's government was unable to implement efficient reforms of the coal industry. Conversely, the oblast administration together with the directors of coal mines went to extreme lengths to frustrate reform in order as they saw it to keep the branch working (*Zerkalo Nedeli*, 2001, No. 13). The view, widely held amongst miners who were thankful for the end of barter and the prompt payment of wages, in favour of Yushchenko's government and, especially, of Deputy Prime Minister Tymoshenko, who was responsible for the reforms, was ignored. At the fourth congress of the NPH in July 2001, the miners joined the opposition organisation, the National Salvation Forum, which was led by Tymoshenko. Later, in September 2002, the NPH joined the protest that had been organised by a group of anti-Kuchma parties including BYUT (Bloc of Yulia Tymoshenko), SPU, CPU and the 'Our Ukraine' Bloc led by Yushchenko.

The 2002 parliamentary election was similar to the 1999 presidential election. The Donetsk elite provided support for pro-presidential forces and prevented opposition parties, especially 'Our Ukraine' and BYUT, from gaining a presence in the oblast. Despite accusations of electoral fraud, the results were recognised by the Central Electoral Committee. The pro-presidential bloc 'For United Ukraine' received 36.83 per cent of the vote in Donetsk oblast while 'Our Ukraine' received only 2.69 per cent and BYUT 1.40 per cent. The national result was somewhat different: 'Our Ukraine' won 23.57 per cent (winning 70 seats in the Verkhovna Rada), BYUT won 7.26 per cent of the vote (22 seats) while 'For United Ukraine' received 11.77 per cent of the vote (35 seats). The high vote in Donetsk oblast gained by 'For United Ukraine' indicates the influence that the oblast '*adminresource*' had, since the next highest vote for the bloc was only 17.05 per cent in Sumy, where the share of 'Our Ukraine' was 18.61 per cent (Tsentrvyborchkom (Central Electoral Committee), 13 April 2002). In order to strengthen the position of President Kuchma, who had been undermined by the parliamentary crisis during the Yushchenko government and the Kolchuga scandal in which diplomatic relations with the USA had been strained over the sale of a radar system to Iraq, Governor Yanukovych was appointed prime minister. He then formed a Cabinet of Ministers in which representatives of the Donetsk elite filled the key portfolios.

Conclusion

In conclusion it can be argued that the Donetsk elite over time developed a workable relationship with the central authorities located in Kyiv. The elite's political support for the presidency in exchange for economic autonomy has become a key feature of the Donetsk–Kyiv relationship. The deepening political crisis in Ukraine nationally resulted in a change in the central authorities' attitude towards the region, which provided the elite with access to top government positions. Within the region this situation creates two problems. First, the concentration of capital is higher in Donetsk than anywhere else in Ukraine. Alternative business groups are not permitted access to the market if their business is perceived to rival the established elite's interests. As the economy is controlled or owned by the same group, there is no competition and consequently little industrial restructuring and modernisation of the economy. Second, there is no evidence of political opposition, of an active civil society or of a free press. The communists in Donetsk oblast have not constituted the main political obstacle to the progress of reform and integration. Moreover, had the oblast elite perceived the communists as a potential electoral threat to reform, they would have lobbied for rapid comprehensive reform programmes in order to protect their position. Rather the Donetsk elite has been protected from electoral pressures and has consequently made only partial progress in reforming the economy. Indeed oblast officials engage in declarative politics in which official positions on issues are articulated irrespective of their connection to reality. The situation in Donetsk is currently highly regarded in Kyiv amongst those who see it as a possible model to be followed after the 2004 presidential elections.

Notes

1   Ukraine, like Russia, Belarus and much of south-eastern Europe, including former Yugoslavia and Romania, inherited many or all of the traits of patrimonial communism. This is characterised by (1) low opportunities for intra-elite contestation and popular interest articulation, (2) low to intermediate rational-bureaucratic institutionalisation, (3) hierarchical chains of personal dependence between leaders in the apparatus and their subordinates, and (4) extensive patronage and clientelistic networks. Owing to the weakness of opposition to communism in these countries during the Soviet era, the transition proceeds through pre-emptive strikes launched by elements of the old elites who are able to impose their preferred constitutional design and consequently establish personalised power relationships. In turn local and national leaders capitalise on their name recognition to develop clientelistic networks. As a result, urgent socio-economic and political transformation questions are ignored (see Kitchelt 1995: 447–72).
2   Almost every issue of local newspapers such as *Socialistichesky Donbass*, *Donetsky Kryazh*, *Donbass* and *Vecherny Donetsk* reported the protest actions between March and November 1993.
3   At the end of March 1993, Chuprun sent a telegram to Kyiv in which he openly criticised top officials (see *Socialistichesky Donbass*, 27 March 1993). In June 1993 the Oblrada passed a resolution of no confidence in President Kravchuk (see *Donetchyna*, 23 June 1993).
4   Zviahylskyi was accused of using state reserves to acquire illegal profits and left Ukraine for Israel. The case having collapsed, he returned to Ukraine two years later and was elected a people's deputy. He is a director of one of the most profitable coal mines in Donetsk.
5   V. Shcherban is the co-owner of a chain of shops and restaurants in Donetsk. In March 1999 President Kuchma appointed him as governor of Sumy oblast in exchange for

providing support in the presidential election of that year. Melnichenko's tapes, the secret recordings made by a former guard of the president, include an episode when V. Shcherban presents President Kuchma with a 25 per cent share plus a 'golden share' in the Sumy chemical plant. Whilst this claim has never been confirmed, neither has it ever been denied.

6   The term 'unofficial economy,' which comprises the white, grey and black economies, is not applicable to Ukraine because of the implication that participants in such activities are criminal. The term 'shadow economy' is more applicable because it refers to illegal practices conducted by the majority of economic actors.

References

Donetsk Oblast Administration (2000) *An Investment Guide: Investing in Donetsk Region*, Donetsk: Donetsk Oblast Administration.

Hellman, J. S. (1998) 'Winners take all: the politics of partial reform in postcommunist transitions', *World Politics*, **50**(2): 203–34.

International Monetary Fund (IMF) (1999) *Ukraine: Recent Economic Developments*, Washington, DC: IMF.

Kitchelt, H. (1995) 'Formation of party cleavages in post-communist democracies: theoretical propositions', *Party Politics*, **1**(4): 447–72.

Kubicek, P. (1996) 'Variations on a corporatist theme: interest associations in post-Soviet Ukraine and Russia', *Europe–Asia Studies*, **48**(1): 27–46.

Office for Democratic Institutions and Human Rights (2000) *Ukraine Presidential Elections, 31 October and 14 November 1999, Final Report*, Warsaw: Office for Democratic Institutions and Human Rights.

Oosterbaan, G. (1997) *Clan Based Politics in Ukraine and Implications for Democratization*, New York: Columbia International Affairs Online, Conference proceedings, http://www. cc.columbia.edu/sec/ciao/conf/ece01/ece01oog.html.

Sorensen, G. (1998) *Democracy and Democratization: Process and Prospects in a Changing World*, 2nd edn, Boulder, CO: Westview Press.

Varfolomeyev, O. (2002) 'Stuck in the Pits', *Transitions Online*, 5 December.

4 The evolution of the industrial structure in Donetsk region

Macroeconomic, microeconomic and institutional factors

Alexander Lyakh

Introduction

Donetsk oblast is currently one of the most politically and economically influential regions in Ukraine. Occupying 4.4 per cent of the territory of Ukraine and accounting for 10 per cent of the population, this old industrial region provided 12.5 per cent of the country's gross value added in 2000 and 12.7 per cent of the gross industrial output in 2001 (Donetsk Oblast Department of Statistics 2002: 19, 24). However, the region has its socio-economic and political problems. The economic power of the region is built on the hollow foundations of heavy industries whose prosperity in the long term is very doubtful. The first sign of the weakness of the heavy industries was the dramatic restructuring of the coal mining industry, which in reality primarily involved mine closures. Donetsk region faced the inevitability of following the same difficult path followed previously by old industrial regions in Western countries. However, the conditions for restructuring in old industrial regions in Ukraine and other CIS countries are different from those in advanced countries. These differences include the structural reform of sectors that are technologically connected, the peculiarity of transforming the economy of Ukraine into a market economy, and processes of regional elite forming (see Chapter 3). This chapter considers the current situation and outlook for economic restructuring in Donetsk oblast in the context of internal mechanisms of structural change and institutional factors.

Ten years of transformation and industrial development in the region: structural change and investment

Macroeconomic factors influencing industrial growth and structural change

During the first six years of independence the economy of Donetsk oblast experienced a sharp recession and structural changes which meant that the proportion of production, employment and regional budget revenues from heavy (so-called 'basic') industries increased. These structural changes were a spontaneous process accounted for by different factors at different times. Between 1992 and 1994 such factors were the high rates of inflation and the monopolistic position of the majority of heavy industry enterprises in the domestic market. Also these enterprises were less affected than final-product manufacturers by the break-up of technological ties among enterprises and the loss of energy resources, cheap raw materials, and sales markets after the disintegration of the USSR. Between 1995 and 1998 the major factors shaping the structure of the regional economy were the impact of rigid monetary restraints that depressed domestic demand, the low quality and price competitiveness of domestically produced consumer goods and machinery compared to imports, and the absence of investment funds to re-equip these industries. At the same time the key basic industries appeared to be quite competitive in external markets mostly owing to low prices (as a result of direct and indirect subsidies), low labour costs and ecological expenses. The only exception among the heavy industries was coal mining, which fell into a deep depression. The production costs of Donetsk coal are higher than prices in the external coal market because of poor geological conditions, obsolete technologies, poor management and the absence of a properly operating coal market in Ukraine. The government attempted to find a way out of the crisis in coal mining by restructuring the sector.

Donetsk region's economic indicators sharply differed in 1999 compared to 1998, in spite of the recession caused by the financial crisis in the autumn of 1998 which carried on through the first half of 1999. Enterprises in the region increased their sales and notably improved their financial position, and some even initiated large investment projects for upgrading production. In 2000 the regional industrial economy showed even better results – in 1999 industrial output increased by 6.7 per cent and by 12.2 per cent in 2000 but fell by 6.1 per cent in 2001.[1] The factors explaining the growth in the regional economy are the following.

Firstly, the high rates of economic growth are a statistical effect because they are compared to a very low base. At the beginning of 1999 the deep recession caused by the financial crisis of 1998 persisted. The core of the regional economy (ferrous metals and related industries) suffered significantly from this economic crisis. By this time the restructuring of the regional economy meant it became increasingly dependent on basic industries and in particular on the extraction and primary processing of raw materials. Whole branches of regional industry (for example light industry, construction materials, glass industries and engineering) nearly disappeared or dramatically reduced in size. Naturally, production growth at those few enterprises still operating made an impact in the regional statistics but the share of heavy industries sharply increased. The data showing changes to the structure of the regional economy and the dynamics of industrial production are shown in Tables 4.1, 4.2 and 4.3.

Up to 2001 the share of ferrous metallurgy in the gross production of Ukraine reached about 27 per cent, whilst in Donetsk region this share exceeded half the regional output. Thus even a small growth in metallurgy is automatically reflected in the regional statistics as a growth of the whole economy. Moreover, owing to a high degree of industrial concentration in Donetsk, regional economic growth is, in fact, ensured by two dozen large enterprises. Indeed two huge metallurgical plants located in Mariupol account for nearly half of the regional profit total and

Table 4.1 Output by sector in Donetsk oblast, 1990–2001

	1990* %	2001** %
Total output	100.0	100.0
Including:		
Industry	59.4	50.6
Agriculture, fishing and forestry	12.8	6.6
Construction	8.0	2.7
Transportation and communication	7.9	12.0
Retail and wholesale trade	3.8	12.6
Payable services and others	1.9	4.8
Public utilities and services	6.2	8.9
Finance and insurance	–	1.8

Source: Donetsk Oblast Department of Statistics 1991: 15; Donetsk Oblast Department of Statistics 2003: 27.

* National income is used as output for 1990. Until 1995 regional statistics were based on the Gross Public Product methodology used in the USSR. This methodology was different from the National Account System used in market economies in that it did not consider public and financial services as a 'productive sector' creating national income.

** Since 1995 GDP statistics in Ukraine have been calculated on the basis of value added plus taxes minus subsidies.

Table 4.2 Industrial output in Donetsk oblast by branch, 1990–2001

	1990 %	1999 %	2000 %	2001 %
Industry, total	100.0	100.0	100.0	100.0
Including:				
Electric power generation	5.1	13.2	10.1	11.2**
Coal mining	16.3	17.3	15.1	13.2
Ferrous metals*	32.6	46.6	52.3	51.9
Non-ferrous metals	1.0	0.4	0.4	0.3
Chemical and petrochemical products	4.0	3.1	3.5	2.8
Subtotal: basic industries	59.0	80.6	81.4	79.4
Machinery, equipment and metal manufacturing	17.0	8.7	8.6	8.6
Construction materials	3.8	2.4	2.3	2.1
Light industry (textiles and apparel, shoes, etc.)	7.0	0.3	0.3	0.5
Manufactured food and kindred products	7.9	5.3	5.3	6.7
Others	5.3	2.7	2.1	2.7

Source: Donetsk Oblast Department of Statistics 1991: 146; Donetsk Oblast Department of Statistics 2000: 113; Donetsk Oblast Department of Statistics 2001: 84; Donetsk Oblast Department of Statistics 2002: 85–6.

* Including coke production.

** Since 2001 this includes water regeneration and supplying which was formerly included in the ferrous metals statistics.

Table 4.3 Index of industrial output in Donetsk oblast by branch, 1990–2001
(1990 = 100 per cent)

	1995	1998	1999	2000	2001
Industry, total	49.4	43.4	46.4	52.2	55.4
Including:					
Electric power generation	56.4	35.9	39.1	39.0	39.3
Coal mining	46.5	46.4	46.7	47.3	45.1
Ferrous metals	42.3	42.4	47.5	54.5	56.9
Non-ferrous metals	12.5	12.7	18.7	39.4	39.2
Chemical and petrochemical					
products	33.0	36.3	36.2	37.1	36.1
Machinery, equipment and					
metal manufacturing	51.2	37.0	37.6	42.7	43.7
Construction materials	27.3	17.1	15.9	15.4	14.2
Light industry (textiles and					
apparel, shoes, etc.)	15.7	13.1	11.5	15.9	19.4
Manufactured food and					
kindred products	33.6	24.6	28.8	38.9	47.2
Others	68.3	38.8	29.3	31.0	33.7

Source: Author's calculations based on Donetsk Oblast Department of Statistics 2000: 115; Donetsk Oblast Department of Statistics 2001: 82; Committee of Statistics of Ukraine 2001: 56; Donetsk Oblast Department of Statistics 2002: 87–8.

36 per cent of the taxes collected from regional firms (*Negotsiant* 2001: 21–5). Obviously, relative stability at several major enterprises results in the improvement of all regional economic indicators.

Secondly, during the second half of 1999 and 2000 there was an improvement of market conditions for the basic export goods of the region, such as ferrous metals, machines and equipment, owing to economic expansion in Russia, Belarus and Western countries. It has been calculated by G. Krauze that a 1 per cent increase in economic growth in the EU results in the growth of Ukrainian exports by 0.8 to 1 per cent, which in turn increases Ukrainian production by 0.2 to 0.3 per cent (cited in Vakhnenko 2000: 8). Obviously, for the Donetsk regional economy the multiplication effect is even more pronounced and reveals the extent to which the entire regional economy depends on the metallurgical industry, which constitutes nearly 70 per cent of the total regional exports.

Thirdly, the hryvnia's depreciation after the financial crisis that lasted until the middle of 1999 increased the competitiveness of Ukrainian goods in both the domestic and the export market, which led to a growth in the output of key exporters and the substitution of imports. Subsequently the substitution of imports was encouraged through non-tariff barriers (especially relating to the purchase of hard currency) and tariff barriers which the Ukrainian government imposed on some goods (Kvizer and Wynzenz 2001: 95, 103).

Fourthly, industrial growth in 1999 and 2000 was primarily caused by monetary factors. Massive settlement of budget arrears, such as social payments, prior to the presidential election and the sale of hryvnia for hard currency in order to service external debt resulted in an increase in the inflation rate from 19.2 per cent in 1999 to 25.8 per cent in 2000 (UEPLAC 2000: 33). However, consumer demand and retail turnover increased, resulting in increased output in economic sectors producing mass consumer commodities. In 2001 the rate of inflation decreased to 6.1 per cent and the growth of the money supply decreased. This, combined with the appreciation of the hryvnia (by 8.2 per cent compared to the US dollar), meant that by the end of 2001 the impact of the increased money supply in generating economic growth was reduced by nearly a half (Pynzenyk 2002: 6). These factors and reduced demand in the foreign metals market led to a fall in ferrous metals output in the region of 4.8 per cent in the first half of 2002. This is why regional industrial output decreased by 2.2 per cent compared to the same period of 2001 (Svetlychnaya 2002: 3).

Fifthly, the non-payment of electricity and gas by heavy industrial enterprises increased their liquidity and encouraged industrial growth. This meant that one branch of Ukrainian industry – electricity generators and importers of gas from Russia and Turkmenistan – was a creditor to all the others sectors of the economy.

The factors listed above explaining growth suggest that industrial growth is unstable not least because the final factor, energy suppliers subsidising industrial enterprises, might result in the collapse of the whole economy of Ukraine. This would have a pronounced effect on the Donetsk regional economy because of its dependence on imported gas and on electricity generators.

Restructuring and investments

The volume and sectoral structure of investment affects the restructuring of the economy of Donetsk region. Gross investment into the real sector (i.e. value added producing) of Donetsk region decreased continuously between 1991 and 1997. The average annual investment was just 1.7 per cent of the value of fixed capital accumulated in the regional economy. At this rate of investment, replacement of fixed capital in the region would take 59 years. Domestic and foreign investment in the real sector of the regional economy started to increase in 1998 but the financial crisis at the end of 1998 resulted in declining domestic investment until the end of 2000. In 2001 the amount of domestic investment grew in both nominal and constant hryvnia terms (see Table 4.4). In 2001 the rate of annual gross investment to the value of accumulated fixed capital increased to 2.5 per cent. However, despite this investment, Donetsk oblast is lower than the average for Ukraine. In 2001 gross investment in the real sector of the regional economy amounted to UAH11.9 per UAH100 of industrial output, which is 18 per cent lower than the average for Ukraine in 2000 (UEPLAC 2000: 22).

More than two-thirds of investment was from firms' own funds. Heavy industries, and especially ferrous metals, dominate the sectoral structure of internal investments because they have greater funds. The share of foreign direct investment (FDI) in total investments increased between 1995 and 1999 from 0.7 per cent to 21.4 per cent (see Table 4.4); however, it halved in 2000 and fell to 5.9 per cent

Table 4.4 Domestic and foreign investment in Donetsk oblast, 1995–2001*

	1995	1996	1997	1998	1999	2000	2001
Total investment (million hryvnias**)	2,040.4	1,193.5	1,078.9	1,155.5	1,310.6	990.1	1,205.9
Domestic investment (million hryvnias**)	2,027.0	1,174.7	1,045.0	1,069.8	1,030.3	885.2	1,134.9
Percentage of total	99.3	98.4	96.8	92.5	78.6	89.4	94.1
Foreign investment (annual) (million USD)	9.1	14.5	26.2	58.5	150.6	54.6	40.1
Percentage of total	0.7	1.6	3.2	7.5	21.4	10.6	5.9
Accumulated foreign investment (million USD)	52.2	76.3	106.2	166.2	259.5	305.3	334.8
Increase to the sum on the end of previous year (%)	20.9	27.8	34.3	55.1	90.6	21.0	13.1

Source: Donetsk Oblast Department of Statistics 2001: 18; Vylenchuk 2001: 18; Donetsk Oblast Department of Statistics 2002: 124, 156.

* These data include direct investment in productive assets in the real sector of the regional economy.

** In constant (1995) hryvnias.

in 2001.[2] As in other transition countries, foreign investors were more likely than domestic investors to pursue deep restructuring, changing firms' organisational structures and management personnel, reducing employment, investing additional capital, altering the product mix, and raising the share of exports in total sales (Danylenko 2000: 52). Domestic investors, typically burdened by having to service debt taken on to acquire enterprises, often lacked resources to upgrade the company's technology and product structure. Consequently these investors frequently had a short-term aim of technological development and market expansion (Bornstein 2001: 5).

Despite the regional economy's industrial potential and the expectation that FDI would play a significant industrial restructuring role, accumulated FDI in the oblast is low even compared to the average for Ukraine. At the beginning of 2002 FDI per inhabitant in Donetsk region was $69 whereas the average for Ukraine was more than $80. Between one-third and 40 per cent of all FDI in the region is in the ferrous metals sector (see Table 4.5). However, FDI in the region is relatively diversified by sector, reflecting the structure of domestic demand. For example, in food processing, flour grinding and forage processing, FDI and domestic and foreign trade are higher than the sector's contribution to total regional GDP. At the same time, FDI has a very weak impact on the development of the innovative sector of the regional economy. Between 1998 and 2001 this sector (comprising engineering, science and scientific services, communication and information technologies) contributed between 4 and 9 per cent of the total FDI in the region.

Table 4.5 Distribution of foreign direct investments in the region by sectors and industries (as percentage of the total accumulated FDI), 1998–2001

Sectors and industries	1998	1999	2000	2001
Industry (total):	**69.8**	**74.8**	**78.4**	**76.9**
– fuel and energy complex	1.4	1.6	1.8	3.9
– ferrous metals	32.3	41.2	40.1	35.9
– non-ferrous metals	3.1	2.0	1.5	–
– chemical products	4.7	3.2	3.0	3.0
– machine building	10.5	7.0	6.1	4.8
– textiles and apparel, shoes, etc.	0.9	0.8	1.5	0.4
– food processing, flour grinding and forage processing	14.6	18.2	23.0	22.5
– other industries	2.3	0.8	1.4	6.4
Agriculture	1.7	2.8	2.9	3.2
Construction	0.7	0.4	0.5	0.3
Transportation and communication	2.3	1.9	2.2	1.7
Domestic trade	11.0	8.0	6.4	13.5
Foreign trade	6.8	7.1	5.7	
Finance, insurance and pension securing	3.5	2.5	2.0	2.6
Others	4.2	2.5	1.9	1.8

Source: Donetsk Oblast Department of Statistics 2000: 34; Donetsk Oblast Department of Statistics 2001: 167; Vylenchuk 2001: 18; Donetsk Oblast Department of Statistics 2002: 155.

To encourage investment in the region the 'Law of Ukraine about the Special Economic Zones and Special Regime of Investing in Donetsk Oblast' was elaborated by the regional authority and passed by the Parliament at the end of 1998 (see Chapter 3). Domestic and foreign investors operating in the territories under this regime have tax privileges and tariff reductions for imported equipment, parts and raw materials. Between 1999 and 2001 the Special Zones Committee approved the implementation of 116 investment projects with an accumulated value of $467.3 million including $199.4 million of FDI. Almost one-third of these investment projects (31.7 per cent) were in the ferrous metals sector in which FDI made up approximately 70 per cent of the investment, whilst 14.7 per cent of the projects were in the coal mining sector and FDI constituted 15 per cent of these projects.

It is noteworthy that the regional authority selected ferrous metals, coal mining and electric power generation to be included in the list of priority sectors and industries in the law. This is because the law does not aim to encourage progressive structural change of the regional economy, which would create an alternative system of jobs and reduce the region's dependency on volatile foreign markets for raw goods. Equally the law encourages only large investments and does not support investment in small business, which can be active agents for effective restructuring. It is necessary to note that stable legal frameworks, predictable macroeconomic policy and an appropriate auxiliary infrastructure are more important for both domestic and foreign investors than the regime of privileges (Mollers 1999: 9). This conclusion is proved by the fact that nearly half of the FDI in Donetsk region originates from offshore financial centres, such as the British Virgin Islands and Cyprus, and suggests that much of this investment consists of capital that has flowed out of the country before returning to the region as FDI. (The structure of FDI by geographical origin can be seen in Table 4.6.) This conclusion is corroborated by the fact that a high proportion of FDI is in heavy industry sectors of the economy; foreign investors tend to avoid enterprises in branches requiring extensive restructuring, such as steel, coal mining, heavy machinery and basic chemicals (Carlin *et al.* 1999: 15).

The financial sector has little influence over investment processes and the prospective restructuring of the regional economy. The share of commercial bank

Table 4.6 FDI in Donetsk oblast by country of origin at the end of 2000

Country	%
British Virgin Islands	42
USA	23
Great Britain	7
Cyprus	6
Germany	6
Russia	5
Other	11

Source: Donetsk Oblast Department of Statistics 2002.

loans and investment funds in investment in the real sector varied from 3.4 per cent to 5.7 per cent between 1996 and 2001. High interest rates remain an obstacle for industrial companies trying to secure credit from the commercial bank sector. Between 2000 and 2001 average bank interest rates fell by 22.8 per cent to 29.2 per cent while the inflation rate fell from 25.8 per cent in 2000 to 6.1 per cent in 2001 (Pynzenyk 2002: 7). However, average profitability of the industrial sector in the region was a little above 10 per cent and in construction about 11 per cent. In the regional economy more than one-third of enterprises and organisations were loss making, and in industry and construction the figure was as high as approximately 40 per cent. It is natural that banks focus their credit policy on sectors and enterprises with a high turnover of working capital and in some cases large heavy industrial enterprises that have sufficient internal funds or are subsidised by the state. Also banks prefer short-term loans because of the high risk associated with long-term loans. Data on the distribution of credits to economic bodies show that 58 per cent was lent to the industrial sector including 29 per cent to the ferrous metals industry and 9.8 per cent to coal mining. However about one-fifth of all credit was to the trade and catering sectors because of their high level of liquidity and the rapid turnover of capital. Very high interest rates combined with low income mean small businesses are not able to secure credit from commercial banks, with the result that the majority of small enterprises do not have the opportunity to expand their businesses. With investment predominantly in heavy industry and with small businesses having little access to credit, the endogenous development potential of the region became weaker.

Microeconomic and institutional factors in the restructuring of the regional economy

The structural shifts in the economy of the region that took place in the last 10 years were in many respects determined not only by macroeconomic factors but also by the relations formed among different sectoral systems, the behavioural stereotypes of enterprise top managers, and other institutional factors. This requires an examination of the behaviour of enterprises in various sectors in the context of the changing economic conditions.

Even during the period of *perestroika* one of the ways of loosening centralised planning and of injecting market relations into the command system was through the creation of co-operatives and other forms of small enterprise. State-owned enterprises (or, to be precise, their top managers) reacted to the liberalisation of the central planning system by formally or informally leasing property and facilities belonging to the state-owned enterprise they managed to various co-operatives and small enterprises. At that time of shortages, centralised price determination and the subsidisation of state-owned enterprise, the newly created small enterprises supplied or serviced or functioned as wholesalers (at prices above the fixed state price) for the associated state-owned enterprise or organisation. The real purpose of creating such small enterprises was to engage in so-called 'skimming' involving the partial withdrawal of surplus value, the privatisation of the cash flow of an enterprise, and earning arbitrage profits as a result of either intermediary activity or the resale of the enterprise's goods.

Later, these 'small surrounding enterprises' (SSEs) were transformed into independent private firms and became the basis for the primary accumulation of capital during the market transformation period. They continued to fulfil intermediary functions using the gaps in government market regulation and state property management that opened up dramatically during the first years of independence. They also used opportunities to receive government subsidies and state guaranteed loans. All these activities were extremely common in the years 1992 to 1994. Naturally, in Donetsk oblast the majority of the SSEs were formed in the fuel and energy sector and in the metallurgical industry. A popular intermediary business was supplying steel, equipment, conveyor belts and other materials to coal mines in exchange for coal (especially coke coal) which was then supplied to coke chemical plants, metallurgical enterprises and power stations (see also Chapter 6). Arbitrage profits in this instance were derived either from the overpriced supply of goods to consumers or by manipulating coal qualitative parameters as well as the actual under-supply of materials in respect of what was stated in the declaration (Radionov 1997: 34). As a rule, current or former senior managers of 'paternal' state-owned enterprises and officials belonging to branch ministries chaired, usually through relatives or trustees, the SSEs (Wittkowsky 1998: 124–5; Yoffe 1995: 27–8).

Gradually, the activities of these small enterprises attracted the attention of the local and regional state authorities. The authorities were able to become involved in such activities because they enjoyed the formal power to appoint the general managers of state-owned enterprises (Zimmer 2000: 58). Local and regional authorities could also affect an enterprise irrespective of its legal form of ownership by making its (or its competitors') operations more difficult through directing subordinate bodies such as the local tax authorities, sanitary inspectors or the fire department to inspect them. Thus this meant that the primary accumulation of capital and the growth of new private enterprises (which underpinned the economic and social development of the region) depended in part on the preservation of traditional mechanisms of state management and close linkages with the state bureaucracy at all levels. This dependency on the traditional institutional paradigm was present across all Ukraine but especially in industrially developed regions (Zimmer 2004; van Zon 1998: 615). This explains why there is not a paradox in the fact that the majority of the 'new economic elite' had no interest in comprehensive market transformation, excluding privatisation, which would have entailed the legalisation of property ownership and the decriminalisation of their activities (Wittkowsky 1998: 125; see Chapter 3). Instead directors of state-owned enterprises preferred forms of privatisation such as the so-called 'lease-with-buy-out' and privatisation that involved the transfer of share certificates to the enterprises' employees. The latter form of privatisation resulted in diffuse ownership that prevented the legal owners from exercising their legal power over the senior management who continued to control the enterprises' cash flow and channel it through SSEs.

The break-up of the former Soviet Union and the disintegration of the central planning system resulted in an economic recession in the region and the country as a whole. However, the extent of the recession varied between sectors and enterprises according to whether they met a real demand and on their capacity to adapt to the changing situation. Changes to the structures of prices and the emergence of trade barriers between countries formerly part of the USSR that disrupted the supply of cheap raw materials and resulted in the loss of traditional markets led to a transformational shock associated with a dramatic fall in demand. Enterprises or industries that suffered the least were those that retained access to relatively cheap raw materials and government subsidies and whose output was competitive and met demand or those that developed new products and/or exploited new markets. The iron and steel industry became the leading exporting branch of the economy, and the coal industry, which had a strong lobby in the upper echelons of authority, received significant direct and indirect state subsidies and loans at negative real interest rates (i.e. lower than inflation). Nevertheless maintaining coal prices that were competitive with imports depended on state subsidies that were a considerable burden on the state budget. As the IMF and World Bank demanded stricter budgetary and monetary policies, the government refused to subsidise the coal industry between 1995 and 1997 and announced the closure of loss-making coal mines. Closure of mines often took place without clarification of the reasons for an individual mine's losses nor consideration of a comprehensive mine closure programme (Grynev 2001: 3). As direct budgetary support to the coal industry decreased, coal mines, the official bankruptcy of which was resisted by central and regional authorities, accumulated payments arrears which effectively compensated for the loss of subsidies.

By the time the restructuring of the coal industry took place, new and relatively powerful 'finance industrial groups' (FIGs) had emerged out of the interdependence between industrial enterprises and intermediary firms. A significant amount of capital belonging to these FIGs was transferred abroad, primarily to offshore financial centres. The main sphere of the FIGs' activity was earning profit through arbitrage activities in two commodity chains: 'coking coal–coke–metal' (leaf or pipes) and 'thermal coal–power–metal' (see Figure 4.1; see also Chapter 6). Whilst the first commodity chain was highly liquid since transactions were made in cash, the second commodity chain depended on 'quasi-money', which entailed the reciprocal clearing of payments arrears.

In 1996 a new commodity chain, 'gas–metal–gas pipes', rapidly emerged, which resulted in reducing the liquidity of the two other commodity chains. In this new commodity chain, gas was paid for with gas pipes but the terms of the barter transactions overvalued the pipes relative to the gas, permitting companies trading gas pipes to accumulate significant profits through arbitrage pricing of the gas. As a result, the largest FIGs in Donetsk entered the highly competitive market to supply gas to iron and steel enterprises by establishing with the Donetsk oblast authorities the Donbas Industrial Union (*Industrialny Souz Donbassa*) (ISD). ISD was set up to compete with Common Energy Systems (*Edyny Energytychnyi Systemy*) (EES), a corporation based in neighbouring Dnipropetrovsk and administered by

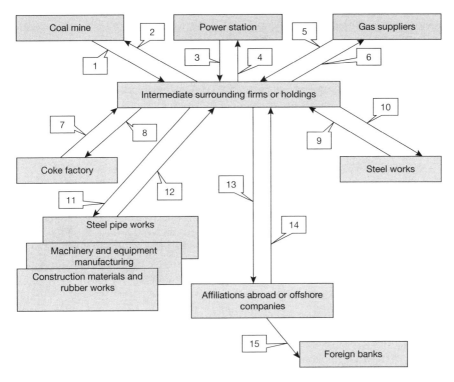

Flows:
1 – coke and thermal coal; 2 – steel, equipment and parts, conveyor belts, construction materials, power, mutual arrears clearing, money for salaries; 3 – power; 4 – thermal coal, gas, mutual arrears clearing, money for salaries; 5 – gas; 6 – money; 7 – coke; 8 – power, gas, mutual arrears clearing, money; 9 – steel; 10 – coke, gas, power, construction materials, equipment and parts, money; 11 – steel, power, gas, mutual arrears clearing, money; 12 – gas pipes, equipment and parts, conveyor belts, construction materials; 13 – steel, gas pipes, equipment and parts; 14 – money, imported equipment and materials; 15 – cashed arbitrage profits.

Figure 4.1 The 'coking coal–coke–metal' and 'thermal coal–power–metal' commodity chains

former Prime Minister Pavlo Lazarenko. The Donetsk Regional Administration ensured that the largest iron and steel enterprises in the oblast purchased their gas from ISD. Following Lazarenko's resignation as prime minister, ISD and its affiliates expanded to control 80 per cent of the regional gas market for industrial enterprises as EES was effectively excluded from the gas market in Donetsk oblast. In effect, Donetsk Regional Administration's regional programme 'Metal–Pipe–Gas' ensured that ISD controlled the commodity chain. ISD supplied semi-finished metal from Azovstal Steel Works located in Mariupol to the Khartsyzk Pipe Plant, which in turn supplied large-diameter pipes to Gascomplectimpex which was affiliated to the Russian company Gazprom (Pak 2001: 43). Subsequently the other two commodity chains, 'coal–coke/power–metal', were revived owing to opportunities offered by the widespread use of barter, the clearing of mutual arrears and tolling schemes.[3] All these commodity chains concentrated profit in the hands of the regional FIGs which was then used to finance capital investment.

Between 1997 and 1998 when there was a shortage of currency, barter transactions, in which output was exchanged for construction materials and equipment, provided the means for capital investment by enterprises. As a result, during this period the construction material industry was one of the top three sectors (with power generation and the coal industry) using barter transactions. The lion's share of tolling transactions were implemented by the iron and steel industry and the chemical industry (*Salon Dona y Bassa* 1998: 23). By 1999 the regional FIGs had accumulated sufficient financial resources to acquire control, in part through the purchase of large shareholdings, of metallurgical, coking-chemical and coal companies as well as machine-building plants that produced equipment for mines and iron and steel works. To control state-owned coking coal mines, the FIGs tried to implement so-called 'shadow privatisation'. The FIGs exerted influence on the mines to purchase power, equipment and materials from companies that were either owned or controlled by the FIGs. Since the mines could not pay for these supplies they became indebted to the FIGs, which through initiating bankruptcy proceedings could take over the mines. The volume of such 'investments' in coal mines by two FIGs up to May 2001 amounted to UAH500 million (Gumenyuk 2001: 5).

An example where shadow privatisation was attempted was Makeevka Steel Works (MakMK). Bankruptcy proceedings against MakMK, which owed almost UAH1,400 million, were initiated but continually postponed at the request of the Ministry of Industrial Policy. The accumulation of debt was in part due to poor management and in part caused by the activities of the FIGs in relation to MakMK. The accumulation of debt by MakMK began in 1992 when the plant took out a DM200 million loan, guaranteed by the Ukrainian government, from a German bank. The loan was used to construct two rolling mills and an ambitious housing project for workers, but none of the projects were completed. Debt increased during the 1990s when five regional FIGs supplied raw materials, energy and gas to MakMK in return for the right to sell its output. The FIGs wanted to acquire the state-owned MakMK but only if the government agreed to write off the company's debt. CJSC Danko, which is affiliated to ISD, continued to deal with MakMK and found a foreign investor, Trans Commodities International (TCI), which was registered in the USA and headed by a Ukrainian émigré, to purchase a majority shareholding in the company. By September 2002, TCI had invested $7.2 million in MakMK but was waiting for further guarantees from the government prior to committing further investment. In particular TCI demanded that the government restructured MakMK's debt in order to form a new firm with a clean balance sheet (*Donbas-Invest* 2002: 14–17).

In general the FIGs, which increasingly operated like holding companies, are engaged in vertically and horizontally integrating production in the region. Moreover, one can observe that the various FIGs are themselves becoming more integrated with one another. Changing ownership structures and the opportunity for further consolidation of existing businesses into business groups together with the uncertain long-term prospects for traditional industrial sectors meant that the FIGs continued to expand organically and through acquisitions. The concentration of finance in the region's integrated FIGs permitted them to make large investments in their priority sectors (Parfenov 2001: 6). Significantly the transformation from being intermediate companies engaged in trading into FIGs that owned production plants was encouraged by the government's efforts to reduce barter payments and mutual arrears clearings. It is striking that between 1998 and 2001 the largest investors in the Donbas economy were Ukrainian investors who had hidden their capital in offshore financial centres. This illustrates the change in the business strategies of entrepreneurs and industrialists. In particular they began to realise that the extraction of profit from the production sphere and then depositing it in offshore financial centres would in the long term result in the depreciation of their productive assets. In addition the authorities accepted the concentration of property in the hands of the FIGs (Pivovarsky 2001: 9).

In 2000, when machine-building enterprises began to be privatised, the regional FIGs operating the 'coal–coke–metal' commodity chain started to acquire large or controlling shareholdings in those companies that produced machinery for the coking-chemical, coal and metallurgical industries. The two largest regional FIGs, CJSC ARS and ISD, established Ukrvuglemash (Ukrainian Coal Machinery) to own and manage four local machine-building plants as well as two plants in Russia owned by ARS. The general director of ARS explained that there were three reasons for acquiring the machine-building plants (see Gumenyuk 2001: 8). Firstly, internalisation of machine building would reduce the company's dependence on external market relationships. Secondly, ARS would be able to provide the capital investment needed to modernise the machine-building enterprises. Thirdly, the new joint venture would enable enterprises engaged in coal mining, coking-chemical and metallurgical equipment to break into the Russian market. Subsequently ARS and ISD promoted the establishment of the Technopark located in the Donetsk Free Economic Zone. This involved co-operation between local machine-building plants, the Innovation Centre of Donetsk Regional Administration, a range of project institutes and institutes affiliated to the National Academy of Science. The chairman of the Technopark explained the purpose of the Park was 'to put the industrial base into order, to restore the coal mines and heavy industry, to provide jobs and wages to the majority of the population, and then to move into high technologies' (Malyuta 2001: 8). This reveals that, even though representatives of the FIGs and local and regional authorities realised the limitations of an economy overly dependent on heavy industry and on the export of low-value-added goods, their vision for the future of the regional economy centred on heavy industry.

The evolution of the regional policy initiatives

In post-Soviet society the political and economic interests of elites are inextricably linked (Segbers 1995: 18–19; see also Chapter 3). The struggle between rival national and regional elites, involving political bargaining and compromises over the mechanisms and institutions that provide these elites with access to economic and/or political resources, has played an important role in Ukraine (Wittkowsky 1998: 3). The majority of the political and economic decisions made by different authorities must be seen in the context of their association with individual and collective rent-seeking strategies in the sphere of business. Decisions by local and regional authorities in Donetsk oblast relating to economic restructuring entirely followed this pattern.

'The Comprehensive Programme for Social and Economic Development of the Donbas (Donetsk and Luhansk oblasts)' for 1994–2000 was the first document of its kind approved in the region. Scholars belonging to local research institutes and universities elaborated the programme. The programme argued that increased dependency on heavy industry would be detrimental to regional development and that it was necessary to accumulate finance and implement mechanisms in order to diversify the regional economy. In particular, the programme prioritised the development of high-tech production, support for SMEs, and the development of recreation zones in the oblast. However, while the programme was being elaborated, figures representing the interests of local industries successfully influenced the final version. As a result, in its final form the programme comprised two thick volumes which consisted of statistical forecasts of the development of different sectors in the oblast.[4] The programme also emphasised the need for the central and regional authorities to provide significant budget support. In reality the programme ulti-mately reflected the interests of the regional elite which sought control over large state-owned enterprises and over the licensing of exports and imports in the region. The regional elite saw the programme not as a way to increase the endogenous economic potential in the long term, but as a tool to monitor cash flow and ensure taxes were paid by local industries. The programme argued that a greater portion of taxes collected in the region should be retained in the region rather than sent to Kyiv so that a special fund to financially support investment projects in accordance with the programme's priorities could be established. One of the programme's priorities was to encourage job creation in sectors other than heavy industry. However, according to the programme's plan the volume of investment allocated to each traditional sector, such as ferrous metals, coal mining and power genera-tion, almost equalled or even exceeded the sum of the taxes collected in the region. Given the influence of the heavy industries lobby, it was easy to forecast that the programme fund would benefit traditional heavy industries.

The programme was agreed by central government in early 1994 when Yukhym Zviahylskyi, who had formerly been a director of a large coal mine and mayor of Donetsk, was acting prime minister. At the same time the interests of the regional elites were expressed in a presidential decree on the 'economic experiment' in Dnipropetrovsk, Donetsk, Zaporizhzhia, and Luhansk oblasts. The decree granted greater powers to the regional authorities over the management of state-owned enterprises and foreign trade in their regions. The decree was a belated attempt by President Leonid Kravchuk to secure the support of powerful eastern elites (especially the 'Red Directors' who had closer ties to regional rather than national authorities) in subsequent presidential and parliamentary elections. After these elections the new Cabinet of Ministers dismissed the programme as an exercise in electioneering. However, the decree on the economic experiment in the eastern oblasts remained in force.

Once Viktor Yanukovych was appointed governor of Donetsk oblast in 1997, a number of other regional initiatives were announced. In early 1998 the regional administration announced the 'Programme of Urgent Measures to Mitigate the Social and Economic Crisis'. The programme, which lacked conceptual coherence, simply comprised a collection of measures designed to increase sales, profits and employment in large enterprises and amounted to a so-called '*skyrda*' (deposit of straw). The purpose of the programme was effectively to re-impose control over the management of enterprises as had been the case in the 'good old Soviet times'. In 2000, the oblast administration elaborated the 'Comprehensive Programme for Social Economic Development of Donetsk Oblast until 2010'. The programme was drawn up in a similar way to previous ones but in this case central government did not approve the programme because of a lack of finance. However, the interests of the regional elite were reflected in a presidential decree on 'Special Economic Zones and the Special Regime of Investing in Donetsk Oblast' that was subsequently superseded by the law mentioned on page 85. In spite of the optimism expressed by regional business and political actors (see Svynarenko 2000: 45–6), some Western and local experts suspected that rent-seeking strategies by the regional elite lay behind the formation of the special investment regimes (Zimmer 2000: 16).

Conclusion

Four conclusions arise from my analysis. Firstly, current economic growth is, and the future development of Donetsk oblast will be, path dependent. The heavy industries, especially ferrous metals, continue to play a significant role in the economy and will continue to do so in the future. However, the regional development pathway is not fixed because regional and industrial policies and the volatility of market competition will shape the future development trajectory. A careful combination of appropriate public policy and regulation of market competition can steer the regional economy away from the stagnation associated with old industrial regions. Secondly, the role of government in ensuring that the regional economy develops is twofold. On the one hand government has to support the economic competitiveness of non-heavy industry sectors. In order to do this it has to use macroeconomic policy to support domestic demand and create an institutional framework to support small business, new business alliances, public–private partnerships (especially in depressed communities) and environmental movements. On the other hand government has to impose hard budget constraints and competitive market relations on the powerful FIGs that have a monopolistic position in the regional economy. Thirdly, the government should support the positive impacts that the FIGs have on the regional economy by encouraging, for example, expenditure on R&D. The state should support the FIGs' innovative initiatives since this is the only way to accelerate the modernisation of the whole of the Ukrainian economy. Finally, the government needs to take into account when elaborating and implementing administrative reform that Donetsk Oblast Administration, in the context of weak regional policy and the absence of citizen oversight, intervenes in business in order to exploit rent-seeking opportunities. However, central government should also encourage initiatives by the regional authorities that are intended to create jobs in new economic sectors and develop an enabling environment for existing and new businesses to invest.

Notes

1 Here and hereafter data of the regional statistics office are used (Donetsk Oblast Department of Statistics 2001; Donetsk Oblast Department of Statistics 2002; Vylenchuk 2001). It has to be taken into account that official statistics do not reflect the informal economy that is caused by high rates of taxation and other institutional factors. According to different publications the shadow economy amounts to between 30 and 60 per cent of overall economic activity in Ukraine. Pynzenyk (2002: 7) has calculated that the proportion of money in circulation outside the banking system was over 43 per cent in 2001. There are sectors and industries where the proportion of revenues hidden from taxes and official statistics is higher than the average. These are sectors where cash payments predominate, such as trade, catering and services, and industries where barter and tolling transactions are common, such as construction materials, coal mining and ferrous metals.

2 The increase in foreign investor activity in 1999 was caused by a number of factors. Firstly, Donetsk metal works completed three investment projects that accounted for almost 43 per cent of the total FDI in the region. Secondly, foreign capital deposited in offshore financial centres was used to purchase large state-owned enterprises that were privatised in 1999. Thirdly, the adoption of the 'Law of Ukraine on Special Economic Zones and Special Regime of Investing in Donetsk Oblast' in late 1998 also encouraged foreign investment from offshore financial centres.

3 A tolling scheme is a form of non-cash payment in which a supplier of a raw material pays for the processing of that input by receiving the processed commodity minus a quantity in lieu of the payment for the processing.

4 The present author was part of the team elaborating the programme and observed the way representatives of the oblast administration and allied industrial groups, engaged in rent-seeking strategies, influenced the content of the final document.

References

Bornstein, M. (2001) *Post-Privatization Enterprise Restructuring*, Working Paper No. 327, Ann Arbor, MI: William Davidson Institute.

Carlin, W., S. Estrin and M. Schaffer (1999) *Measuring Progress in Transition and towards EU Accession: A Comparison of Manufacturing Firms in Poland, Romania, and Spain*, Working Paper No. 40, London: European Bank for Reconstruction and Development.

Committee of Statistics of Ukraine (2001) *Ukraina u tsyfrakh u 2000 rotsy: Derzhkomstat Ukrainy*, Kyiv: Tekhnyka.

Danylenko, A. (2000) 'Tendencyy y perspektyvy pryamogo ynozemnogo investuvannya u promyslovyst` Ukrainy', *Financy Ukrainy*, 8: 50–5.

Donbas-Invest (2002) 'Teny ystcheznuvshykh investorov', 3–4: 4–17.

Donetsk Oblast Department of Statistics (1991) *Social`no-economycheskoe razvytye Donetskoy Oblasty za 1986–1990 gody*, Donetsk: Donets`koe Oblasnoe Upravlynnya Statystyky.

Donetsk Oblast Department of Statistics (2000) *Donetskaya oblast v tsyfrakh v 1999 godu. Kratky statystychesky spravochnyk*, Donetsk: Donets'koe Oblasnoe Upravlynnya Statystyky.

Donetsk Oblast Department of Statistics (2001) *Statystychesky shorychnyk Donets'koy oblasty za 2000 ryk*, Donetsk: Donets'koe Oblasnoe Upravlynnya Statystyky.

Donetsk Oblast Department of Statistics (2002) *Statystychesky shorychnyk Donets'koy oblasty za 2001 ryk*, Donetsk: Donets'koe Oblasnoe Upravlynnya Statystyky.

Donetsk Oblast Department of Statistics (2003) *Statystychesky shorychnyk Donets'koy oblasty za 2002 ryk*, Donetsk: Donets'koe Oblasnoe Upravlynnya Statystyky.

Grynev, V. (2001) 'Restrukturyzatsyya ugol'noy otrasly', Unpublished paper presented at the Donetsk Public Debates on the Government Programme 2002, 24–25 July.

Gumenyuk, I. (2001) 'Investytsyy kak osoznanaya neobchodymost'', *Salon Dona y Bassa*, 29 May: 5, 8.

Kvizer, W. and F. Wynzenz (2001) 'Integratsya Ukrayny u svytovy ekonomyku. Yakym tchynom, yak shvydko ta navysho', in *Ukrayna na shlyakhu do Evropy*, Kyiv: Phenyks.

Malyuta, Ya. (2001) 'Post-industryal'ny Donbass: v Donetskoy oblasty reshily zanyatsya technologyamy', *Salon Dona y Bassa*, 29 May: 5–8.

Mollers, F. (1999) 'Foreign direct investment in Ukraine: experiences taken from reality', in A. Seidenberg and L. Hoffmann (eds), *Ukraine at the Crossroads: Economic Reforms in International Perspectives*, Heidelberg: Physica-Verlag, pp. 138–60.

Negotsiant (2001) 'Donbass' 2001: Reytyngy promyshlennykh predpryyaty Donetskoy oblasty', 20 June: 21–6.

Pak, V. (2001) 'Donetsk: tchuzhye zdes' ne khodyat', *Energetycheskaya Polytyka*, 7–8: 39–47.

Parfenov, G. (2001) 'Ekonomyka Donbassa: tochky rosta y tochky padenya', *Salon Dona y Bassa*, 29 May: 5–7.

Pivovarsky, A. (2001) 'How does privatization work? Ownership concentration and enterprise performance in Ukraine', IMF Working Paper, WP/01/42 (April).

Pynzenyk, V. (2002) 'Otsynka tendentsyi ekonomychnoy dynamyky u 2002 rotsy', *Ekonomychny Isse: Institute Reform Vypusk*, **1**(12): 5–13.

Radionov, S. (1997) 'Tcherny treugol'nyk', *Business*, 50, 15 December: 34–5.

Salon Dona y Bassa (1998) 'Donbass 50: 50 krypneyshykh promyshlennykh predpryyaty Donetskoy oblasty/Reytyng', 12 May: 19–25.

Segbers, K. (1995) 'Systemic transformation in Russia: a critical revision of methods and a new agenda', in K. Segbers and S. De Spiegeleire (eds), *Post-Soviet Puzzles: Mapping the Political Economy of the Former Soviet Union*, Vol. 1, Baden-Baden: Nomos.

Svetlychnaya, L. (2002) 'V Donetskoy oblasty nametylsya economytcheskyi spad', *Salon Dona y Bassa*, 30 July: 3.

Svynarenko, T. (2000) 'Rol' investytsyi u rozvyazany social'no-ekonomytchnych problem Donbasy', *Financy Ukrainy*, 8: 44–7.

Ukrains'ko – Europe'sky Consultativnyy Center z Pytan' Zakonodavstva (UEPLAC) (2000) *Tendentsyy Ukrains'koy ekonomyky*, Kyiv: UEPLAC.

Vakhnenko, T. (2000) 'State debt of Ukraine: current condition and evolution', *Ukrainian Economic Trends*, February.

Vylenchuk, R. (2001) 'Region osobogo naznachenyya: Monytoryng social'no-ekonomytcheskogo polozhenya Donetskoy oblasty v 2000 gody', *Negotsiant*, 20 June: 15–20.

Wittkowsky, A. (1998) *Pyatyletka bez plana. Ukraina: 1991–1996. Formirovanye national'nogo gosudarstva, ekonomyka, elity*, Kyiv: Sphera.

Yoffe, Y. (1995) *Odyn na odyn s systemoy: vospomynanyya y razmyshlenyya byvshego premier-ministra Ukrainy*, Luhansk: Lugan`.

Zimmer, K. (2000) 'Donetsk case study', Unpublished paper on the research project 'Akteure und Institutionen in der regionalen Entwicklungspolitik in Polen, Rumanien, Ungarn und der Ukraine'.

Zimmer, K. (2004) 'The captured region: actors and institutions in the Ukrainian Donbass', in M. Tatur (ed.), *The Making of Regions in Post-Socialist Europe: The Impact of Culture, Economic Structure and Institutions*, Vol. 2, Wiesbaden: VS Verlag, pp. 231–348.

Zon, H. van (1998) 'The mismanaged integration of Zaporizhzhya with the world economy: implications for regional development in peripheral regions', *Regional Studies*, **32**(7): 607–18.

5 Trapped in past glory

Self-identification and self-symbolisation in the Donbas

Kerstin Zimmer

Introduction

Culture is a common theme in treating regional differences in Ukraine, especially in explaining election results and political orientations (Åberg 2000; Åberg and Sandberg 2002; Kubicek 2000; Shulman 1998, 1999a, 1999b). But generally, this is a macro-view, taking the east and the west of the country as opposite poles. The studies mostly rely on election results and opinion polls, whereas the specific content of the cultural resources at the regional level proper is hardly ever researched (for a partial exception see Hrytsak 2001) and – most importantly – their impact on political and economic development remains unclear.

Various arguments have been put forward to explain the lack of reform or the erratic reform path in Ukraine. They mostly deal with the structure of the political system, the entanglement of political and economic power, and enrichment strategies at the national level (Åslund 1999, 2002; Kubicek 1999; Levitsky and Way 2001; Matsuzato 2001; Siedenberg and Hoffmann 1999; Wilson 2001; Wittkowsky 1998). Within the Ukrainian context, Donetsk as an old industrial region plays a special role. Its economic, social and political development after Ukrainian independence has been described (Friedgut 1994; Lyakh and Pankow 1998; Lyakh 1999a; Volovodova 1999a), and special social groups such as the coal miners and industrial workers have been the subject of several contributions (Borisov and Clarke 1994; Crowley 1997a, 1997b; Crowley and Siegelbaum 1995; Siegelbaum 1997). But these studies rarely refer to the cultural basis and precondition of the observed development.

The major task of this chapter is to explicate under what circumstances economic restructuring might succeed or under what circumstances its success is forfeited. Its central thesis is that the recent economic development of Donetsk region can be explained by two interrelated factors: culture and actors. This contribution emphasises the interplay between culture and political and institutional traits and introduces the concept of region capture.

By using an approach that owes much to Grabher (1993, 1994) this contribution examines the interplay between local actors' patterns of thinking and self-symbolisations, understood as social constructs, that are created and modified by the elite and the population at large (Berger and Luckmann 1967). Regional cultural resources – provided by a stock of symbols (Berger and Luckmann 1967) accumulated throughout history – may vary substantially from one place to another and create unequal potential for the re-invention of a locality's future development. In the context of political and economic transformation in central and eastern Europe, the specific content and form of a local or regional identity – in particular the narratives relating to the region's traditions – can turn into a symbolic tool to facilitate change or else become a trap of self-idealisation. Discourses, however, cannot be separated from the political, social and economic powers that create them; and it is constellations of actors that condition the use of the available cultural resources.

The first part of this chapter addresses theoretical reflections about the links between culture, identity and development as well as the constellation of actors. The second and main part of the chapter deals with the empirical case study[1] and puts special emphasis on the development blockades in the region. After a short introduction to Donetsk region, it considers dominant actors and institutional patterns up to 2003. Then, the identity discourse in Donetsk region is analysed on the basis of 60 interviews with regional actors[2] conducted in 1999 and 2000. The material was analysed for shared symbols and a common semantic that might integrate the region and possibly facilitate collective action. By way of conclusion the interplay between culture, actors and development is reassessed.

Culture, actors and development

This section examines the role of culture and actors for the potential development of an economically and socially depressed region. Regions are distinguished by historically developed production patterns and dominant strategies of individual and collective actors, who are embedded in a web of networks and a cultural setting. For the purpose of this chapter, 'culture' is defined as symbols, stories, codes, cognitive models and world views rather than values and norms. The relation between culture, identity and development is conceptualised with regard to symbolic resources that signify the stock of knowledge (Berger and Luckmann 1967; Schütz and Luckmann 1979) and the stock of symbols at the disposal of a society or group. In this sense, a 'region' is a multi-layered and contradictory space that is not to be understood in territorial terms, but as socially constructed by the actors' discourse as well as their action and interaction (Berger and Luckmann 1967). Regional identity discourses are the symbolic reflection of the region as an imagined community (Anderson 1998) and they generate a semantic space for communication. Symbolic universes (Berger and Luckmann 1967) objectify themselves through the symbolically mediated interactions of members of society and structure actors' behaviour. Groups develop a stock of significant symbols that enable members to make sense of their world or rather to create and to sustain a world. A shared regional identity potentially forms a common basis for co-operation. Symbolic resources accumulated throughout history can be disregarded or activated; they can be re-constructed and reshaped in communicative interaction. But all memory is connected to the present and serves a political purpose in its broadest sense. Recollections affect present perceptions, but today's actors purposefully select which events are to be remembered in order to constitute their identity.

Evidently, discourses are inseparable from their creators and bearers. Regional identity and specialisation have a high degree of resilience, particularly if they are backed by strong interest groups. North (1990) gives an explanation: if a development path once moves into a certain direction, the learning processes of the participants and the historically acquired subjective interpretations of reality confirm it. Thus, even unproductive paths can be further pursued. Both the interests and the cognitive models of the participants rationalise the existing institutional structure, and they produce an ideology which explains the social order and justifies its bad performance. Whether the perceptions are correct or false is irrelevant, as they are the basis of action. Yet, informational and relational redundancy (Grabher 1994) at the regional level facilitates potential for action as well as adaptability. Relational redundancy refers to loose coupling, i.e. an abundance of relations and loose networks that are based on co-operation and trust. They offer the possibility to recombine single elements in always-new constellations and to make use of different interpretations of reality as well as processes of learning and unlearning. Whereas relational redundancy concerns the constitutive preconditions of regional adaptability, informational redundancy refers to cognitive preconditions of the creative use of these possibilities. In this context, Grabher (1994) pointed to the relevance of regional identity, understood as a specific semantic – in the sense of Berger and Luckmann – for regional development. For Grabher this denotes not only the conscious acceptance of history – and not its idealisation or eradication – but also the ability to relate oneself to different contexts, to express oneself, to communicate and to react suitably. Redundancy allows not only for adaptation to certain external changes, but also for questioning the appropriateness of this adaptation (Grabher 1993, 1994). Moreover, Grabher's concept conveys a positive attitude towards conflicts as forms of communicative work with 'regional identity' understood as a by-product of conflicts rather than as a consensus restricting conflicts. In addition it introduces a reading of supra-regional functional interlocking and trans-regional linkages as enrichment and not as a threat to regional identity.

This general framework has special implications for old industrial regions, as Grabher (1993) showed for the German Ruhr. This type of region achieved growth by adapting to a highly stable economic environment, leading to an ever-stronger specialisation and an extreme preference for such innovations, which reproduced the existing regional economic, political and cultural setting. The symbiotic relationship between the political-administrative system and the industry impedes the reorganisation and paralyses political innovation as it promotes the emergence of common orientations and shared cognitive models that decide which phenomena are perceived and which are ignored (Grabher 1993). The lack of relational and informational redundancy triggers the simultaneous occurrence of functional, cognitive and political lock-ins. The system loses its ability for internal reorganisation and can no longer react to unanticipated changes in the environment.

But the Old Industrial Region Paradigm is not sufficient to explain the recent development in Donetsk region. It is problematic to apply the concept to the post-Soviet context, as it implicitly assumes functionally differentiated spheres of action which are typical of democratic market systems but are not present in the neo-patrimonial transformation regime of Ukraine (Šabić and Zimmer 2004; van Zon 2001). As I have argued elsewhere (Zimmer 2002, 2004), the region is a captured one that has fallen victim to its own economic and political elite. The capture includes not only the control of the political arena and the economic realm, but also the determination and imposition of public discourse by that regional elite.

The shadow of the past

The city of Donetsk was founded in the nineteenth century under Russian rule, and developed into an industrial centre, which retained its frontier character until the beginning of the twentieth century. From the 1920s it belonged to the Soviet Union, and for several decades it served as the industrial hub of the country. The Soviet leadership celebrated the Donbas[3] as the showcase of socialism, referring to the industrial achievements and the hard work performed by miners and heavy industrial workers. The region was tightly integrated into the Soviet inter-republic division of labour, but gradually lost its importance to the coalfields of the Soviet far east. Economic decline set in during the 1970s, but only became publicly visible during the *perestroika* phase. Spontaneous and extensive miners' strikes erupted in 1989. The general feeling that the region was disadvantaged in the Soviet system fostered support for Ukrainian national independence in 1991.

In the sense of path dependency, history has left the following structural and cultural traces on Donetsk region: its history is characterised by industrialisation from above, in the course of which the region has persistently been dominated by an exclusive power structure, consisting of the industrial elite and political actors who were strongly linked to the political power centres in the respective capitals while reigning in their own 'principalities'. The region underwent repeated waves of immigration of diverse origin, leading to cultural and linguistic russification. Workers commonly articulated their discontent by leaving their workplaces or by revolts, but they never arrived at sustainable associations that would stand for their class interests. The population's historical experience is made up of continuous economic expansion and repeated violent devastations, with the latter being excluded from public memory. The Stalinist purges and the famine of the 1930s contributed to the disintegration of the population as they completely destroyed the local rural population and obliterated integrative structures. In this context, industrial enterprises turned into places of refuge but sustained societal weakness.

Who owns Donetsk region?

At first sight, Donetsk is a rather typical old industrial region. Presently its economy is based on coal mining, metal and steel production, machine building and chemicals. Since 1991 the share of heavy industry has steadily increased. The regional share in national production is steady at 20 per cent. Large enterprises dominate production and employment. Simultaneously many industrial companies and coal mines are unprofitable and depend on state subsidies. The region accounts for a third of Ukraine's export revenue, with the metalworking industry accounting for much of that volume. Russia continues to be the main trading partner. Donetsk as an old industrial region plays a special role in Ukraine's economic and political system, and it occupies a special position as earner of export revenue and creator of a political power base. The region numbers roughly 5 million inhabitants, and with a rate of 90 per cent it is considered the most urbanised region in Ukraine. The city of Donetsk, with about 1 million inhabitants, is the uncontested centre. Other important cities are Mariupol, with its important seaport and steel industry, and the industrial cities of Kramatorsk and Gorlovka.

This one-sided economic development of the 1990s is mirrored by the emergence of dominant actors at the regional level. Neither the recent nor the present constellation of actors allows us to speak of relational redundancy. But the neo-patrimonial character of the regional regime goes beyond the scope of the concept of lacking relational redundancy. Not only are actors linked by rigid hierarchical ties, but they fuse spheres of action, thus obliterating the formal separation of economic, social and political spheres. After Ukrainian independence, a distinct political and economic regime encompassing important economic and political players gradually matured in the region. In the Ukrainian discussion, the dominant group is mostly referred to as the 'Donetsk Clan',[4] but owing to their bridging of spheres the expression 'administrative-economic groups' (Turchinov 2000) with a neo-patrimonial character seems appropriate to convey the regime's character. The actors' position can be viewed as state capture (Hellman *et al.* 2000) at the regional level. They control the hardly separated economic and political spheres, including the political infrastructure, and the rule setting process at the regional level.

In order to secure and strengthen their businesses and influence, the Donetsk actors tried to augment their political presence in the 'corridors of power' in Kiev, including the Parliament. In 1998 Donetsk Mayor Vladimir Rybak set up the Party of Regional Revival of Ukraine and thus laid the foundation for a regional Party of Power.[5] In 2000 and 2001 this Party of Power was formalised under the formal leadership of the former regional *nomenklatura* and some Red Directors, when the Party of the Regions, the members of which are predominantly from the Donbas, was founded. Today, this Party of Power dominates the regional political playing field as the regional council and the mayors' offices have virtually been taken over by its members (*Ostrov*, 24 June 2003). At the national level, the party has gained much influence since the parliamentary elections in March 2002, and experienced another boost after the appointment of the former Donetsk governor Viktor Yanukovich as prime minister. In April 2003, Yanukovich was elected chairman of the party. Obviously, it is to serve as a political machine for the next presidential elections in 2004. The local/regional Party of Power in fact served as a collective political machine, in the sense of a *komanda*, whose common denominator is its members' belonging to the region and shared interest in favourable conditions for economic success. The leading actors have established new companies and financial industrial groups that exhibit a high degree of vertical integration of the mining, metalworking and energy complex. Thus, they have power over the entire value chain in the heavy industrial sector. In addition, they include financial intermediaries and various offshore companies. During recent years the financial industrial groups have also expanded into agriculture, food processing and telecommunications and have started to establish their own – still rather small – media empires.

In Ukraine the absence of freedom of the press and expression is a continuing problem. Although freedom of speech is legally guaranteed, most official and formally independent media are disinclined to publish stories criticising the government. Most of the print media use the state-owned publishing houses and distribution system, and broadcasters use state-owned frequencies and air time. Moreover, financial pressures have taken the place of unconcealed censorship, and media outlets have been forced into the arms of political patrons in order to survive. Independent and critical journalists lead a dangerous life. In addition to the well-known case of Georgii Gongadze, several other journalists have been murdered.

This control signifies a lack of informational redundancy which is especially severe in Donetsk region. In Donetsk region a number of print media outlets as well as television and radio stations are owned or financed by the public authorities, both at the city and the regional level (Lyakh 1999b).[6] Others are owned or controlled by big businesses. The real owners of other newspapers are hard to discover as the newspapers are often officially owned by the staff. As those journalists are as a rule poorly paid, one can assume that there are real owners who prefer to remain unknown. Control of the regional political infrastructure combined with control of the media allows this narrow circle of actors to determine the identity discourse. Deviant views hardly ever reach the public domain.

The region on their mind

This section attempts to characterise, interpret and assess the symbolic universe – related to the region – that prevails among the interview partners and the population at large. It dissects the significant symbols that materialise in the discourse of the regional elite and their assessment of regional potential. It considers whether and how the actors' re-construction of the past creates a vision of the region's future. It examines the formal characteristics of regional identity discourse, its openness with regard to supra-regional and trans-regional communication and the appraisal of conflict as a form of communicative work.

The industrial heartland

Although my interview partners never specified the spatial boundaries of the region, one can indirectly conclude that 'region' can be both Donetsk oblast and the (Ukrainian) Donbas or occasionally even eastern Ukraine. The region is neither imagined nor portrayed in territorial terms but rather as a homogeneous space, distinguished by a uniform socio-economic situation.[7] When asked about the region, only a few interview partners started to talk about its history.[8] But those who did recall history always did it in terms of industrial history, referring to economic and socio-economic criteria which have 'always' been valid in the region. The city was portrayed as 'the largest industrial centre in Ukraine' and as 'the miners' capital'. Nearly all interviewees repeatedly accentuated the outstanding role and significance of the region within a larger (national) context: tsarist Russia, the Soviet Union and today's Ukraine. 'It is an industrially developed region. A fifth of the gross domestic product is produced here. By this indicator alone one can assess the strength of the region.'[9] The region is considered as *primus inter pares*, which is also the title of an official publication about it.[10] The assumed and celebrated uniqueness, strength and supremacy of the region in the Soviet Union are used as an argument for the region's unquestionable present and future role. Most interview partners have internalised the picture of their region as a successful one and presented it accordingly. Several of them postulated the supremacy of an industrialised, urbanised region which is simultaneously the stronghold of the working class and a cadre factory.[11] One interview partner stressed its mission in the context of a general world-wide development and illustrated the exceptional role of the region as follows:

> in Donetsk oblast the civilisation of this world has accumulated a splendid level of knowledge, has created a really strong position in relation to technology, and from this a substantial mass of sociocultural infrastructure has developed. That is an achievement of world civilisation. And if today Donetsk oblast's weight is declining, then that is a loss for world civilisation. This is not some village in Africa; this is an educated region with 5 million trained workers who are so well trained that their spirit can operate in any production process, starting from coal mines which are one and a half kilometres deep, to the open sea (we have a sea), and in steel plants where there are fires, where the lava flows. For our people no production process is too difficult.[12]

Tutoshnii-*ness*

People in Donetsk region strongly identify with their region. This intense attachment is the strongest feeling related to a home region in Ukraine (Hrytsak 2001). The self-definition and self-symbolisation of the Donetsk regional elite and its typical inhabitants are local in nature and set the region apart from the rest of Ukraine. My interview partners' imagined community is a construct of the regional population that is defined and stylised in socio-economic rather than ethnic terms. The Donbas used to be an attractive region for migration during the industrialisation of the nineteenth and twentieth centuries, when people arrived from different parts of Ukraine, Russia and the Soviet Union. In the 1989 Soviet census, 50.7 per cent of the regional population defined themselves as Ukrainians, 43.6 per cent as Russians (Zadorozhnyuk and Furman 1997: 90) and 5.7 per cent belonged to other nationalities. In 2001, this ratio had changed: 56.9 per cent defined themselves as Ukrainians and 38.2 per cent as Russians (*ForUm*, 6 February 2003). But many of the people who define themselves as Ukrainians are Russian-speaking, and a closer look at Donetsk region reveals that the Russian–Ukrainian dichotomy is misleading because it conceals the multi-layered and – at first sight – contradictory identities many people in Donetsk region have. The identification with both nationalities is not perceived as contradictory (Liber 1998). Whereas eastern and western Ukrainians identify equally with other Ukrainians, only 11 per cent of western Ukrainians but 47 per cent of eastern Ukrainians assert that they have things in common with Russians (Miller *et al.* 1998: 266). In fact one could describe most inhabitants of the Donetsk region as *tutoshnii* (Lieven 1999: 79), that is people whose main identification is with their locality rather than with the state or nation. When residents of Donetsk refer to their 'homeland', they primarily think about their own region and hardly ever any larger unit (Hrytsak 2001: 272). This identity is socio-economic and – according to my interview partners – the imagined community comprises all national and ethnic groups. Thus, the region is described as multi-ethnic.[13] One could, however, characterise this understanding as non-ethnic, pan-ethnic or even pre-ethnic. Kuzio (1998) maintains that the western and eastern regions of Ukraine are at different stages of the nation-building process, with the eastern part lagging behind owing to it having belonged to tsarist Russia. Later, Soviet rule produced strong identification with the locality on the one hand and the whole Soviet Union on the other, but only feeble identification with Ukraine (Lieven 1999: 79). This was especially pronounced in the Donbas, which was celebrated as the showcase of socialism. Lieven quotes the Ukrainian scholar Grigorii Nemiriya: 'The fact that you came from the Donbass was more important than that you were Russian or Ukrainian; so of course the break-up of the Soviet Union also meant a raising of this regional identity and loyalty' (Lieven 1999: 80).

The regional identity has extremely positive connotations. In 2002 more than two-thirds of the local population expressed their pride in being residents of the Donbas, 18 per cent were undecided and only 12 per cent were not proud to belong to the region (DIATs 2002). People derive their self-consciousness and a feeling of power from their self-identification as heroes and members of a vanguard, the way the workers of the region used to be portrayed. They do not accept the role of victims – understood as russified, alienated Ukrainians – which Ukrainian nationalists would like them to adopt (Wilson and Khmelko 1998). The strong local identity is also embodied in the importance attached to local holidays. Miners' Day, which is celebrated on the last Sunday in August, is further upgraded by the city anniversary on 27 August. The coinciding festivities have led to a fusion into a week-long celebration, in the course of which Ukrainian Independence Day (24 August) turns out to be the least important.[14]

Creating signs of identity

Manifestations of industrial identity can also be traced at the visible level. The regional council chose the Mertsalov palm tree as a symbol of Donetsk region. Aleksei Mertsalov forged this piece of metal sculpture in 1896.[15] It was displayed at the all-Russian exhibition, where it was awarded the first prize. Today it decorates the regional coat of arms, which itself is a bizarre mixture of tsarist, Soviet and Ukrainian symbols. Although the palm tree can be interpreted as a symbol of ties with Russia, it is blue with a yellow background, representing Ukraine's national colours. According to information found on the official website of the regional state administration,[16] the yellow or golden colour is a symbol of wealth, justice and generosity. The blue is the symbol of hope, happiness, abundance and the development of the agricultural sphere. The black colour of the original palm tree embodies the profusion of mineral resources. The palm tree itself symbolises the basic professions of Donbas – mining and metalworking. But first and foremost the new emblem signifies the state of development of the region at the end of the nineteenth century and the recognition it received both at the national and at the international scale. The inscription on the coat of arms is related to a story. In 1897 the Russian Academy of Sciences sent Dmitrii Mendeleev to the Donbas to assess the development prospects of the region. Mendeleev was impressed and recorded: 'The former desert has come to life. It is a complete success. *Vozmozhnost' dokazana delom* [The possibility is proved by a deed].' This reference to deeds, however, proves that at present the inscription was selected with particular concern for (Russian and) Soviet principles. In the first half of the nineteenth century, Vladimir Dal' had already asserted that 'deeds, and not words, reveal the man, indicate his real face and his real person'. Kharkhordin (1999) points to the importance of deeds in Russian and Soviet ideology, and he emphasises the fact that the Soviet practice of 'self-criticism' and self-exposure was mainly directed to 'revealing the real person by his or her deeds' (Kharkhordin 1999: 214). Currently, this way of thinking is also reflected in the motto '*delat' konkretnoe delo*' (to do concrete things), which is often evoked by key regional actors eager to show that they are taking care of and solving pressing problems.[17]

Street and district names and monuments are further embodiments of self-identification and self-symbolisation. In Donetsk, they allude to the socio-economic traits of the city. Numerous streets and monuments bear the names of (formerly) prestigious professions such as *shakhter* (miner) or *metallurg* (steel worker). Other symbols either are of Soviet origin or make reference to it. Monuments to Lenin continue to occupy central locations in all cities in the Donbas. Several streets in the city centre bear the names of important Soviet politicians, including those of local leaders who were in office during the famine of the 1930s;[18] others make reference to Soviet celebrations and anniversaries. But public announcements are also tokens of Soviet identity. The slogans and billboards that were on display in Donetsk in the autumn of 2000 took one back to the 'good old days': '*Vmeste vosrodim Donbass*' (Together we will revive the Donbas) or '*Donchane, nam est chem gardit'sya*' (People of Donetsk, we have something to be proud of).

Back to the USSR?

As has become apparent, the region's Soviet past continues to be of overriding importance. Many members of the local population continue to see the region as an integral part of the pan-ethnic Soviet Union, that is to say a bigger unit in which the regional self-understanding as an industrialised hub acquired meaning. Opinion polls confirm that part of the regional population continues to describe itself as 'Soviet' (Malanchuk 1999; Subtelny 1995: 199; Volovodova 1999b). My interview partners did not portray themselves in this way, but references to an identification with the Soviet system can be traced in many interviews, predominantly in those with state and quasi-state actors. Today, it is becoming apparent how intensely the official propaganda, which presented the Donbas as the showcase of socialism and the engine of industrial development, was internalised. The above-mentioned interviewees mainly drew on examples, symbols and yardsticks from the Soviet period, referring to – among other things – the socialist myth of manual labour, equating it with 'qualification', which points to a materialist understanding of work.[19] In many interviews, the region was portrayed within a larger (national) framework where it always assumed the role of the vanguard and hero, which is inextricably linked with the myth of physical work and the Soviet cult of miners and steel workers. Thus, socio-economic identity is inextricably linked with Soviet symbols and beliefs.

In 1989 and 1991 the miners criticised the Soviet system because they felt exploited and believed that the allegedly resource-rich Ukraine would be better off on its own. Ironically, the strikes contributed to the demise of the Soviet Union, the very state in the framework of which the miners' identity had been shaped and acquired sense (Lieven 1999: 95). In 1995, almost half of the respondents of a survey conducted in Donetsk would have voted against independence if they had had the chance to decide again (Golovakha and Panina 1997: 267). My interviewees' statements pointed neither to a real nor to a symbolic detachment from the Soviet Union. Most likely the Soviet identity will fade away in the long run. It is not clear, however, what will take its place.[20]

Significant others

The way one perceives others reveals much about one's self-perception and correlating strategies. One's own identity always includes the 'other', often constructing a dichotomous image of the world. The structure/formal characteristics of the identity discourse are relevant here. Its openness and the actors' capacity for empathy, i.e. their ability to place themselves into other actors' positions, tell us something about their ability to view themselves from the outside and acquire a more accurate picture of their situation and to question their own position and strategies. Two images will be considered here: Russia and the West.

To Russia with love?

Russia has become an outside factor for many people in the Donbas. Today, fewer people in Donetsk region identify as Russians than a decade ago. Their percentage fell from 43.6 per cent in 1989 to 38.2 per cent in 2001 (*ForUm*, 6 February 2003). Nevertheless, in 2000 and 2001, between 81 and 93 per cent of the polled local population favoured granting the Russian language official status as the second state language (DIATs 2001). Young people in Donetsk mainly speak Russian in their daily life (91.7 per cent) and at work or in school (75.8 per cent), and most of them advocated Russian as a second state language (DIATs 2000). The majority of my interview partners did not want to commit themselves to a native language and said that they spoke both Ukrainian and Russian.[21] But even though the state language is Ukrainian and it is used in the regional state administration, Russian continues to dominate in public and private everyday life. These language habits reflect regional history, which in turn is shaped by in-migration and cultural and linguistic assimilation.

At the same time, the regional power elite uses and politicises the issue of the status of the Russian language in order to present itself as the advocate of the regional population and to exert pressure on the national centre. Thus, it perpetuates the importance attached to the Russian language. But there has not been any political mobilisation of the Russian-speaking population since they do not consider themselves as *rossiyany* (citizens of Russia or the Russian Federation), even though more than a few of them might identify themselves as *russkie* (Russians defined by culture and language). As mentioned before, the strong regional identity overshadows other modes of identity and inhibits mobilisation in national terms.

But Russia is not only relevant as a cultural point of reference, but also valued in economic and political relations. In 1997, most people in the region perceived the development of economic and trade ties with Russia (62.3 per cent) and with the CIS (49.2 per cent) as beneficial for Ukraine. Among those who advocated stronger ties with Russia, 27 per cent favoured the re-establishment of the Soviet Union, 28 per cent the conclusion of a political union within the CIS, and 12 per cent a union with Russia (Tsentr Politologicheskikh Issledovanii 1997: 13), although it remains unclear what the shape and substance of such a union would be. In 2001 between 78 and 81 per cent expressed a positive attitude towards a possible union of Ukraine and Russia with Belarus (DIATs 2001). In general, people looked favourably at the intensification of cultural (88.1 per cent), economic (83.7 per cent) and military ties (58.4 per cent) with Russia (DIATs 2000).

Although many people in Donetsk oblast are in favour of stronger ties with Russia and other CIS countries, none of my interview partners mentioned that they wanted their region to be part of the Russian Federation today and none questioned the right of the Ukrainian nation-state to exist. Relevant local actors, including most of my interview partners, have accepted the Ukrainian *derzhava* (state) as a framework for action. Many of them have helped to shape it and together with other regional actors they have material interests in the continuance of that state, towards which their 'lobbying' and rent-seeking strategies are directed.[22] It remains, however, an empty structure without symbolic strength or potential for identification, because '[sovereignty] is simply an established fact to be reckoned with, like the weather' (Garnett 1999: 44).[23] Along these lines, none of my interview partners mentioned the emergence of an independent Ukrainian state as an important stage in the region's history. In this sense, Ukraine as such has not yet become the prevalent imagined community for people in Donetsk region.

In the business sphere, the attention paid to CIS markets is also conditioned by difficulties encountered on other international markets and Ukraine's dependence on energy imports from former Soviet Union countries. Some interviewees doubted whether Ukrainian producers have any prospect of penetrating Western markets, as those markets have already been divided up.[24] Hence Ukraine, and especially Donetsk region, should concentrate on the 'lost' markets in the east. Several interviewees held the dissolution of the Soviet Union responsible for the region's economic problems. They consider the Soviet phase to have been positive, and because the Donbas has always been connected with Russia – and later the Soviet Union – numerous participants regard today's separation into two independent economic spheres as unnatural and harmful. For them, the rapprochement between Russia and Ukraine signifies the gradual re-creation of the former order.[25]

There are also close linkages and real interest in co-operation with Russian firms and political actors in several fields. Several official agreements on co-operation both with the Russian Federation and with single federal subjects or cities have been concluded. There are close ties with Moscow, where a Donbas diaspora (*zemlyachestvo*) is even active.[26] During Soviet times many people from the Donbas moved to Moscow, and some of them today hold high positions within the federal or city government. Allegedly 200,000 people from the Donbas reside in Moscow. The diaspora mainly serves as a mediator between the political establishments of Donetsk and Moscow. The relationship between the two mayors, that is Vladimir Rybak (until March 2002) and Yurii Luzhkov, is considered 'comrade-like'.[27] For the time being the old friends are actively exchanging symbolic souvenirs. A copy of the newly conceived symbol of Donetsk region, the Mertsalov palm tree, was unveiled on Moscow's Manezhnaya Square. In return the city of Donetsk was given a copy of the famous Pushkin Gun, which is a symbol of Russian statehood.[28] The discourse and symbolic actions such as festivities construct and re-construct the image of Russia by drawing attention to the mutual relations and by reviving them time and again.

The West

This section makes transparent the interviewees' perception of Europe and the United States of America. Regarding their assessment of foreign actors and their actions, one can discern some differences among the interview partners. Whereas NGO representatives by and large exhibit a more positive attitude, interviewees from state organisations and a part of the business and scientific community articulate rather sceptical to negative attitudes. But all of them prefer self-reliance and refuse to wait for 'help' from the outside. Asked about foreign assistance to the development of the region, a respected academic and consultant to different public authorities painted the following picture: 'I have the impression that, for America and Europe, Ukraine is not a subject but an object. It is not a partner, with whom one should work and whom one should support, but something to be exploited and observed.' In his view the West takes advantage of Ukraine's position, only gives credit but does not invest in spite of allegedly favourable conditions such as cheap labour. Asked about the reasons, the interviewee replied:

Well, because nobody in Europe is interested in Ukraine's being an independent state. Because Ukraine is a big state, a huge territory with a large population. It is a new competitor. They are afraid of competitors . . . What should we do? Well, it is necessary to work oneself and not to hope for help . . . What does the help consist of? The foreigners flood our market and aggravate the situation. Our industry lies idle, salaries decline, the capital stock decays, unemployment rises, because foreign goods are imported in large amounts . . . Thus, so far, America and Europe have helped us with the decline of our economy and not with its development.[29]

Other actors from public administration and educational institutes agreed and expressed their distrust of Western economic and lending organisations. Their general scepticism towards foreign financial and technical assistance is partly linked to first-hand experience, but also to a conviction that one knows one's own backyard, in which outsiders should not interfere. Some interviewees assumed that Western organisations want to turn Ukraine into a peripheral state that supplies raw material and semi-finished products and that imports consumer goods.

When asked about their assessment of international co-operation within the region, NGOs and others who benefit from concrete projects and grants mostly regarded it as substantial and positive. Others criticised the character of international help or claimed not to know of or perceive any assistance. An employee of the regional state administration expressed his disdain about co-operation with international donors:

Yes, there are programmes of TACIS and programmes of the international banks. But to tell the truth, in my opinion, frankly, it does not pay to put one's faith in them . . . Yes, to some extent they have influence, but it is necessary to accomplish things on one's own . . . We already know what needs to be done. It is necessary for the economy to become stable – and we must accomplish it.

When asked about joint projects, he responded: 'I do not expect much from it. If you don't do it yourself, nobody will come and do it. At the official level it is all promoted, but informally I do not believe in it.'[30]

One public official described the work of foreign consultants in the region as follows:

Well, I would not say that [the international advisers' work] inspires me very much. They do not know our specifics . . . We know more, we know our way around here and we know the European experience . . . Therefore, it seems to me that the foreign experience with its offers . . . is on a very low level, personally for me. My higher education allows me to understand the economic problems of all the countries in the world. I am proud of this education, which I received during Soviet times . . . All these programmes, they might be normal for China or maybe for Africa. But the region of Donetsk has a huge potential and produces many goods. Here we have trained personnel, a valuable *intelligentsiya*, scientific personnel, 80 scientific institutes that invented devices to fly into space or to drive under water . . . And they come here to tell us how to organise companies in order to get things going. So far the [rest of the] world hasn't produced techniques such as those, that are known to the scientists of Donetsk and produced here. And they come to us and talk to us as if we were natives of Africa or New Zealand. Well, for me this is just ridiculous. In such cases I just sit there politely, listen quietly to what they have to tell me . . . Unfortunately, it is like this.[31]

On the basis of the above interviews and assessments given by foreign consultants on the spot,[32] one can conclude that there is little commitment to co-operation at the regional and local level, especially on the part of some of the beneficiaries such as the regional state administration. The perception of foreign actors and organisations rationalises the increasing structural closure of the region vis-à-vis foreign influence. This mind-set is the complement of the regional actors' accommodation to the international economic competition, in which they take advantage of favourable internal conditions and structures conducive to the economic success of specific sectors. In other words, the ideological justification of protectionism reflected in the identity discourse provides the financial industrial groups with a privileged position compared to foreign investors.

Assessing the assets

A decisive part of the actors' regional identity is their perception of the present value of their region. The question of how to assess and use the regional potential revealed apparent substantial cleavages among the different interview partners. Taking the assessment of the region's potential and proposed strategies for the future as a guiding principle, one can roughly discern three different groups of interview partners: the Old Boys, the Ambivalent and the Progressives. The Old Boys and the Progressives represent opposed points of the compass. Yet, the quantitative balance is very unequal as most interview partners can be characterised as oriented towards the past. These conservative and backward-oriented Old Boys can mainly be found in public administration, at both the local and the regional level, as well as in big (state-owned) companies and the traditional trade unions.[33] They portrayed their region in affirmative terminology and conveyed an image of a dynamic industrial region that will rise again and rescue Ukraine. In most of these interviews, processes of decay were denied, played down or described as transition phenomena from one positive status to the next. If the interviewees did mention processes of decay, they described them as events which have their roots outside the country or in 'natural' conditions. In the eyes of these respondents, these are beyond their control and do not entail a need for the development of new strategies. Interviewees pointed to recent statistics that showed relatively high growth rates and interpreted them as a proof of the aptness of their vision and strategy.[34]

The second group, the Ambivalent, form a medium-sized group of actors who are hard to generalise about. They include some open-minded public officials, some NGO representatives and representatives of new and independent trade unions. Their views are a mixture of thinking in terms of preservation of the old structures and thinking of new ways of solving problems. Several of them have adopted new ideas and have some vision of what should change in the region. However, occasionally the new ideas seem to have been adopted from international programmes and sound like catchphrases, with a strong personal commitment and interest lacking. These actors have embraced new ways of solving problems, which makes their approach less hierarchical and constraining and more collaborative. In general they favour more democratic procedures within organisations and in dealing with others. Their organisations are more transparent and accessible to outsiders. Many of them have created a job for themselves by establishing their 'own' NGO, but their organisations are barely rooted in society. As they depend on outside sources of funds, satisfying their foreign donors becomes more relevant to them than securing real changes. Through their international connections they have access to alternative sources of information. They often view the local situation differently from the Old Boys, having adopted different yardsticks and long-term objectives. At the same time some of them, on the very basis of their foreign contacts, have come to argue that Ukraine – and especially the Donbas – inherently differs from Western countries and therefore has to seek its own specific solutions. Thus they are sometimes prepared to endorse the way the regional elite acts. Open criticism of regional rulers does not belong to their repertoire, at least not during recorded interviews. Moreover, they inevitably become involved with the local authorities through their work and thus become more careful and prepared to compromise in their actual behaviour – a fact which is, on occasion, exacerbated by their dependence on the state.

The final group, the Progressives, includes some NGO representatives but is mainly made up of new private entrepreneurs who are not closely connected to the authorities and/or have retained some autonomy. They exhibit both new ways of thinking about regional potential and new visions for the region's future. Their perceptions are related to their own status and corresponding interests. However, they have neither decision-making power in the political or legislative sense nor a distinct lobby to influence decisions. Although they perceive their region in almost the same way as the well-established actors, their conclusions are different and they criticise the current situation. They see ambivalences in the industrial structure of the region and question the prevalent way of thinking:

> On the one hand [the economic potential of the region] is enormous and this is good, but on the other hand it is enormous and this is bad. Who needs these steel plants with this consumption, with these inefficient production cycles, irrational structures and so on? This applies to all gigantic companies, of which we have many.[35]

The Progressives criticise public revenue and expenditure policies. In their opinion, most major enterprises pay no taxes and do not contribute to the national budget, which is financed by the new private entrepreneurs. Moreover, they object to the behaviour of the political and economic elite and decry the character of the system:

> They are all the same people who used to govern, who used to steal. What can they do, except for stealing? Nothing, and they do not want to do anything else . . . This happened to us. They came across a huge amount of money that lay at their feet in 1991. This mountain was seen by the young and ruthless . . . and they took it.[36]

The Progressives voice a general critique of the system and formulate a counter-project and exhibit thinking in terms of generalised rules. Even though they are well aware of the fact that the regional power structures have come to control the vital parts of the productive and non-productive spheres, several independent interviewees called for reforms of the regional economic and political structure:

> Well, many big companies are still state-owned. They are joint stock companies, but still state-owned. Therefore, there is strong control of the business. This is very bad, because the state should regulate the economy by money flows but must not manage enterprises. But they are engaged in such things . . . Where the state has a controlling share, the influence on the company is great.[37]

Nevertheless, the progressive actors are quite isolated, and their contacts with the more numerous conservative actors are extremely limited. Their views hardly reach the public domain as they have little access to the media. Instead they often derive and maintain their standing by establishing viable contacts outside the region, often with foreign partners.

What needs to be done? The future is in the past

All the actors' aforementioned dispositions lead to specific ideas for the future development of the region. Most respondents – with the exception of the Progressives – constructed historical continuity and linearity, from which they derived both the present and the future role of the region, which does not differ significantly from that of the past. Historically available and current options were excluded. Times of crisis were omitted and breaks and ambivalences in the historical development were not perceived. The extremely selective perception of regional history allows Soviet historiography to persist. For example, the devastating famine of the 1930s was not mentioned in a single interview[38] and most interview partners did not mention a break with the Soviet system.[39]

But in the economic sphere, one has to mention that historical models of a different economic structure in the form of small and medium-size enterprises are indeed not present. In this regard, the regional actors have a limited reservoir of symbolic resources to choose from. The only structures that can be regarded as typical and historically developed are those which entail little or no growth in the long run, but depend on subsidies and are exposed to fluctuations on the world market, i.e. above all the steel industry and its domestic suppliers. In this situation actors who are close to state structures rationalise the existing structure and reject models that are proposed from the outside:

> Small companies do not suit Donetsk oblast – it consists of large, gigantic companies. Like a sponge, these companies have absorbed the people, and they are tied to the companies like rowers on Turkish galleys: they cannot escape anywhere from this ship . . . And what should the small companies do, if it is the large ones that are profitable? In general people work in large companies. There must be a director, there must be engineer services, and everyone must fulfil his function. Well, it happened that our people want to do things this way . . . Why should one give that up? Is one to take a mine, close it and open small mines? Or close a factory and open small metalworking companies? No, that is not normal. One must understand Donetsk oblast and understand the general situation in Ukraine. In other oblasts it is exactly the same. This is the way things are here.[40]

The historical development and people's habits are portrayed as a barrier to any alternative policy and serve as a justification for and explanation for not leaving the beaten track. Such a conservative attitude is discernible with regard to industrial policy as well. In the view of people linked to the coal sector, coal is Ukraine's only 'own' (i.e. domestic) energy source and therefore needs to be sustained, developed and subsidised. In turn, it is thought to spur the development of other sectors.[41] The actors most closely connected with state structures assume that everything will remain as it is and that the region will rise again on the basis of the 'old orientation' and in new (equals old) splendour, because 'in the future it will be exactly the same'.[42]

Conclusion: regional identity and region capture

The research revealed that the self-descriptive discourse mirrors the economic development tendencies and strategies. Both highlight the role of heavy industry and restrict the region and its inhabitants to the 'traditional role' as an industrial centre. The image feeds itself mostly from Soviet times, but is projected on to the present situation and into the future. Drawbacks or dangers pertaining to the one-sided economic structure are not considered. The appropriateness of the regional economic adaptation is not questioned. Most respondents explained the region's economic problems with reference to the disintegration of the Soviet Union and systemic transformation. They perceive the crisis as temporary rather than as structural, which means that real reforms appear unnecessary. At the same time, they – successfully – demand investment in old structures. Resources are re-directed and invested to secure and expand their own power base.

Alternative models are discarded as inadequate, which is justified historically and by reference to the habits of the population. The actors rationalise the current

structure and related actions. Hegemonic and isolated organisational and communicative practices do not allow us to speak of relational or informational redundancy.
For that reason the diagnosis is a grave cognitive lock-in. The homogeneous
and coherent regional discourse is rarely disrupted by deviant interpretations.
However, even though there is a consensus on what the region is, there is disagree-
ment among – weakly interrelated – groups of actors on how this regional potential
is to be evaluated and used and/or transformed for the future. Instead the Progressives
are marginalised or – on occasion – co-opted and silenced (Zimmer 2004).

The regional identity has an integrative power, and it also incorporates the
regional population, whose achievements form the very basis of that identity.
Potentially such a marked regional identity can serve as a common ground for
co-operation and progress, and as a resource for endogenous development. But in
the post-Soviet context in the Donbas, this feature proves to be problematic. As in
many other old industrial regions, it relates to an idealised icon of the region, which
has become detached from reality (Grabher 1993, 1994) and cannot be instrumen-
talised for conceiving and implementing inclusive development projects. The
narratives and thinking of most interview partners lack reflexivity and a proper
long-term assessment of regional potential in the context of worldwide competition. There is no historical stock of ideas which transcend the attachment to the
'here and now'. This lack of a rich symbolic resource derived from history impedes
the re-invention and envisioning of the region.

The cohesiveness of the regional alliance is time and again reinforced by
emphatic appeals to the productive mission of the region (Grabher 1993), which
symbolically includes the regional population and serves as an ideological way of
impeding the emergence of new industries. The dominant ideology vis-à-vis
the outside world, especially the West, rationalises the structural closure and the
unsatisfactory development of the region. The cognitive lock-in has been frozen
into an ideology that regards the region not as a hostage of its own power elite
and of the powerlessness of society, but as a victim of global forces that either
show an interest in the region or stay away, and are criticised whatever they do. It
is a self-centred discourse. In contrast to those in western Ukrainian regions, the
actors in Donetsk region do not consciously delineate themselves from other parts
of the country (Šabić 2004). They simply do not need the outside for their self-
identification. They are not able to relate to other regions. The only outside actors
that enter the scene are Kiev as the political centre and other countries, in the context
of which the West is conceived of negatively.

The fact that the regional discourse has not changed decisively can be explained
by the lack of qualitative changes to the elite at the regional and local level. Many
nomenklatura members continue to hold important positions in the administrative
and economic sphere. But the newly emerged actors also take advantage of and
sustain this discourse. They appease the population and pretend to be their advo-
cates, both in the region and – more importantly – in the national centre and against
foreign exploiters.[43] This discourse is advantageous to them as it corresponds to
their immediate aims related to power and wealth. The emphasis on the region's
uniqueness and achievements allows them to derive their claim for power and

decision-making rights. Lately, one can notice a tendency to integrate this regional identity into a Ukrainian identity (or, possibly, vice versa), mixing regional symbols with symbols of Ukrainian statehood. This strategy is mainly advocated by the regional elite that wants to prove its loyalty to the central authorities, mainly President Kuchma, and thus officially promotes the process of Ukrainisation. Recently, the regional discourse is officially extended by national Ukrainian elements, because the regional elite's claim for power is asserted and effected in the Ukrainian national context.

I do not conclude that all future development of Donetsk region is predestined. For the time being, it is difficult to assess the likelihood of new development directions as many uncertain events at the international, national and regional levels affect them. But undoubtedly the present structural and cognitive disposition of the region precludes its adaptability to external changes and prospects for sustainable development. The economic basis continues to be heavy industry, which is inextricably linked to the present discourse. Nevertheless, the discourse might change in the medium term. Important economic actors have started to shift their economic power base away from heavy industry.[44] But the question remains whether only the content will change (imposed from above) or whether the structure of the discourse will change as well and become more open.

Notes

1 The empirical findings of this chapter are based on in-depth analysis of the regional discourse as well as political and economic processes in Donetsk region. The field research (1999–2000) was conducted within the research project 'Local and Regional Development Policy in Central and Eastern Europe: Actors and Institutions in Poland, Hungary, Romania and Ukraine' led by Professor Melanie Tatur, University of Frankfurt am Main, and funded by the Volkswagen Foundation.
2 Interviewees consisted of representatives of regional governments, assemblies and related organisations, regional representatives of the central state, activists of economic interest organisations, cultural associations and NGOs active in the field of local and regional development, scholars and several private entrepreneurs as well as managers of state-owned companies. The interviews were semi-structured, and they were all taped and transcribed. In the section of the interviews that the present chapter is based on, interviewees were asked to talk about their region. Most interviews were conducted in the city of Donetsk, and a few in Artemovsk, a medium-sized city in the north of Donetsk region.
3 The Donbas, abbreviated from 'Donetsk Coal Basin', historically comprises large parts of eastern Ukraine and part of the Rostov oblast in today's Russia. The Ukrainian Donbas includes almost all the territories of the Donetsk and Lugansk oblasts, as well as the eastern rim of Dnipropetrovsk and Zaporizhzhia oblasts (Lyakh 1999a).
4 The notion of 'clan' is rather problematic and not well defined in the Ukrainian context. It is preferable to use the concept of 'administrative economic groups' as it exposes the lacking delineation of the political and economic sphere.
5 In the Russian context the notion of Party of Power is used to label a specific type of informal power structure (Ryabov 1998) that has access to the inner circle of political decision-making, that is the president and his surroundings, and is organised as a network of followers – the *komanda* – that cuts across all kinds of formal institutional differentiation linking administration and Parliament, different political parties, the media, and economic organisations and corporations.

6 The fact that the former director of the regional television and radio station was dismissed when the governor was ousted in 1996 indicates the importance of this position, or rather the importance the state structures attribute to the mass media and their influence on the population in both a discursive and an informational sense.

7 The dominant portrayal of the area as industrialised and urbanised is appropriate only to the agglomeration in the centre of the region, whereas other parts are sparsely inhabited and less industrialised. None of the respondents touched upon the disparities in the economic and social structure within the region or the tremendous contrasts between the city and the countryside.

8 Those referring to history were mostly related to the city administration or the heavy industry sector. In Donetsk some of them referred to the founding history of the city, which is centred around the Welsh entrepreneur John Hughes, who managed the first steel factory of Novorossiiskoe Obshchestvo. At the time of the first interviews this was present in a special way, as the city was officially celebrating its 130th anniversary.

9 Interview with a head of department, Donetsk Regional State Administration, 1999.

10 *Donbass: Primus inter Pares*, published by Kardinal Publishing House, Donetsk, 1996.

11 The Russian term *kuznitsa kadrov* refers to the intellectual and technical potential and educational facilities of the region that produced highly qualified cadres for the Soviet bureaucracy and economy. This notion also includes aspects of indoctrination and loyalty to the party line.

12 Interview with a representative of the Secretariat of the Council of Free Economic Zones, Donetsk, 1999. By and large, the interviewees' yardstick for the classification of the region continues to be the Soviet Union and criteria connected with the Soviet system. For example, size and output continue to be yardsticks by which the value of a company is measured.

13 Some respondents, mainly from the business sphere, compared the Donetsk region with America in its function as a settlement and its frontier character as well as a melting pot of cultures. They referred to different immigration waves from Russia and later the whole Soviet Union. This nationality mix is evaluated positively today, since it is perceived as preventing national tensions from arising. Western Ukrainian nationalism and the national policy of Ukrainisation are opposed by people who delineate themselves by stressing their own tolerance and multiculturalism. Yet, this understanding of the region's make-up is also a product of Soviet propaganda and historiography, which always portrayed the Soviet Union as a multi-national country where national and/or ethnic differences were allegedly insignificant. Donetsk continues to serve as an embodiment of this perception.

14 Many inhabitants associate few positive connotations with Independence Day. Many, especially older people, associate it with the demise of the Soviet Union and the beginning of economic decline. In 1991 they hoped that economic improvement would set in, and they are hardly ready to accept further hardship for the sake of an independent Ukraine (Wittkowsky 1998). In eastern Ukraine, many people thought Ukrainian independence would be attained within a (changed) Soviet context and involve political autonomy and economic independence from Moscow. They had not anticipated a separate state having international borders with other (post-) Soviet states, the severance of economic ties, or the introduction of a separate currency (Lieven 1999: 48).

15 Mertsalov was employed at the Novorossiiskoe Obshchestvo, which owned the first and most important steel factory in the city.

16 Website of the regional state administration: http://www.oda.dc.dn.ua/simbol.html.

17 Ivzhenko (2001) also pointed to this usage. Former Donetsk Governor Viktor Yanukovich often employed this motto.

18 In 2001 a monument to the first secretary of the Communist Party in Donetsk during the 1970s was set up in one of the areas of the city.

19 For the miners' perception, see Siegelbaum and Walkowitz (1995), Siegelbaum (1997: 13–14) and Crowley (1997a).

20 Some authors contend it could be a non-ethnically defined (civic) Ukrainian identity, i.e. an identification with the Ukrainian state (not the nation). But currently, this seems quite unlikely, because of the bad performance of the Ukrainian state.

21 This might partly be a politically correct answer in line with the state policy of Ukrainisation, which is officially uncontested by the Donetsk political decision makers, who would like to prove their loyalty towards the national leadership in Kiev. On the other hand, they favour the Russian language as well in order to appease the regional population.

22 Rent-seeking strategies are discernible with regard to the coal mining industry and the establishment of free economic zones in Donetsk region as well as the introduction of a so-called experiment in the metallurgical sector. All these privileges have been received in exchange for loyalty to the president and pro-presidential forces.

23 As mentioned above, the regional elite strives to be particularly Ukrainian in order to demonstrate its loyalty towards the national centre.

24 Low product quality and competitiveness were not discussed during the interviews. Thus the interviewees – mostly from the big businesses and semi-public structures – perceived Western markets as 'politically' allocated.

25 The present governor of Donetsk region Anatolii Bliznyuk made similar statements during a public speech in 2001.

26 It can be regarded as an organisation dominated by former *nomenklatura* actors. The Donetsk-based Organisation for the Enhancement of the Popularity of the Donbas, the 'Golden Skythian', as well as the 'political dinosaurs', former Donetsk mayor Vladimir Rybak and Efim Zviagilskiy, one of the Red Directors, who used to be Ukrainian prime minister in 1993–1994, were actively involved in the upgrading of the earlier established diaspora organisation.

27 Interview with a head of department, Donetsk City Administration, Donetsk, 2000; *ForUm*, 21 September 2001.

28 But in addition to these mostly symbolic events, there are hard business interests that partly take advantage of these diaspora ties (one could also claim that the latter are merely of an instrumental character) and extend them to other spheres and circles of actors. But – as is not uncommon in the post-Soviet context in Ukraine – they are difficult to trace.

29 Interview with a head of department, Academy of Sciences, Donetsk, 1999.

30 Interview with an employee of the Donetsk Regional State Administration, 2000.

31 Interview with a representative of the Secretariat of the Council of Free Economic Zones, Donetsk, 1999.

32 Several – unrecorded – interviews with foreign consultants were conducted as well.

33 The present Ukrainian trade union movement is basically split into two major groups: the big old (former Soviet) trade unions and the much smaller new trade unions, several of which emerged during and after the strike movement of 1989–1991. In the coal sector these groups are represented by the Trade Union of Workers in the Coal Industry (Profsoyuz Rabochikh Ugol'noi Promyshchlennosti Ukrainy – PRUP) and the Independent Coalminers' Trade Union of Ukraine (Nezavissimyi Profzoyus Gornyakov Ukrainy – NPGU).

34 This made evident the interviewees' inclination to treat production increase as an end in itself and not as a means towards public welfare and the sustainable development of the region.

35 Interview with a private entrepreneur, Donetsk, 1999.

36 Interview with the owner of a publishing house, Donetsk, 1999.

37 Interview with a private entrepreneur, Donetsk, 1999.

38 This is both a manifestation of the eradication of that collective memory and a sign of a failure to reappraise the Soviet past. The topic of the famine in the 1930s continues to be taboo in the east of Ukraine, where the famine took place and cost many lives. Recent interviews about family and local history in the Donbas show how little younger

generations know about the life of their parents and grandparents. Often, they only found out about certain events during the course of the interviews. The famine was not mentioned in a single interview (Agentstvo Regional'nogo Razvitiya 'Donbass' 2000). In contrast the famine is widely discussed in western Ukraine, the area that was not affected by it. But here it is used as further evidence of Russian dominance and oppression of the Ukrainian people.

39 If they did perceive a break, they did not relate it to national independence in 1991 but to the beginning of economic reforms in 1995, for example, interview with a head of department, Donetsk Regional State Administration, 1999.

40 Interview with a representative of the Secretariat of the Council for Free Economic Zones, Donetsk, 1999.

41 Interview with the deputy director of a coal mine, Donetsk, 2000. This view was supported by several other interview partners from the state structures and (former) state-owned companies.

42 Interview with the deputy director of a metal processing company, Donetsk, 1999.

43 The paternalistic attitudes of many people in Donetsk region support this strategy.

44 Recently, the financial industrial groups have been forcefully expanding into food processing and telecommunications.

References

Åberg, M. (2000) 'Putnam's social capital theory goes east: a case study of western Ukraine and L'viv', *Europe–Asia Studies*, **52**(2): 295–317.

Åberg, M. and M. Sandberg (2002) *Social Capital and Democratisation: Roots of Trust in Post-Communist Poland and Ukraine*, Burlington, VT: Ashgate.

Agentstvo Regional'nogo Razvitiya 'Donbass' (2000) *Zhiznennye Strategii Grazhdan Donbassa: Perekhodnoe Sostoyanie*, Donetsk: ARD.

Anderson, B. (1998) *Imagined Communities: Reflections on the Origin and Spread of Nationalism*, London: Verso.

Åslund, A. (1999) 'Problems with economic transformation in Ukraine', Conference paper: Fifth Dubrovnik Conference on Transition Economies, Dubrovnik, Croatia, 23–25 June, http://www.ceip.org/people/aslDubrovnik.html.

Åslund, A. (2002) *Why Has Ukraine Returned to Economic Growth?*, Working Paper 15, Kyiv: Institute for Economic Research and Policy Consulting.

Berger, P. L. and T. Luckmann (1967) *The Social Construction of Reality: A Treatise in the Sociology of Knowledge*, New York: Anchor Books.

Borisov, V. and S. Clarke (1994) 'Reform and revolution in the Communist National Park?', *Capital and Class*, 53: 9–14.

Crowley, S. (1997a) 'Coal miners and the transformation of the USSR', *Post-Soviet Affairs*, **13**(2): 167–95.

Crowley, S. (1997b) *Hot Coal, Cold Steel: Russian and Ukrainian Workers from the End of the Soviet Union to the Post-Communist Transformations*, Ann Arbor, MI: University of Michigan Press.

Crowley, S. and L. H. Siegelbaum (1995) 'Survival strategies: the miners of Donetsk in the post-Soviet era', in L. H. Siegelbaum and D. J. Walkowitz (eds), *Workers of the Donbass Speak: Survival and Identity in the New Ukraine, 1989–1992*, Albany, NY: State University of New York Press, pp. 61–96.

Donets'kii Informatsionno-analiticheskii Tsentr (DIATs) (2000) *Press Reliz*, Donetsk, www.diac.dn.ua.

Donets'kii Informatsionno-analiticheskii Tsentr (DIATs) (2001) *Press Reliz*, Donetsk, www.diac.dn.ua.

Donetskii Informatsionno-analiticheskii Tsentr (DIATs) (2002) *Press Reliz*, Donetsk, www.diac.dn.ua.

Friedgut, T. H. (1994) 'Perestroika in the provinces: the politics of transition in Donetsk', in T. H. Friedgut and J. W. Hahn (eds), *Local Power and Post-Soviet Politics*, Armonk, NY: M. E. Sharpe, pp. 162–83.

Garnett, S. W. (1999) 'Ukraine and Russia', in Center for Strategic and International Studies (ed.), *Ukraine in Europe*, Washington, DC: Center for Strategic Studies, pp. 42–9.

Golovakha, E. and N. Y. Panina (1997) 'Rossiisko-Ukrainskie Otnosheniya V Obshchestvennom Mnenii Ukrainy I Rossii', in D. E. Furman (ed.), *Ukraina I Rossiya: Obshchestva I Gosudarstva*, Moscow: Prava cheloveka, pp. 259–77.

Grabher, G. (1993) 'The weakness of strong ties: the lock-in of regional development in the Ruhr area', in G. Grabher (ed.), *The Embedded Firm: On the Socioeconomics of Industrial Networks*, London/New York: Routledge, pp. 255–77.

Grabher, G. (1994) *Lob der Verschwendung: Redundanz in der Regionalentwicklung: Ein Sozioökonomisches Plädoyer*, Berlin: Edition Sigma.

Hellman, J. S., G. Jones and D. Kaufmann (2000) *'Seize the State, Seize the Day': State Capture, Corruption and Influence in Transition*, World Bank Policy Research Working Paper, 2444.

Hrytsak, Y. (2001) 'National identities in post-Soviet Ukraine: the case of Lviv and Donetsk', in Z. Y. Gitelman, L. Hajda, J.-P. Himka and R. Solchanyk (eds), *Cultures and Nations of Central and Eastern Europe: Essays in Honor of Roman Szporluk*, Cambridge, MA: Harvard Ukrainian Research Institute, pp. 263–81.

Ivzhenko, T. Y. (2001) '"Donetskii Klan" Uverenno Vkhodit Vo Vlast'. Sleduyushchii Prezident Ukrainy Mozhet Okazat'sya Predstavitelem Kraya Uglya I Metally', *Nezavisimaya Gazeta*, 149, 15 August, http://www.ng.ru/cis/2001-08-15/5_donetsck. html (last viewed 31 October 2002).

Kharkhordin, O. (1999) *The Collective and the Individual in Russia: A Study of Practices*, Berkeley, CA: University of California Press.

Kubicek, P. (1999) *Unbroken Ties: The State, Interest Associations, and Corporatism in Post-Soviet Ukraine*, Ann Arbor, MI: University of Michigan Press.

Kubicek, P. (2000) 'Regional polarisation in Ukraine: public opinion, voting and legislative behaviour', *Europe–Asia Studies*, **52**(2): 273–94.

Kuzio, T. (1998) *Ukraine: State and Nation Building*, London: Routledge.

Levitsky, S. and L. Way (2001) 'Competitive authoritarianism: hybrid regime change in Peru and Ukraine in comparative perspective', Conference paper: Annual Meeting of the American Political Science Association, San Francisco, CA, 30 August–2 September.

Liber, G. O. (1998) 'Imagining Ukraine: regional differences and the emergence of an integrated state identity, 1926–1994', *Nations and Nationalism*, 2: 187–206.

Lieven, A. (1999) *Ukraine and Russia: A Fraternal Rivalry*, Washington, DC: United States Institute of Peace Press.

Lyakh, A. and W. Pankow (eds) (1998) *The Future of Old Industrial Regions in Europe: The Case of Donetsk Region in Ukraine*, Warsaw: Foundation for Economic Education.

Lyakh, O. (1999a) 'The Donbas: actors, agendas and strategies in regional policy', in M. Tatur (ed.), *The Challenge of Regional Policies: Actors and Institutions on the Local and Regional Level in Post-Socialist Europe*, Eschborn: GTZ, pp. 147–59.

Lyakh, O. (1999b) Regional profile: region of Donetsk. Unpublished data, gathered within the framework of the research project 'Actors and Institutions of Regional Development Policy in Poland, Romania, Hungary and Ukraine'.

Malanchuk, O. (1999) 'Social identification versus regionalism in contemporary Ukraine', Conference paper: 'Local Troubles, Global Problems': Conference on Social Problems and Transition around the Baltic Sea, Helsinki/Tallinn, 26–28 August.

Matsuzato, K. (2001) 'From communist boss politics to post-communist caciquismo: the meso-elite and meso-governments in post-communist countries', *Communist and Post-Communist Studies*, **34**(2): 175–201.

Miller, A. H., T. F. Klobucar, W. M. Reisinger and V. L. Hesli (1998) 'Social identities in Russia, Ukraine, and Lithuania', *Post-Soviet Affairs*, 3: 248–86.

North, D. C. (1990) *Institutions, Institutional Change, and Economic Performance*, Cambridge/New York: Cambridge University Press.

Ryabov, A. (1998) '"Partiya Vlasti" v Politicheskoi Sisteme Sovremennoi Rossii', in M. McFaul, S. Markarov and A. Ryabov (eds), *Formirovanie Partiino-Politicheskoi Sistemy v Rossii*, Moscow: Carnegie Center, pp. 80–96.

Šabić, C. (2004) 'The Ukrainian Piedmont: the L'viv region', in M. Tatur (ed.), *The Making of Regions*, Wiesbaden: VS Verlag für Sozialwissenschaften, pp. 131–229.

Šabić, C. and K. Zimmer (2004) 'Ukraine: the genesis of a captured state', in M. Tatur (ed.), *The Making of Regions*, Wiesbaden: VS Verlag für Sozialwissenschaften, pp. 107–30.

Schütz, A. and T. Luckmann (1979) *Strukturen der Lebenswelt*, Frankfurt: Suhrkamp.

Shulman, S. (1998) 'Cultures in competition: Ukrainian foreign policy and the "cultural threat" from abroad', *Europe–Asia Studies*, **50**(2): 287–303.

Shulman, S. (1999a) 'Asymmetrical international integration and Ukrainian national disunity', *Political Geography*, 18: 913–39.

Shulman, S. (1999b) 'The cultural foundations of Ukrainian national identity', *Ethnic and Racial Studies*, **22**(6): 1011–36.

Siedenberg, A. and Hoffmann, L. (1999) *Ukraine at the Crossroads: Economic Reforms in International Perspective*, Heidelberg/New York: Physica-Verlag.

Siegelbaum, L. H. (1997) 'Freedom of prices and the price of freedom: the miners' dilemma in the Soviet Union and its successor states', *Journal of Communist Studies and Transition Politics*, **13**(4): 1–27.

Siegelbaum, L. H. and D. J. Walkowitz (1995) *Workers of the Donbass Speak: Survival and Identity in the New Ukraine, 1989–1992*, Albany, NY: State University of New York Press.

Subtelny, O. (1995) 'Russocentrism, regionalism, and the political culture of Ukraine', in V. Tismaneanu (ed.), *Political Culture and Civil Society in Russia and the New States of Eurasia: The International Politics of Eurasia*, New York/London: M. E. Sharpe, pp. 189–207.

Tsentr Politologicheskikh Issledovanii, S. S. (1997) *Proekt 'Izuchenie Obshchestvennogo Mneniya Kak Sotsial'nogo Faktora Razvitiya Donetskoi Oblasti'*, Donetsk: Tsentr Politologicheskikh Issledovanii.

Turchinov, O. (2000) 'Peciliarities [*sic*] of oligarchy in Ukraine', *Political Thought*, **7**(3–4): 51–7.

Volovodova, E. (1999a) 'Razvitie Territorii V Raionakh Zakritiya Shakht', *Biznesinform*, 7–8: 10–12.

Volovodova, E. (1999b) 'Report on the situation in the coal settlement near the Pravda Mine, Proletarskii Raion, Donetsk' (unpublished), National Academy of Sciences, Donetsk.

Wilson, A. (2001) 'Ukraine's new virtual politics', *East European Constitutional Review*, **10**(2/3).

Wilson, A. and Khmelko, V. (1998) 'Regionalism and ethnic and linguistic cleavages in Ukraine', in T. Kuzio (ed.), *Contemporary Ukraine: Dynamics of Post-Soviet Transformation*, Armonk, NY: M. E. Sharpe, pp. 60–80.

Wittkowsky, A. (1998) *Fünf Jahre ohne Plan: Die Ukraine 1991–1996. National-staatsbildung, Wirtschaft und Eliten*, Hamburg: Lit.

Zadorozhnyuk, E. and D. E. Furman (1997) 'Ukrainskie Regiony i Ukrainskaya Politika', in D. E. Furman (ed.), *Ukraina i Rossiya: Obshchestva i Gosudarstva*, Moscow: Prava cheloveka, pp. 88–129.

Zimmer, K. (2002) *'Einheit, Eintracht und Wiedergeburt': Zur Rolle und Relevanz des Donezker Clans. Der politische Einfluß von Wirtschaftseliten in der Ukraine. Nationale und regionale Oligarchen*, Arbeitspapiere und Materialien, Bremen: Forschungsstelle Osteuropa.

Zimmer, K. (2004) 'The captured region: actors and institutions in the Ukrainian Donbass', in M. Tatur (ed.), *The Making of Regions*, Wiesbaden: VS Verlag für Sozialwissens-chaften, pp. 231–348.

Zon, H. van (2001) 'Neo-patrimonialism as an impediment to economic development: the case of Ukraine', *Journal of Communist Studies and Transitions Politics*, **17**(3): 71–95.

Part II

The restructuring of the coal mining industry in the Donbas

6 The Donetsk clan and the demise of the coal industry

Oleg Bogatov

Introduction

The current situation in the coal industry in Donetsk oblast, which accounts for 50 per cent of Ukraine's coal production, proves the inadequacy of the reforms implemented since 1996. Instead of a promised competitive coal market, Ukraine has a poorly disguised monopoly. Western aid programmes, aimed at restructuring the coal industry, have turned out to be ineffective and have not been fully implemented (see Chapter 8). On the one hand, the state as nominal owner of the coal mines, has lost all the mechanisms to control them. The Ministry of Fuel and Energy (MFE), which took over responsibility from the Ministry of the Coal Industry, attempts to govern the sector. The MFE's formal role is to close mines with a low level of output, set indicative prices in order to influence the coal market and provide financial aid for loss-making mines. However, its informal role appears to be to lobby for the coal sector within government, particularly when it comes to determining the size of government subsidies to the industry. The MFE also attempts to resolve crises and emergencies at individual coal mines where necessary. On the other hand, private capital, through the operation of intermediary firms (see Chapter 4), regards the coal industry as a cost that has to be minimised in order to maximise profits in the production and export of iron and steel. Moreover, the MFE is in part controlled by representatives of these private intermediary firms and seeks to maintain the status quo because it serves the purposes of private capital. Together these factors mean that the coal industry is in a state of paralysis.

In order to analyse the coal industry in the Donbas it is necessary to distinguish between the two types of coal mine. The first type of mine extracts energy or steam coal and the second type of mine extracts coking coal. The coking coal sector has experienced a renaissance with growing extraction and sales, while the energy coal sector is in a deep recession. Figure 6.1 shows the output of energy and coking coal in Donetsk oblast between 1995 and 2001. Figure 6.1 shows that from 1996 onwards the extraction of coke coal constantly increased and the extraction of energy coal constantly declined, with the exception of 1998. The figures indicate that these two sectors should be analysed separately, while also examining the differences and common tendencies in both sectors. In the first section of this chapter the development in the coking coal sector is analysed. This is then followed by an

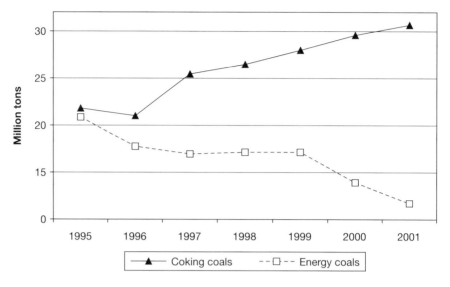

Figure 6.1 Extraction of coking and energy coal in Donetsk oblast, 1995–2001
Source: Ministry of Fuel and Energy of Ukraine.

analysis of the energy coal sector. The final section of the chapter considers government policy and support for the coal industry as a whole.

The coking coal industry

Consumption patterns

The main reason for the relative success of coking coal mines is their role in the 'coal–coke–metal' commodity chain (see also Chapter 4). This chain generates considerable export revenues and supports Ukraine's large iron and steel industry. During the era of the USSR, Donetsk oblast produced 80 per cent of the total supply of coking coal in Ukraine, which made it the main resource base for the steel industry. In turn, the steel industry plays a key role in the economies of both Donetsk and Ukraine. The share of metallurgy in Ukrainian industrial production in 2001 was 22.6 per cent (see Donetsk State Regional Department of Statistics 2002). In Donetsk oblast, metallurgy accounted for 52 per cent of industrial output in the same year. In 2001, four-fifths of Ukrainian steel production was exported, which represented 33.9 per cent of the country's total exports. Heavy metallurgy accounted for 21.6 per cent of industrial employment in Donetsk. The steel industry in Donetsk oblast consists of three metallurgical *combinats* (plants combining smelting and coke chemical plants), four steel plants, two pipe producing enterprises and several other metal processing plants. Iron and steel products contributed 65 per cent of the exports of Donetsk oblast in 2001 (Donetsk State Regional Department of Statistics 2002).

Largely because of its export orientation (to the CIS, South-East Asia, Europe and North America), the steel industry has been the main source of revenue during the economic crisis that unfolded in the 1990s. A portion of the earned revenue was transferred by the steel producers down the 'coal–coke–metal' commodity chain, namely the coke chemical plants and mines extracting coking coal. Frequently iron and steel producers ignored invoices from other less important suppliers, such as electricity and natural gas suppliers. Their invoices were either not paid at all or were paid using non-monetary transactions, such as barter. Under these circumstances the coking coal mines were in a more favourable position than energy coal mines (see Table 6.1).

Coking coal mines were also positively affected by the fact that the corporate strategies of the steel producers entailed increasing production. In recent years the steel industry twice experienced serious shortages of coking coal. The first shortage occurred in 1998 when iron foundries produced 947,000 tons of cast iron. Facing favourable conditions in the world market, the Donetsk Oblast Administration planned to increase cast iron production to 1.1 million tons. The planned increased was to be achieved by commissioning additional production capacities which were at the time under re-construction. However, in September 1998 it became evident that owing to the deficit of coke the steel producers were not only unable to increase production but also unable to maintain production at a constant level. In that month, average daily production decreased 10 per cent in comparison to the previous month. In October 1998 output fell by a further 15 per cent. The main reason for this decline in output was the shortage of coking coal at the coke chemical plants.

The second time a coke supply crisis hit the industry was in late 2000. According to Anatoly Starovoit (the director of the UkrCoke Association, which since the early 1990s has coordinated all the coke chemical plants in Ukraine), the shortage was caused once again by an unexpected increase in cast iron production. By mid-October 2000 most major iron and steel producers had started to reduce their cast iron output. Anatoly Starovoit stated that the

> Russians simply are not able to satisfy our needs. Polish coal is too expensive – more than $40 per ton on DAF [delivered at frontier] – while usually coke plants buy coking coal mix for $32 per ton. Anyway, Polish coal is also in shortage.
>
> (quoted in Parfenov 2000: 35)

It thus became clear that Ukrainian steel producers could not rely on imported coking coal.

The shortages of coke coal led to discussions about ways to prevent further shortages in the future. The first option involved decreasing the amount of coke used per ton of cast iron produced (in 2000 this figure stood at 628 kilograms of coke per ton of iron) (Parfenov 2000: 35). The second option involved increasing the output of coking coal. However, in order to achieve this, huge investment in coke coal mines was required. According to estimates made by Donetsk Oblast

Table 6.1 The supply and payments for coal, 1999–2002

Type of coal	1999		2000		2001		2002 (11 months)	
	Supply (US$ m)	Percentage paid	Supply (US$ m)	Percentage paid	Supply (US$ m)	Percentage paid	Supply (US$ m)	Percentage paid
Coking	370.6	75.5	634.2	80.0	631.2	94.0	441.9	93.4
Energy	649.3	21.9	730.6	41.9	711.0	90.5	704.0	89.3
Total	1,019.9	41.4	1,364.8	59.6	1,342.2	92.1	1,145.9	90.7

Source: Ministry of Fuel and Energy of Ukraine.

Administration, in order to maintain current production levels approximately $800 million would have to have been invested annually for ten years.

However, the consumers of coking coal did not want to pay increased costs for coking coal. According to Vladimir Boiko, director of the Illyich Steel Works located in Mariupol, the introduction of auctions for coking coal in the summer of 2000 led to a 25 per cent increase in prices. As a result the profitability of the largest Ukrainian steel producer, KrivorozhStal, declined by 80 per cent. The profitability of Illyich Steel Works nearly halved, and producers such as ZaporozhStal and Makeevka Steel Plant posted net losses (*Pravda Ukrainy*, 4 April 2001: 1). It should be noted that the prices posted on the auction were calculated by experts of the Ukrainian government and were supposed to include not only current costs but also capital investment costs. The steel producers wanted to increase output but continue to purchase under-priced coal from loss-making mines.

In this conflict of interests between the steel and coal producers, the state supported the former. Government sources stated that:

> during the first three-quarters of 2000, coal extracting enterprises lost between $100 million and $110 million in profits owing to an unreasonable decrease by the Fuel and Energy Ministry of the indicative prices of coking coal . . . In 1999 such losses totalled $80–90 million.
>
> (Parfenov 2000: 35)

A proportion of the losses was compensated by government subsidies. In other words, the government ended up subsidising the steel industry by covering the losses inflicted upon coal producers. This was surprising because the government has no interest in low prices for coking coal.

In contrast the intermediary companies, the so-called Donetsk Financial and Industrial Groups (FIGs), derived most of their profits from price disparities in the commodity chain. These FIGs, such as the Industrial Union of Donbass (IUD), Energo, UkrBallBearing and Radon, enjoyed a monopoly in the Ukrainian coking coal market. The largest FIG, IUD, together with affiliated companies such as ARS and Danko, controlled 80 per cent of the market for coking coal (see Table 6.2). IUD and its affiliates controlled three steel enterprises in Donetsk and Lugansk oblasts, two coke chemical plants, the Khartsizsk Pipe Plant (which was a main supplier to Gazprom in Russia) and a number of machine-building and fireproof materials enterprises.

ARS owned the Avdeyevka Coke Chemical Plant, which was the largest in Europe, the coal mine Komsomolets Donbassa, and the ore enrichment factory Oktyabrskaya. The extent of the collusion between IUD and ARS was indicated by the fact that the two groups kept a common balance sheet for all coal-related operations. Moreover, IUD and ARS established the trading company UkrUgle-Mash, which owned four machine-building enterprises in Ukraine and two in Russia which produced equipment for coal mines (see Chapter 4). Danko owned the Enakiyevo Steel Plant and had an interest in the Makeevka Steel Plant. UkrBallBearing Corporation controlled not only the majority of the ball bearing

Table 6.2 The corporate structure of the largest Financial Industrial Groups in the Donbas

Head company	Enterprises owned or controlled			
	Heavy metallurgy	*Coke chemical industry*	*Coal industry*	*Machine building*
Industrial Union of Donbass	Mariupol Steel Plant, Azovstal, Alchevsk Steel Plant (controlled together with InterPipe), Kramatorsk Metallurgical Plant, Khartsizsk Pipe Plant	Alchevsk Coke Chemical, MarkoKhim	Coal holdings: KrasnodonUgol, KrasnoarmeyskUgol, DonUgol, DopropolyeUgol, MakeyevUgol; mines: Komsomolets Donbassa and Krasnolimanskaya; central ore enrichment factory: Oktyabrskaya	EnergoMAshSpec-Stal, AzovMash, Novokramatorsk Machine-Building Plant; company: UkrUgleMash (holds majority stakes at DonetskGorMash, Donetsk Energy Plant, Druzhkovka Machine-Building Plant, Gorlovka Machine-Building Plant, Krasny Luch Machine-Building Plant, and two machine-building plants in Russia: in Shakhty and Kamensk)
ARS		Avdeyevka Coke Chemical Plant		
UkrBall-Bearing Corporation		OAO DonetskCoke		
Danko	Enakiyevo Steel Plant, Makeyevka Steel Plant			
Energo and JVC CABI	Parts of Donetsk Metallurgical Plant capacities and those of KrivorozhStal	Yasinovskiy Coke Chemical Plant	Mines: Krasnoarmeyskaya-Zapadnaya and Zhdanovskaya	

Source: Bogatov 1999; Parfenov 2000; Malyuta 2001.

factories in the region but also owned one coke chemical plant. (UkrBallBearing subsequently sold its coke chemical plant to ARS and withdrew from the coal market.) Together these companies controlled virtually the whole market for coke.

Somewhat separate from the other companies, the Donetsk-based company Energo, established in 1992, traded coal and controlled coal enterprises in Ukraine, Kazakhstan and Russia. In 2003 Energo owned the Krasnoarmeyskaya-Zapadnaya coal mine, which was the most modern in Ukraine. However, Energo's influence was reduced following the privatisation of coal mines in Russia, which led to Energo being excluded from the Russian market. Energo responded by acquiring the Kostromskaya coal mine located in Kemerovo. Other relatively independent companies in the coke market are Radon (which controlled one steel and one coke chemical plant), Europa (which was affiliated with Sergey Tulub, the president of Energoatom, the national nuclear energy company) and Zasyadko mine, which was controlled by the member of parliament Efim Zviagilskiy.

Investment processes in the coking coal sector

The FIGs entered the market for coking coal after they had gained control over several coke chemical and steel plants. By taking control over the coal mines, they pursued three main objectives: to impose effective management, to increase output and to eliminate small and medium-sized competitors. The FIGs were not able (or were unwilling) to acquire the mines and preferred to use financial levers to control them. For example, there were only two mines officially owned by the FIGs: Komsomolets Donbassa was owned by ARS and Krasnoarmeyskaya-Zapadnaya was owned by Energo.

At the end of 1998 ARS, IUD and the Donetsk Oblast Administration proposed an investment plan for coking coal mines. However, the effectiveness of these investments is rather open to question. According to Yulia Timoshenko (ex-vice-prime minister of Ukraine responsible for energy), the Donetsk traders sold over-priced equipment to coal mines in return for coal paid for at the government's indicative prices, which did not cover the full costs of extracting the coal (Malyuta 2001: 90). Timoshenko's successor, Oleg Dubina, was also sceptical towards this form of investment:

> What kind of investment is that, when one buys a hryvnia's worth of equipment, sells it to a mine for two hryvnia, takes back a hryvnia's worth of coal, covering the costs, and then keeps the hryvnia of investment, which does not even exist?
>
> (quoted in Malyuta 2001: 90)

Planned investment in coal mines was $350 million in 1999, $400 million in 2000, and $450 million in 2001 (UNIAN, 8 February 2001). In 2001, ARS and IUD invested around $75 million in coking coal mines and intended to have returns on their investment in between five and seven years (Malyuta 2001: 90). The director of ARS, Igor Gumenyuk, stated that the primary goal of his company was not immediate returns on its investment, but rather to increase coking coal output to meet the demand of the metallurgy industry: 'We are satisfied with our investments. If we did not invest in expanding production, we would have lost much more from importing coal' (quoted in Korablev 2001: 9). He also pointed out that the directors of steel enterprises were ready for further co-operation with coal mines and had agreed to provide additional investment.

Investment by the Donetsk FIGs was a means of exercising control over coal enterprises. As the mines accumulated huge debts to the FIGs and became dependent on them for the supply of equipment, they became subject to the FIGs' influence. The investors, rather than the mines, took all management decisions relating to purchases and sales and in reality appointed and dismissed senior management. In certain respects this situation had positive effects on coking coal mines. The investors improved discipline amongst the workforce and increased efficiency. The FIGs also effected the appointment of new managers; in 1998, 40 top managers at coal mines were replaced. In return for improved management and efficiency, the formally state-owned mines lost their capacity to participate in the coke market as independent companies. Gradually some of these coal mines became part of the highly vertically integrated 'coal–coke–metal' commodity chain.

Owing to the special position that the FIGs enjoyed in the regional economy and connections to local and regional authorities, the commodity chain was closely controlled. It has been stated that:

> In recent years the Donbas has become a stronghold of the domestic elite, which has a monopoly control over virtually every aspect of regional life, administration and industry. Any new business in the region can be launched only with the 'family's' blessing… The Donetsk group led by (as observers state) Rinat Akhmetov, Igor Gumenyuk and Vitaly Gayduk is currently one of the most powerful economic entities in Ukraine. It distanced itself from the political struggle in the centre, concentrating instead on its own development, skilfully bargaining with other groups, when their interests intersect (such as co-operation with Interpipe at the Alchevsk Steel Plant). It has political representatives in Parliament, who belong to different political factions. Recently, the political representatives of this group have reformed around a new parliamentary faction, the Party of the Regions… which signals their entrance in the political arena as an independent political force. The group influences virtually all industry in Donetsk oblast and some enterprises in the oblasts Lugansk and Dnipropetrovsk. Under the direct control of the Industrial Union of Donbass (the main pillar of the group with USD750 million profits) and its affiliates fall four coke chemical plants, eight steel plants, two ore enrichment factories, banks, five coal-extracting holdings and a number of mines in Donetsk and Lugansk oblasts. IUD controls hundreds more enterprises through its control over gas supplies in the region… [IUD] controls public administration in the oblast, has representatives in the highest places in government, has support of shadow elements and controls the trade unions.
>
> (Yar 2001)

There is indirect evidence to suggest that the largest players on the coking coal market are also the major bosses running industry in Donetsk oblast. For example, total sales of the six largest members of the largest FIGs in the region were more than $3.35 billion, a figure that accounts for two-thirds of industrial output in the oblast (see Table 6.3).

Table 6.3 Sales volumes of companies of the vertically integrated Financial Industrial
Groups in Donetsk oblast, 2001

Name	Sales US$ million
Industrial Union of Donbass	1,303.6
Donetsk Industrial Union	529.7
ARS	527.1
Danko	513.0
Concern Energo	239.8
UkrUgleMash	228.5
Total	**3,341.7**

Source: *Top-100* Ukrainian investment newspaper, 2002.

Note: The Industrial Union of Donbass and the Donetsk Industrial Union are holding companies belonging to the same business group.

Moreover, according to Menshakov (2000: 9), a characteristic of vertical integration is the systematic underreporting of the profits of steel enterprises. Steel works purchase raw materials and equipment from intermediary firms at above cost price whilst steel is sold at low prices to offshore companies. This means that rather than the steel works accumulating significant profits they are channelled to numerous offshore companies. It can be assumed that similar schemes occurred in other industries controlled by the Donetsk FIGs.

Monopoly in the coking coal market

The director of Illyich Steel Plant in Mariupol, Vladimir Boiko, said 'We all know how the coal is distributed. Before I worked with mines, but now I work only with ARS.' In March 2001 the Anti-Monopoly Committee of Ukraine started to investigate the coking coal market after numerous complaints by consumers of coke that were not connected to the Donetsk FIGs. This involved an audit of coking coal mines, coke chemical plants, intermediary businesses and the steel enterprises. However, after the chairman of the Anti-Monopoly Committee was replaced in the summer of 2001 the investigation stalled. Fearing that they might lose their monopoly, the Donetsk FIGs started to actively oppose ex-Vice-Premier Yulia Timoshenko's efforts to reform the coal industry. Attempts to introduce coal auctions and a payments system which involved monetary transactions through a limited number of authorised banks threatened to undermine the mechanisms intermediaries used to control the mines. This was because if the reforms were implemented the coal mines would become independent actors on the market and take over the control of transactions from intermediary firms. As a result the Donetsk business elite did everything it could to discredit and remove Yulia Timoshenko from office. However, the reforms indicated to the FIGs that their control over the coal mines was weak. Consequently, the head of ARS, Igor Gumenyuk, said his company was ready to formally take over the management of the mines it controlled and was even prepare to buy some of them (Korablev 2001: 9).

One of the most disturbing problems with the coking coal monopoly was that it was impossible to calculate the 'true' price of coal. It has already been noted that the indicative prices set by the ministry were unfair to the mines because they did not take into account the cost of capital investment. Currently investment in the coke coal mines is controlled solely by the intermediary firms who serve their own interests and their own vision of the development of the coal industry. This results in severe under-investment in the coal industry. For example, the $75 million invested by ARS in mines compared poorly with the estimated required capital investment, $750 million. The absence of a competitive coal market meant that the consumer did not pay the true price for coking coal – this is even acknowledged by representatives of the FIGs. Neither the mines, the intermediary companies nor the government were able to establish what the price for coking coal, covering the capital costs of the coal mines, should be. Currently there are only three profitable coal mines in the country; these are Zasyadko, Krasnolimanskaya and No. 1 Industria. Currently the intermediary companies do not assess the viability of coal mines according to profitability but rather according to the volume of production. It should be noted that, in 2000, 61 out of the 190 mines in the country collectively produced 3 million tons of coal, which was less than the volume extracted by Zasyadko mine in Donetsk. The FIGs do not have a business interest in these mines because of the low level of output. Without effective price formation via a competitive market, it was impossible to evaluate the efficiency of coal mines and to identify which mines should be invested in and which should not.

Traditionally, vertically integrated commodity chains are opaque and disguise the real production costs and therefore make it difficult to determine the required level of subsidies (Rothbard 1970: 247). Government policy had made it impossible to change this situation. The government has established very low indicative prices for coking coal and subsidises coal mines, which provides an incentive to increase output rather than efficiency. It thus appears that the government supports the Donetsk FIGs. Therefore the only way to liberalise the coking coal market is if the government ceases to provide political support to the FIGs. The inefficiency of the vertically integrated commodity chain linking the coal and steel industry in the Donbas results in economic problems in the regional and national economy. The Donetsk regional economy has become increasingly dependent on the steel industry (see Chapter 4). In 1998 the share of metallurgy in the oblast's industrial production was 47 per cent but this had increased to 52 per cent in 2001. This means that the economy becomes ever more dependent on volatile world markets. According to the Ukrainian Agency for Human-Centred Technologies, 'neither heavy metallurgy nor the chemical industry and a number of machine-building and energy enterprises have a chance in a globalised economy. Their ability to survive will depend solely on the government's policy' (Part.org.ru, 18 May 2001).

The energy coal industry

The creation of the Donbass Fuel-Energy Company

Even though the large intermediary companies had long been involved in the coking coal sector, until recently they had ignored the energy or steam coal sector. Primarily this was because the electricity generators had accumulated significant payments arrears and had systematically not paid for coal. However, beginning in early 2000 the situation in this industry started to improve. Whilst Viktor Yushchenko was prime minister, between December 1999 and April 2001, payments for electricity became more regular and subsequently there was an increase in payments for energy coal (see Table 6.1). Nevertheless, the improvement in the financial situation of the energy coal sector was not the main feature that attracted the attention of the big vertically integrated companies. Beginning in 1998, Donetsk Oblast Administration attempted to establish a centralised market for electricity in the Donbas by linking suppliers and consumers of electricity in the region. This was in part to increase the utilisation of spare electricity generating capacity in the region. On the one hand the region experienced a permanent shortage of electricity and yet on the other hand its power stations worked at only 35 per cent of their capacity. To resolve this situation, in early 2000 President Kuchma decreed that DonetskOblEnergo, which was the main supplier of electricity in Donetsk oblast, and DonbassEnergo, which was the main electricity generating company in Donetsk and Lugansk oblasts, both majority state owned, would be merged and transferred to the oblast administration. Under this arrangement 51 per cent of the stock in the new merged company was owned by the state with the remaining stock owned by the FIGs. It was planned to privatise the merged firm completely once the rate of cash electricity payments had reached 100 per cent. However, according to Malyuta (2001: 89):

> investments in the coal industry are possible only when the investor either controls or is directly represented in every step of the technological chain. In the coking coal case this chain is 'coal–coke–metal', and in the case of energy coal we have 'coal–power generation–electricity'. Otherwise scams and non-payments are guaranteed.

In the summer of 2000 implementation of the presidential decree was blocked by Yushchenko's government, which argued that the merger would increase the proportion of electricity payments that took place in the informal economy. Originally the government had planned to privatise controlling stakes in a number of electricity companies, including DonetskOblEnergo and DonbassEnergo, between 2000 and 2001. However, Yushchenko's government firmly opposed the privatisations and stopped the process. Nevertheless the Donetsk FIGs, which appreciated the opportunities of a single regional energy company, in an example of so-called 'shadow privatisation', created the new company in any case. On 11 May 2000, part of DonetskOblEnergo's property was confiscated on the grounds of debts it owed to OblAvtoDor, a major transportation company. The $4.5 million debt had been accumulated by non-payment of road fees but appeared insignificant compared to the $350 million debt DonetskOblEnergo owed to power stations as of January 2001. Skilfully using laws and court procedures, OblAvtoDor was able to win a court ruling that 7 per cent of the shares in DonetskOblEnergo should be auctioned. Among purchasers of these shares was a company called Service-Invest, which was a joint venture owned in part by UkrBallBearing, and the Avdeyevka Coke Chemical Plant, which was majority-owned by ARS.

In late 2000, Service-Invest obtained a licence to supply 7 billion kilowatt-hours of electricity annually (accounting for 43 per cent of the oblast's consumption) to a number of districts in Donetsk and Dnipropetrovsk oblasts. In this way Service-Invest became the supplier to some of the largest and richest corporate consumers of electricity. Indeed 86 per cent of its electricity was sold to cash-rich steel plants. Between September and December 2000 the payments of customers amounted to 104 per cent of delivered electricity. In other words these customers not only paid for the electricity they consumed but also repaid some of their outstanding arrears (Kinash 2001). By the end of April 2001, despite objections by the government, three power stations, Kurakhovskaya, Zuyevskaya and Luganskaya, which were owned by DonbassEnergo, were auctioned in lieu of payments arrears. The power stations were purchased by an unknown company, TekhRemPostavka. Following this sale DonbassEnergo was left with only two power stations and with payments arrears comprising payables worth $407 million and receivables worth $277 million. Efforts by the government to annul the auctions were unsuccessful and in late 2001 the government recognised the new owners of the power stations. If, as seems likely, Avdeyevka Coke Chemical Plant, TekhRemPostavka and Service-Invest are controlled by the Donetsk FIGs, a large regional energy company had been formed. In this way the FIGs had finally gained control over electricity generation, another important industry in Donetsk oblast. In 2001, Donbass Fuel-Energy Company was established by the FIGs to coordinate the energy industry in the region.

Donetsk's geographically peripheral position in Ukraine meant that the new company enjoyed a local monopoly. This was because the position of Donetsk oblast in the country's national electricity network meant generators in other oblasts were prevented from supplying customers located in Donetsk. This in turn raised the prospect that the Donetsk FIGs could use their control over electricity supply to artificially reduce energy costs in order to enhance the profitability of their steel works. The prospect of such a development simply encouraged the numerous dumping accusations against Ukrainian steel producers.

A Russian alternative to the Donbass Fuel-Energy Company

The only real threat to the Donbass Fuel-Energy Company was the possibility that the Russian and Ukrainian electricity grids might be reunited. There was a degree of co-operation between the two national grids during the 1990s. The Russian energy monopoly, United Energy Systems (UES), supplied electricity to the north-eastern regions of Ukraine, whilst power stations in the Donbas supplied electricity to the north Caucasus. A preliminary agreement between the Russian and Ukrainian presidents to reunite the grids, in which electricity could be transferred from one to the other, was signed at a summit in Dnipropetrovsk in 2001 in order to create a larger and more stable system for supplying electricity. However, following the summit the situation altered. In mid-2001 the Russians began commissioning the Rostov nuclear power plant in part to supply the north Caucasus. Once the new power plant is fully commissioned it will be able to export electricity to the Donbas and the rest of Ukraine. This was significant because Russian electricity was relatively inexpensive, at approximately $0.011 per kilowatt-hour compared to $0.023 per kilowatt-hour for Ukrainian electricity (Maskalevitch 2000: 59). This suggested that Russian electricity generators could in time become competitors to the Donbass Fuel-Energy Company.

Investment processes in the energy coal industry

The creation of the Donbass Fuel-Energy Company led the Donetsk FIGs to reconsider its use of coal resources. According to the National Electric Energy Regulating Commission, the cost of coal accounted for 58.15 per cent of the final price of electricity generated by DonbassEnergo in 2000 (Maskalevitch 2000: 60). In addition DonbassEnergo purchased 99 per cent of its coal from mines in Donetsk and Lugansk oblasts (Maskalevitch 2000: 60). Therefore the FIGs' control over coal mining, through the supply of investment capital, meant they could also influence to a large extent the price of electricity. In 1999 the Donetsk FIGs identified a new system of investing in energy coal mines. As almost all the mines had accumulated payments arrears, including to the state, they were not eligible to claim the special investment tax reductions offered by the government. In order to circumvent this restriction and claim the tax benefits, a novel form of property relations was established at several mines. In 1999 at Zhdanovskaya mine a new company was formed which leased some coal seams from the mine, re-equipped them and used the mine's workforce and infrastructure to extract coal from them. However, because this new company was not in arrears to the state it was entitled to receive the tax reductions.

It should be noted that a number of foreign investors commenced several investment projects in the energy coal sector. For example, in 1999 the Slovak company KIMEX used an arrangement similar to the one discussed above as a vehicle to invest in Komsomolets Donbassa mine. In this case KIMEX leased a coal seam in return for supplying $7.8 million worth of equipment. Another foreign investor, the Czech firm Metalimex, provided a $0.5 million loan to Trudovskaya mine, which belonged to the DonUgol regional holding company based in Donetsk city, to purchase new equipment and prepare new coal faces. Subsequently Metalimex began negotiating similar arrangements at other coal mines. Most investments by foreign companies involved the mining of anthracite for export to European countries.

State support for the coal industry

Coal is Ukraine's only domestic energy source, and the maintenance and expansion of output are the only means the country has to reduce its dependence on Russian energy supplies. Moreover, it should be noted that Russia's so-called 'gas age', which began in the 1970s, is drawing to a close, as Gazprom has indicated that the supply of gas will fall and prices will increase. Many of Gazprom's large gas extraction sites are near the end of their life and require between $30 billion and $40 billion investment up to 2020. However, Gazprom has not been able to attract the investment it requires (Novoselova and Sivakov 2002: 23). This means that the shortage of gas in the Russian market is likely to grow whilst the demand for coal will increase. Whilst coal accounted for 23 per cent of Russian energy requirements in 2000 this is expected to increase to 54 per cent by 2020. Therefore Ukraine cannot rely on Russian gas and coal to meet its energy needs and needs to provide incentives to continue to develop its coal reserves. However, this is very difficult to achieve without a functioning market for coal to form true prices. Nevertheless world market prices for coal provide a guide for future planning. Currently exports of Russian coking coal cost $40 per ton (Vinkov and Sivakov 2001: 23) whereas on the London exchange one ton of coking coal (of mark G) costs approximately $60. Table 6.4 shows how these prices compare with the wholesale prices of coal mines in the Donbas. It shows that in 2001 Zasyadko mine sold its coal for $36 per ton, the highest in the Donbas.

The low price of coal from the Donbas explains why coal mines have accumulated significant losses over several years. The coal mines use their losses to make the government increase state subsidies in order to cover production costs. In effect government support for the coal industry simply benefits the steel producers and electricity generating companies. Indeed the iron and steel industry is in effect subsidised twice through cheaper coke and through cheaper electricity. However, government subsidies assist in maintaining social stability in the region, because most of the subsidies are used to pay wages and reduce wage arrears, according to data from Donetsk Oblast Administration (see Kinash 2001).

In circumstances in which the mines are almost never audited they underreport revenues and exaggerate losses in order to obtain subsidies that are higher than required. In early 2001, the Ukrainian Accounting Chamber reported the following:

> The budget subsidies received by the coal industry did not stabilise but merely slowed the deterioration in its financial situation. The Ministry of Fuel and Energy failed to create a subsidy mechanism to stimulate coal mines to meet their planned production volumes and increase revenues. As a result of this failure, during 1999 and the first three-quarters of 2000, the mines that did not fulfil their obligations received almost $37 million in undeserved subsidies.
>
> (Kinash 2001)

The ministry regularly allowed mines to purchase materials and equipment at 30 per cent above normal prices as part of the barter transactions. Whilst it is

Table 6.4 Wholesale prices of the coking coal extracted by the mines and mine holding companies in the Donbas, 2001

Enterprises	Prices US$/ton
DonUgol	20.88
DonetskUgol	16.35
Zasyadko mine	36.61
Mine Butovka Donetskaya	13.08
Mine Petrovskaya	16.14
Mine 17-17 bis	15.82
Oktiabr Rudnik	17.32
YushnoDonbasskaya 1	15.42
YushnoDonbasskaya 3	29.29
MakeyevUgol	28.61
KrasnoarmeyskUgol	30.18
Mine Krasnolimanskaya	33.60
Krasnoarmeyskaya Zapadnaya 1	20.49
SelidovUgol	26.97
DobropolyeUgol	21.29
ArtemUgol	18.89
Gayevoi mine	29.02
DzerzhinskUgol	21.01
OrdzhonikidzeUgol	18.97
ShaxterskAnthracite	20.32
OktyabrUgol	21.51
Mine Komsomolets Donbassa	26.06
TorexAnthracite	20.50
SnezhnoyeAnthracite	27.83
Average in Donetsk oblast	**25.32**

Source: Ministry of Fuel and Energy of Ukraine.

necessary to support the coal industry, such an inefficient allocation of state subsidies only serves to exacerbate the crisis in the industry. Indeed the mechanisms of state support for the coal industry were not only inefficient but also contributed to preserve the financial crisis in the industry and served the interests of the large consumers of coal.

It was stated in the Kiev Forum Report of the World Energy Council held in 2000 that the main cause of unprofitability in eastern European mines was related to:

> delays in the industry's restructuring. Government policies that lead to regulated and artificially low coal prices, the granting of production subsidies and the merging of efficient mines with loss-making mines prevented the potentially efficient coal producers from making profits and investing in further development.

> (Shein 2000: 44)

This explanation is applicable to the situation in Ukraine. An alternative government policy must be devised that will generate sources of finance, other than from the state, for the industry. Government regulation of the sector must provide the means and incentives for mines to invest their own funds in capital investment and also to encourage the FIGs to invest in the industry. However, there are at least two obstacles which prevent coal mines from tapping into sources of investment. First, without a clearly determined fair price for coal, mines will not earn sufficient revenues that can be used for capital investment. Second, to date, investment by the larger FIGs has been insufficient and confined to the coking coal sector.

Other potential investors, such as banks and venture capitalists, have to date not been willing to invest in the industry. This is because they have not believed that the state would be able to protect their interests. Consequently coal mines have had to rely almost entirely on the region's vertically integrated FIGs. The example of the 'shadow' privatisation of the most valuable assets belonging to DonbassEnergo and DonetskOblEnergo in which assets were privatised not through a formal privatisation process but through a debt-for-equity swap demonstrates that the state cannot provide protection to potential investors. The activities of the so-called 'Donetsk oligarchs' resulted in a fall in the value of blue-chip Ukrainian companies on the stock exchange. For example, DonbassEnergo, which had been widely regarded as a blue-chip stock in the late 1990s, ceased to be quoted on the Ukrainian Stock Exchange after losing ownership of three of its power stations. However, there may be a number of other FIGs as well as foreign investors that may decide to invest in the Donbas coal industry. Nevertheless the Donetsk FIGs, which will not easily give up their monopolistic position, will remain powerful.

Conclusion

Since the beginning of the restructuring of the coal industry in 1996 the state has entirely lost control over the industry. The function of the state has become confined to that of a financial donor to non-viable mines. A state monopoly has been replaced by an emerging monopoly controlled by the Donetsk FIGs. The FIGs have already monopolised the coking coal industry and are in the process of establishing a monopoly in the energy coal industry as well. Moreover, these groups consider coal mines as one stage in the metallurgical commodity chain and therefore as providing the potential to reduce short-term costs. The groups ensured that coal prices were minimised in order to give their steel plants a competitive advantage on the world market. State-regulated coal prices and state subsidies are such that they do not provide mines with sufficient revenues for capital investment. To date, in the rare instances where mines have made capital investment it has been insufficient. Monopolisation has blocked the development and growth of coal mines. It has prevented the emergence of a competitive coal market and the formation of prices that would cover both production costs and future investment needs. In addition, the business groups that control the market also enjoy a monopoly over external investment flows into the industry. The Donetsk FIGs have a firm grip on the coal industry, and the development of the sector will depend entirely on them.

References

Bogatov, O. (1999) *Donbass-100. Kto Est Kto v Regione*, Donetsk: Lybid.

Donetsk State Regional Department of Statistics (2002) *Socialno-ekonomicheskoe polozhenie Donetskoy oblasti v 2001 godu*, Donetsk: Donetsk State Regional Department of Statistics.

Kinash, A. (2001) 'Donbass Stroit Energeticheskuyu Vertical', *Forum* (http://www.for-ua.com), 21 May.

Korablev, S. (2001) 'Druzhba Donetskogo Bisnessa s Pravitelstvom: Realniy Mif ili Mificheskaya Realnost', *Zerkalo Nedeli*, 2 February: 9.

Malyuta, Y. (2001) 'Kak Privatizirovali Ukrainskiy Ugleprom', *Fuel and Energy Complex Journal*, 6: 88.

Maskalevitch, I. (2000) 'Atomniy Pasyans: Dvoe Sboku – Nashih net', *Fuel and Energy Complex Journal*, 12: 56.

Menshakov, A. (2000) 'Poslednie Shansi', *Kievskiye Vedomosti*, 22 September: 9.

Novoselova, Y. and D. Sivakov (2002) 'Bolshay Nugda Gazproma', *Expert Journal*, 48: 22.

Parfenov, G. (2000) 'Ukrainskay Metallurgiya: Rost pod Ugrozoy', *Expert Journal*, 47: 34.

Rothbard, M. (1970) *Man, Economy, and State*, Los Angeles, CA: Nash Publishing.

Shein, L. (2000) 'Ot Virtualnoy k Deystvitelnoy Rentabelnosti Shaht', *Fuel and Energy Complex Journal*, 8: 41.

Vinkov, A. and D. Sivakov (2001) 'Pyat Ugolnih Dram', *Expert Journal*, 19: 21.

Yar, A. (2001) 'Energiya dlya Donetskoy Eliti', *Partorg* (http://www.part.org.ua), 13 April.

7 The social consequences of coal mine restructuring

Olena Popova

Introduction

In recent years the Ukrainian government has pursued a radical coal industry restructuring programme. Prior to the beginning of the programme in 1996 the industry faced a number of severe problems. These included the legacies of many years of under-investment, obsolete technologies, low productivity, over-manning and very poor health and safety standards. Reform of the coal industry has occurred in the context of an economic crisis related to post-Soviet economic and political transition. The government faced a decision as to whether to continue subsidising the coal industry – which was likely to become an increasing burden on the state budget – or whether to radically reform the sector. In late 1995 the government adopted a coal industry restructuring programme under which 80 loss-making coal mines were to be closed. According to the World Bank, which helped to elaborate the programme and provided loans to finance it, during the programme 260,000 mine workers were to leave the industry, including 64,000 between 1996 and 1999. Since coal production in Ukraine is geographically concentrated in the Donbas, reform required not only the closure of loss-making mines but also measures to mitigate the adverse social impacts of mine closures and the strengthening of the system of social protection for redundant miners and their families.

Beginning in 1997, the Kyiv International Institute of Sociology (KIIS), with the financial, organisational and methodological support of the World Bank, carried out research in the Donbas to assess the negative social impacts of coal industry restructuring. A variety of research methods were employed including face-to-face interviews, in-depth interviews, focus-group discussions and participant observation. Former miners as well as those who had not worked at mines were questioned during the research. In addition, local experts such as mine directors, representatives of local governments, specialists from social services and representatives of different social programmes were interviewed. In sum a combination of quantitative and qualitative research methods were used to form a comprehensive scientific understanding of the issues.

The research project, entitled 'Negative Social Impacts of Coal Industry Restructuring in Ukraine', was carried out in 1997 and repeated in 1999. The project included a variety of components. Firstly, quantitative research was carried out with redundant coal miners and the inhabitants of settlements where coal mines had closed to examine living standards and the pattern of employment. Secondly, a survey of local experts from government and non-government organisations (NGOs) involved in coal mine restructuring was undertaken to reveal their activities in coal mine settlements. Thirdly, in-depth interviews with former miners from different categories (male and female as well as those who were employed, were unemployed, had retired or had migrated to look for work) were used to form models of redundant miners' behaviour. Fourthly, in-depth interviews with representatives of mines, regional associations of coal mines, municipal executive committees, social workers and trade unions were undertaken to examine the transfer of social assets from coal mines to local governments. Fifthly, in-depth interviews were carried out with representatives of successful local private businesses and of organisations dealing with employment issues (such as the employment service and NGOs) in order to investigate the prospects for private business development in the region. Sixthly, the project involved participant observation, using local observers, to monitor the social situation in mining communities. Seventhly, a case study of one mining settlement entirely dependent on a mine that was in the mine closure process was undertaken. Finally, mass media and other publications related to the industry restructuring and employment trends in the region were analysed.

Beginning in late 2001 a research project on the 'Long-Term Impact of Coal Industry Restructuring on Municipal Development of Mining Communities' was carried out. This project entailed using primarily qualitative research methods to examine two municipalities, Stakhanov and Gorlovka, dependent on the coal industry in the Donbas. The two settlements were selected according to the following criteria: the proportion of those employed in the coal industry had fallen considerably because of the closure of at least one coal mine and the presence of the development (or potential for the development) of alternative economic activities. This first stage of this project involved in-depth interviews with experts at the national, regional and local scale. The second stage of the project involved interviews with people who had been affected by the closure of coal mines in the two municipalities as well as interviews with 'control groups', such as local entrepreneurs, who had not been directly affected by the closures. Quantitative methods were used to compare employment and living standards in the two coal miners' settlements and with the country as a whole. In the remainder of this chapter some of the results of these research projects are presented.

Background information

The coal industry and its consumers (electricity generators and metallurgical works) form a key part of the Donbas economy. In order to comprehend the scale of the impact of mine closures on the region, we made an analysis of statistical data at the regional scale. Between 1996 and 2001 employment of the economically active population (15–70 years old) in Donetsk and Lugansk oblasts decreased from 62.4 per cent to 54.3 per cent.[1] These figures closely mirror the situation in Ukraine as a whole; during the same time period employment fell from 64 per cent to 55.8 per cent. Official registered unemployment in 1997 at the beginning of the coal sector restructuring programme was 0.9 per cent in Donetsk oblast and 1.2 per cent in Lugansk oblast. This compared to an official registered unemployment rate in Ukraine as a whole of 1.3 per cent. By 2001 registered unemployment in Donetsk oblast had increased to 2.7 per cent and 3.3 per cent in Lugansk. This compared to some oblasts in western Ukraine where the rate ranged from 4.8 per cent to 6.5 per cent and a rate of 3.7 per cent for Ukraine as a whole. It should also be noted that the official unemployment rate was significantly lower than figures calculated according to the ILO's methodology. The average monthly salary of the working population of Donetsk and Lugansk oblasts was 126 per cent and 106 per cent of the Ukrainian average respectively. By 2001, when 70 per cent of the mines that were due to close had been closed, the situation in the Donbas, relative to the situation in Ukraine as a whole, had not changed. Thus, in 2001 the average monthly salary in Donetsk and Lugansk oblasts was 110 per cent and 108 per cent of the Ukrainian average, and cash income in the Donbas constituted approximately 110 per cent of the Ukrainian average.

A range of other recent statistical data also shows that the situation in the Donbas is similar to the situation in other Ukrainian oblasts. This means that, in the context of a nation-wide economic crisis that affected living standards and conditions in all oblasts, the statistics do not reveal a specific effect of coal industry restructuring in the Donbas. However, social research during the period 1997–2001 in the settlements in the Donbas where mines were closed shows an extremely difficult social situation amongst both former coal miners and their families and the population of miners' settlements as a whole. Experience of coal industry restructuring in other countries, including in developed countries, suggests that the impact of coal mine closures will be felt for at least 20 years. Consequently the social situation in miners' settlements and the region as a whole should be constantly monitored in order to capture a comprehensive picture of the long-term consequences of restructuring. In addition, such research is needed in order to assist in the design of more effective measures to provide social protection for the most vulnerable social groups in mining communities.

Expenditure level

The expenditure level is certainly one of the main indicators of economic and social changes in miners' communities. In Ukraine, per capita expenditure by households on food and non-food goods has traditionally been used to measure well-being. Indicators of household expenditure were included in the 1997 and 1999 surveys, while the survey of 2001 included only indicators of subjective evaluation of well-being. Therefore, only data from the 1997 and 1999 surveys are presented in this section. In the research the most vulnerable social groups were defined on the basis of a classification of individuals according to expenditure. The deciles showing the distribution of family spending per capita were used for this purpose.[2] Deciles one to three were categorised as families with low expenditure levels; deciles four

Table 7.1 The distribution of per capita monthly expenditure for households, 1997 and 1999

Expenditure level	1997 US$	1999 US$	Difference of dollar equivalents at a commercial rate
Low (deciles 1–3)	11.1	6.6	–4.5
Average (deciles 4–7)	24.0	13.7	–10.3
Above the average (deciles 8–10)	56.2	29.3	–26.9
Mean	**29.5**	**16.2**	**–13.3**

Source: KIIS 2000.

Note: The fall in expenditure between 1997 and 1999, in dollar terms, is in part due to the devaluation of the hryvnia after the Russian financial crisis in 1998.

to seven were categorised as having average expenditure levels; deciles eight to ten were categorised as having above-average expenditure levels (see Table 7.1). The per capita spending of households in mining communities differs substantially. The richest households (decile 10) account for 22 per cent of all expenditure – almost as much as the total expenditure for households in deciles 1–4.

Vulnerable groups

A comparison of the expenditure levels of different families and individuals allows the identification of the factors which have the most substantial effect on consumption (see Table 7.2). The social-demographic structure of vulnerable groups in 1999 did not change substantially compared to 1997. Households with a low social-demographic loading, such as households without disabled people or single-person households of able-bodied age or households comprising couples without children, were in the most favourable situation. This is because household members did not need to care for children or the elderly or infirm and therefore could more easily work.

Among households of average prosperity one can find single-pensioner households and those that comprise couples with adult children. The fact that 50 per cent of single pensioner households have an average expenditure level is explained by the relatively high value of pensions and other benefits by Ukrainian standards. Families with adult children have several generations of working age and, accordingly, the opportunity to obtain income from a variety of different sources, such as wages, extra earnings, grants and pensions. The survey showed that families with children under 16 have the lowest expenditure level. Among this group single-parent families run a greater risk of pauperisation.

Among the factors influencing expenditure level are gender and age. Figure 7.1 shows that in both 1997 and 1999 the ratio of females in the group with a low expenditure level is much higher, regardless of age. This can be explained by the fact that the female ratio among working people is much lower – 46.3 per cent

Table 7.2 The distribution of households of different demographic types according to
expenditure level, 1999

Demographic type of household	Number	Expenditure level (%)		
		Low	Average	Above average
Single:	58	20.7	37.9	41.4
Able-bodied age	32	25.0	28.1	46.9
Pension age	26	15.4	50.0	34.6
Full families:	618	28.2	40.9	30.9
Couple without children	155	20.6	36.1	43.2
Couple with children under 16	139	33.1	33.8	33.1
Couple with children of 16 and older	167	23.4	47.9	28.7
Couple with children under 16 and other relatives	157	36.3	44.6	19.1
Single-parent families:	106	45.3	31.1	23.6
Single-parent family with children under 16	35	54.3	22.9	22.9
Single-parent family with children of 16 and older	71	40.8	35.2	23.9
Other type of family	25	32.0	60.0	8.0
All households	**807**	**30.0**	**40.0**	**30.0**

Source: KIIS 2000.

compared to the male ratio of 52.8 per cent – and the female ratio among the
unemployed is much higher (28.3 per cent for women compared to 18.4 per cent
for men).

Moreover, Figure 7.1 shows that expenditure is higher for the age group 50 to
59, for both men and women. Men in the age group 50–59 are least likely to be in
the group of low expenditure because 63.5 per cent of them receive a pension.
However, despite the fact that the pension of miners exceeds the average Ukrainian
pension it is not always paid on time and in full. Moreover, despite the difficulty
of finding a job, 38.5 per cent of this age group still have a job. The 16 to 29 age
group experience an extremely complicated financial situation as this group has a
high level of unemployment. In this group 34.2 per cent of men and 46.2 per cent
of women are looking for work. Between 1997 and 1999 the expenditure level of
the elderly had somewhat decreased (see Figure 7.1). Even though the 30 to 39
age group contains the highest proportion of women in work (63.8 per cent),
expenditure in this age–gender group has decreased.

Comparative analysis of data from 1997 and 1999 confirms that paid work
reduces the risk of pauperisation (see Table 7.3). Among those who had a job, the
share of persons with above-average expenditure was 34.8 per cent and the share
of those with a low expenditure level was 24 per cent in 1999. It can also be observed

(a) Men

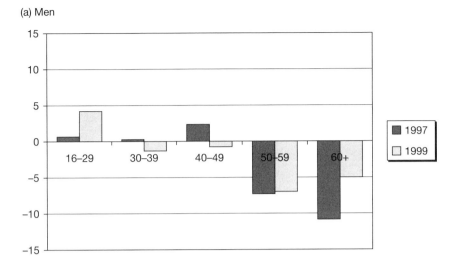

(b) Women

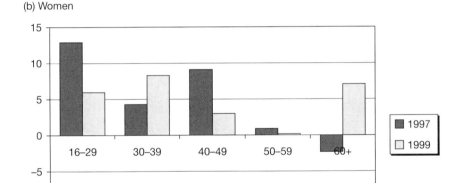

Figure 7.1 The ratio of people with a low level of expenditure by age and gender, 1997 and 1999

Source: KIIS.

Note: The location in relation to the X axis shows how much above or below the average the share of people with a low level of expenditure is in each age group.

that between 1997 and 1999 the impact of pensions as a poverty reducing measure fell. It can also been seen that, although most redundancy payments had been paid by 1999, these payments appear not to have had an effect on the proportion of unemployed or those with a low income.

Table 7.3 Influence of employment on level of expenditure, 1997–1999

Employment	Expenditure level (%)		
	Low	Average	Above average
Have a job:			
1997	26.5	36.0	37.5
1999	24.0	41.2	34.8
Retired:			
1997	27.3	51.6	21.1
1999	31.5	40.1	28.4
Looking for a job:			
1997	41.2	34.4	24.4
1999	38.3	38.9	22.9

Source: KIIS 2000.

Subjective evaluations of the expenditure levels

The subjective assessment of expenditure levels by the population of miners' settlements shows that they perceive their situation to be worse than for the country as a whole (see Table 7.4). In evaluations of their financial situation in 2001, 87 per cent of respondents thought that they barely made ends meet and satisfied their needs for food only. Moreover, of those people, 44 per cent reported that they did not have enough money even for food. This compares with a figure of 30 per cent for Ukraine as a whole.

According to various sociological surveys, people in Ukraine are inclined to evaluate their financial situation negatively and are pessimistic about their prospects for the future. It is important to note that the self-evaluation of their financial situation is based not only on their actual financial situation but also on their expectation of living standards and their understanding of social equity. Although we do not have data that show that the actual expenditure level in the Donbas is lower than in the rest of Ukraine, we can understand why people in miners' settlements evaluate their income level more negatively. This is because former miners compare their income with the relatively high salaries paid to miners during the Soviet era. Nevertheless, a positive tendency has recently emerged both in the country as a whole and more in particular in miners' settlements. The subjective evaluation of expenditure levels has somewhat improved, though in miners' settlements this improvement is less pronounced than in the country as a whole (see Figure 7.2).

Survival strategies

Rapidly changing economic and social circumstances have a particular impact on the most vulnerable groups within society. In order to cope with these changes these groups adapt traditional survival strategies and adopt new ones. Respondents were asked a range of questions related to the survival strategies employed by their

Table 7.4 Subjective evaluation of household's financial situation in coal mine settlements and in Ukraine

	Miners' settlements 1997 %	Miners' settlements 1999 %	Miners' settlements 2001 %	Ukraine 2001 %
We do not have enough money even for food	53.7	48.0	43.8	30.2
We have money for food, but we cannot afford to buy clothes and footwear	41.1	47.0	43.4	50.7
We have enough money for food and clothes, and we can make savings, but we cannot afford to buy such things as, for example, a refrigerator or a TV set	4.3	4.5	11.1	14.1
We can afford some expensive things (e.g. a TV set or refrigerator) but we cannot afford everything we want	0.7	0.5	1.6	4.0
We can afford everything we want	0	0	0	0.4

Source: KIIS 2000; State Statistics Committee of Ukraine 1998, 2000, 2002.

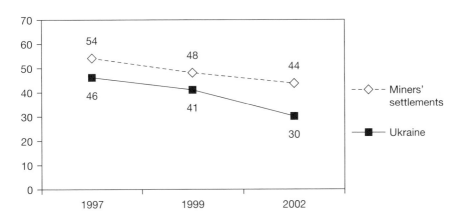

Figure 7.2 The percentage of people who said they did not have enough money for food in miners' settlements and Ukraine as a whole

Source: KIIS.

families (see Table 7.5). During the whole period between 1997 and 2001, the most common strategies were 'exhaustive' or temporary strategies. This included denying oneself essential products, selling property and postponing payments for housing services and utilities. Second in importance were 'reproducible' strategies oriented toward self-provision of products through kitchen gardens. Survival

Table 7.5 Comparative analysis of survival strategies among the population of miners' settlements and Ukraine as a whole

During the last year, did you need to take the following steps to overcome financial difficulties?	*Miners' settlements 1997 %*	*Miners' settlements 1999 %*	*Miners' settlements 2001 %*	*Ukraine 2001 %*
To save on or deny oneself in essential products, things and drugs	–	92.2	87.5	77.1
To postpone housing and utilities' payments	68.9	77.6	62.7	55.8
To borrow money or sell personal things or property to make ends meet	–	65.4	60.2	49.6
To cultivate agricultural products for one's own consumption or sale	58.9	56.9	48.8	71.4
To process documents for receiving allowances	–	12.4	25.3	29.4
To leave for other cities, settlements or countries in search of a job (seasonal work, shop tours, etc.)	7.0	9.2	11.2	8.2
To get additional job/work (or to have to work at pension age)	18.0	12.3	8.8	17.0
To raise the professional level or to acquire a new profession/ qualification	11.6	3.7	8.8	12.5
To be engaged in individual commercial activities: selling or small-scale production of products and services	3.2	5.6	6.4	11.0
To initiate one's own enterprise – firm, shop, workshop	0.4	0.7	0.8	2.9
To do something else to improve one's own well-being	–	2.2	2.4	8.4

Source: KIIS 2000; State Statistics Committee of Ukraine 1998, 2000, 2002.

strategies that are aimed at enhancing knowledge and skills, such as searching for additional jobs and improving educational qualifications, are considerably less common.

It is important to note that the population of Ukraine as a whole tends more often to choose active strategies aimed at improving their professional opportunities and less often to choose exhaustive strategies than the population of miners' settlements. The 'passivity' of the population of the Donbas can be explained by the lack of job opportunities in the region owing to a decrease in production and employment in all economic sectors. Owing to the fact that many declining industries, such as steel and machine building, are geographically concentrated in the Donbas, a lot of manual workers have been made redundant. In addition, low educational levels act as a barrier to retraining and the acquisition of new qualifications, not to mention the limited opportunities that exist in the private sector for such people. Also because of poor conditions for agricultural production in the region, in which only an insignificant part of the land is suitable for cultivation, the opportunities to work in agriculture or on plots of land are less prevalent in the Donbas than in the rest of Ukraine.

Migration

Migration as a survival strategy is difficult to measure through standard sociological surveys. Nevertheless, in the 2001 survey, KIIS attempted to measure migration in an indirect way. In the two miners' settlements, Stakhanov and Gorlovka, 1,618 addresses were randomly selected. If there was nobody at the selected address during the interviewer's visit, neighbours were questioned about the whereabouts of the residents. At 28 per cent of the addresses that were selected the residents had either left for good or left for a long-term period in order to work elsewhere. In the remaining cases where there was at least one resident, interviewers were asked to record the composition of the household. Thirteen per cent of these households had members who were living and working elsewhere. Together these data suggest that migration in miners' settlements is a very significant factor and that the proportion of those who migrated away may have been as high as 40 per cent in 2001.[3] Beyond any doubt, people of working age constitute the majority of those migrating out. When we compared the gender–age structure of registered households with official statistics it confirmed that a substantial proportion of the working age population of these settlements is absent (see Table 7.6). A substantial proportion of absent people are men and younger people; the average age of those remaining significantly differs from official statistical data. On the basis of our data, it is not possible to conclude whether permanent or temporary migration is most common and what circumstances are decisive in making a decision to leave.

Qualitative research in 2001 showed that a new phenomenon had emerged, namely return migration. The main reason for returning was connected to 'push' factors in the destination of migration, such as poor housing conditions, bad working conditions and lack of social insurance. Migrants often faced extortion by criminal

Table 7.6 Age–gender structure of the population of two mining settlements compared with statistical data, 2001

Demographic variable	Official statistics, 1 January 2001 (%)	Survey, January–February 2002 (%)	Difference (%)
Gorlovka:			
Gender: Men	44.8	40.6	−4.2
Women	55.2	59.4	+4.2
Age: 18–29	21.4	12.0	−9.4
30–44	27.7	23.9	−3.8
45–59	22.6	22.8	+0.2
60 and older	28.3	41.3	+13.1
Total (population of age 18 and older)	236,011	1,053	
Stakhanov:			
Gender: Men	44.0	40.6	−3.4
Women	56.0	59.4	+3.4
Age: 18–29	20.6	14.1	−6.5
30–44	28.7	20.8	−7.9
45–59	23.7	24.5	+0.8
60 and older	27.1	40.6	+13.5
Total (population of age 18 and older)	80,298	1,083	

Source: KIIS 2000; State Statistics Committee of Ukraine 2002.

groups, because work for migrants is mostly illegal. Unfortunately, the reasons for returning are not related to 'pull' factors in the miners' settlements.

Employment and job placement models

As mentioned above, paid employment is one of the most important sources of income. Fifty-three per cent of the working age population in miners' settlements did not have a job in 2001. The average figure for all Ukrainian settlements of a similar size (less than 5,000 inhabitants) was 45 per cent. Sixty-five per cent of miners who were made redundant because of the coal mine restructuring programme did not have a job in 1999. Thirty-five per cent of these people without a job were economically active pensioners. The employment level amongst former miners is only low at first sight. The majority of unemployed miners of working age deliberately do not work, because of the high level of unemployment and other benefits. Redundancy payments are often larger than wages and for many there is a disincentive to undertake paid work in the two years following dismissal.

In the first three months after redundancy, former miners receive 100 per cent of monthly earnings. This is then reduced to 75 per cent of earnings for the following nine months. After 12 months, former miners are entitled to 50 per cent of earnings for a further 12 months. Moreover, the majority of vacancies on the labour market are for jobs at public enterprises where the salary is often lower than unemployment benefit and often paid very irregularly. In 1997 the average salary of a miner was UAH264 per month compared to an average salary of UAH170 in non-mining enterprises. By 1999 the respective figures had risen to UAH313 and UAH200 and in 2001 to UAH524 and UAH360. In these circumstances there is little incentive for former coal miners to deprive themselves of a guaranteed benefit that is paid regularly by taking paid employment. Among those former miners who had been made redundant more than two years before the research took place, 74 per cent of working age respondents had found a new job. In comparison only 32 per cent of those who had been made redundant less than two years before were employed.

Our research shows that 44 per cent of the miners who had found permanent or temporary employment after having been made redundant in the course of a mine closure found work at other coal industry enterprises. Thirty-three per cent of redundant mine workers who had found work had done so at public enterprises in other sectors of the economy. Twelve per cent had found employment in private enterprises and approximately 9 per cent were engaged in individual commercial activity or had opened their own firms. In addition, 20 per cent of the surveyed families had one or more family members in paid work in other settlements – this indicates a high level of intra-regional migration. These issues will now be considered in more detail.

The most common job search strategies amongst former mine workers are as follows. Firstly, redundant coal miners search for similar jobs at other coal mines. As already mentioned, approximately 44 per cent of all dismissed workers found new employment at another coal mine. This strategy is especially common for underground workers – 70 per cent of those who found a job in another mine after mine closure were underground workers. Vacancies for surface workers are practically non-existent. As the restructuring programme progresses, the opportunity for miners to find employment in their speciality in other mines continuously decreases. Secondly, more than 30 per cent of former miners who found a job found work at non-mining enterprises.

Whilst the above-mentioned strategies were the two most common for former coal mine workers, these strategies do not solve the employment problem in the Donbas because of the overall economic crisis in Ukraine. Therefore, the following tendencies are apparent in the employment structure of mining regions, as in Ukraine in general. Firstly, the unemployment rate has increased. Among all those unemployed in the Donbas only 56 per cent were actively looking for a job in the sense that they had replied to job advertisements placed in the mass media, had directly visited enterprises to find work or had learnt about job vacancies through acquaintances and relatives. The 'inactivity' of former miners is temporary because, as already mentioned, for the first two years following redundancy they receive a number of state allowances which are a small but constant source of income. In most cases active job searching only commences after the two years of benefits.

Secondly, one of the most popular survival strategies in Ukraine is for families to use a private plot of land to produce food. However, the Donbas does not have enough land suitable for cultivation owing to the high geographical concentration of industrial enterprises and industrial waste dumps and the poor ecological condition of the soil. The shortage of kitchen gardens is an additional burden for the population. Thirdly, the proportion of people employed temporarily has increased. According to experts, quite a number of inhabitants of miners' settlements have seasonal jobs in collective farms. The experts noted that this is a convenient type of irregular earnings, especially for those who are registered at the job centre and receive unemployment benefits. Since doing seasonal agricultural work does not require official registration, the registered unemployed undertaking such work do not lose their entitlement to unemployment benefits. Therefore, the majority of such earnings amongst the unemployed are concealed. Individual commercial activity can also be considered as a temporary form of employment. Such activities create a number of problems, including the degradation of the traditional skills base, the formation of a labour force without social protection and the rise of illegal economic activities entailing tax evasion and racketeering.

Municipal services

Most miners' settlements were only built to accommodate miners in newly sunk mines. This meant that mines not only provided employment but also were the main contributor to the municipal budget and even undertook functions associated with local government. This meant that the coal mines financed either directly or indirectly through the municipal budget the social sphere of settlements. For example, coal mines often constructed and maintained the housing stock as well as transportation and communications such as telephone systems. Even in settlements where there were enterprises besides mines, coal mines often paid for a substantial proportion of the municipal budget. Therefore the closure of mines had an impact not only on the labour market and income levels but also on the development of these settlements as a whole, including their outlook as municipalities, as well as the housing, day care centres, schools and hospitals in the locality. In many respects the municipality is the successor organisation of a closed mine and bears a double burden in which it loses a major source of revenue and is obliged to increase spending because of the transfer of social assets from the mine to the local authority.

There is no doubt that this has an impact on the quality of municipal services and, consequently, on the standards of living of the population. Thus, in 2001, people in miners' settlements negatively evaluated the housing and communal services, day care centres, hospitals, and cultural and educational institutions. The situation in Ukraine appears to be better than in the Donbas on almost all these indicators (see Table 7.7). The poor quality of housing and municipal services is indicated by the fact that only 79 per cent of families have constant electricity, 20 per cent have uninterrupted central heating, 39 per cent have a systematic cold water supply and 1 per cent have a systematic hot water supply (see Table 7.8). Moreover, in 2001 the respondents in miners' settlements offered a more negative evaluation

Table 7.7 Evaluations of the quality of municipal services by the population of miners' settlements and the population of Ukraine as a whole, 2001

How would you evaluate . . .		*Evaluative coefficients[a] of the quality of services*	
		Miners' settlements	*Other towns of Ukraine[b]*
the quality of housing and communal services?	Mean Valid N	−0.8 N=501	−0.3[c] N=616
the quality of medical institutions?	Mean Valid N	−0.3 N=459	−0.3 N=608
the quality of kindergartens?	Mean Valid N	−0.4 N=136	−0.1[c] N=220
the quality of education in schools?	Mean Valid N	0.0 N=187	0.2[d] N=325
the quality of public transport?	Mean Valid N	0.2 N=421	0.2 N=599
the quality of culture institutes?	Mean Valid N	−0.6 N=203	−0.1[c] N=365

Source: KIIS; State Statistics Committee of Ukraine 2002.

Notes:
a Coefficient ranges from −1 to 1: 1 corresponds to a good quality of services, 0 to neither good nor bad, and −1 to a poor quality of services.
b Only settlements that correspnded to the miners' settlements, i.e. those with a population of 20,000–50,000, were referred to as other towns of Ukraine.
c Difference significant at 0.05.
d Difference significant at 0.01.

Table 7.8 Share of population that is provided with high-quality housing services in mining settlements and Ukraine as a whole, 2001

Do you have uninterrupted functioning...	*Mining settlements*	*Ukraine as a whole*
electricity?	79.0	90.9
central heating?	19.9	26.1
cold water supply?	38.2	64.8
hot water supply?	1.1	12.2

Source: KIIS 2000; State Statistics Committee of Ukraine 2002.

of their living conditions than for the population of Ukraine as a whole. Forty-six per cent of those living in apartments reported that their apartments were either in a poor condition or in a state of disrepair requiring major refurbishment or demolition. The comparable figure for the all-Ukraine sample was 21 per cent.

Social self-perception of the people in mining communities

A higher level of professional unity and readiness to stand up for their rights was characteristic of the Donbas even before coal mine restructuring commenced compared to other industrial branches and regions of Ukraine. This is because, first, during the Soviet era coal mines enjoyed a high social status and high wages and thus felt threatened by the restructuring programme. Second, hard working conditions and the high level of industrial injuries were reflected in the levels of pay and helped to produce distinctive communities. Third, the level of unionisation was higher in the coal industry than in any other branch of industry. For these reasons a strong collective identity and sensitivity to social injustice exists among coal miners, which has resulted in a high level of preparedness to collectively defend their rights through mass protests. Therefore, in the 1997 and 1999 surveys we included a set of questions to uncover self-perception. We asked about the significance of the different spheres of life for respondents' general satisfaction with life, about the extent and cause of stress, and respondents' readiness to defend their rights through participation in different protest actions. General satisfaction with life and the degree of stress were entirely comparable with national indicators (see Table 7.9), although the national-level data were collected only for April 2000.

Comparing the data of the miners' survey and the population in general in 1997 (see Table 7.9) we found the biggest difference to be in the proportion that were unemployed (31 per cent in the miners' settlements compared to 12 per cent in Ukraine). However, this should not be a surprise since the surveys took place in areas where mines had been closed. More surprising was that the difference between the mine settlement surveys and the national data for other indicators did not exceed 5 per cent, a figure that can be entirely explained by the sampling error. The nature of stressful situations was very similar in both the miners' settlements and Ukraine as a whole.

In contrast the readiness to fight for their rights is stronger amongst miners and inhabitants of coal mine settlements than for Ukraine in general (see Table 7.10). By 1999 the share of those who were prepared to participate in lawful and moderate political activities (such as electoral campaigns, collection of petitions and lawful meetings) had increased. However, the share of those who were prepared to participate in more radical activities (such as strikes, intimidation, hunger strike, occupation of buildings and groups of self-defence) had decreased (see Table 7.10).

One can conclude that in general the situation in miners' communities is adverse and that the level of satisfaction with life in general and its components in particular is low. Eighty per cent of people experienced stressful situations and approximately 20 per cent experienced severe stress due to unemployment, disease and bereavement. Many inhabitants were also prepared to articulate and defend their rights. However, the social self-perception did not worsen; indeed it improved a little between 1999 and 2001. The degree of dissatisfaction with various spheres of life decreased, and the level of social tension, associated with the level of well-being, nourishment and clothing, also decreased. In addition, the proportion of those who experienced severe stressful situations decreased. Most importantly, the level of

Table 7.9 A comparison of stress factors' prevalence among the population of miners' villages and the population of Ukraine

Stress factors	Mining settlements 1997 %	Mining settlements 1999 %	Difference %	Ukraine 2000 %
Experienced severe disease, operation	19.3	13.3	−6	17.8
Experienced severe disease in the family	26.0	21.1	−4.9	21.3
Experienced bereavement	21.4	14.0	−7.4	16.0
Was in a state close to suicide	2.7	2.0	−0.7	2.2
Lost job and was involuntarily unemployed	31.0	27.0	−4	12.5
Suffered from an attack or robbery	3.7	2.9	−0.8	2.5
Suffered from theft or fraud	6.4	5.1	−1.3	4.8
Found oneself without means of subsistence, was almost starving	16.1	15.5	−0.6	14.9
Felt one's helplessness in the face of the wilfulness of the authorities	22.2	24.4	2.2	16.1
Addressed the court, public prosecutor's office or lawyer for help	6.1	6.3	0.2	3.6
Lost one's faith in the people, was confronted with villainy or betrayal	12.3	12.8	0.5	11.4
Lost one's faith in one's abilities to the extent of losing the desire to do anything	13.6	16.1	2.5	12.5
Was in far-reaching conflict with one's associates	3.4	7.7	4.3	3.7
Experienced other stress-generating situations	19.5	16.7	−2.8	17.3
Did not have any stress-generating situations last year	20.1	21.1	1	22.3
Number of respondents	**1,273**	**807**	–	**2,097**

Source: KIIS 2000; State Statistics Committee of Ukraine 2002.

Note: Respondents were asked the following: 'Please indicate which of the following situations you experienced last year.' The figures are percentages of all respondents.

Table 7.10 Readiness to stand up for one's rights (percentage of respondents)

If your rights are violated and interests are ignored, are you ready to defend them by participation in . . .	Mining settlements 1997 %	Mining settlements 1999 %	Ukraine 1997 %
electoral campaigns?	40.0	43.1	32.6
collection of signatures for collective letters?	45.4	50.8	36.2
lawful meetings and demonstrations?	40.6	45.2	32.6
strikes?	29.0	25.5	19.6
boycott (refusal to abide by decisions of public authorities)?	17.8	18.3	14.5
non-authorised meetings and demonstrations?	11.3	10.2	9.8
unlawful strikes?	9.9	6.9	7.4
hunger strikes?	9.7	7.6	5.7
picketing of governmental institutions?	15.3	16.6	9.8
seizure of buildings?	5.5	3.3	3.5
creation of armed groups for self-defence?	7.7	4.3	6.0
Number of respondents	**1,273**	**807**	**1,969**

Source: KIIS 2000; State Statistics Committee of Ukraine 1998.

social self-perception did not substantially deviate from the self-perception nation-wide. The situation in coal mining regions differs only from the general situation in Ukraine in that the inhabitants are much more willing to defend their rights. This is proved by official data which show that 95 per cent of all financial losses caused by strikes in 1999 took place in Donetsk and Lugansk oblasts. Moreover, the majority of strikes in Donetsk and Lugansk were in the coal mining industry.

Conclusions

During the first stage of the coal mine restructuring programme, special attention was paid to mitigating the adverse impacts of redundancy on former coal miners through the provision of redundancy payments, unemployment benefits and access to services on preferential terms. Gradually it became clear that the negative impact of mine closures was not confined to former miners but included all spheres of economic and social life in coal mining regions. Coal mine closures led to a deterioration in the level of income of the population, resulting in migration, changes to the employment structure and a deterioration in the standard of housing and municipal services as well as high levels of social tension.

The problem of employment remains one of the most serious and long-lasting impacts of mine closures even five or more years after mass employment loss in the industry. Miners' settlements face a labour market lacking in vacancies for permanent jobs, and those vacancies that do exist are for relatively low-paid jobs with salaries that are not sufficient for a decent living. This results in a deterioration of living standards, changes in the character of employment, and the development of unofficial forms of employment with lower salaries and fewer social and legal guarantees. Owing to high competition in the labour market, some social groups within the population become excluded.

Migration out of miners' settlements has a favourable impact on the local labour market and the social situation as a whole. Since a considerable number of the working age population of miners' communities leave for prolonged periods in search of jobs, the shortage of jobs in miners' settlements decreases, allowing the government time to resolve the problem of job creation in those communities. According to regional experts,[4] migration processes in the region should be supported by the state even though migration will always be limited since there are no regions in Ukraine where there is a labour shortage. Support for entrepreneurial activities is an important component of the measures designed to increase employment. In miners' settlements the number of small-scale and individual enterprises increases every year. However, according to experts the jobs these enterprises create are merely 'a drop in the ocean' in the context of mass unemployment. Low purchasing power and the absence of people with the qualities and skills necessary for being successful entrepreneurs are barriers to business development. The social situation in the Donbas is aggravated by a high level of social tension. Therefore, a range of measures should be designed to encourage a positive evaluation of the current situation and future prospects of coal miners' communities to reduce the likelihood of the population engaging in protest. Along with state institutions, public organisations may play an important role in this respect.

Finally, the role of local bodies in implementing the programmes to mitigate the adverse impact of reforms should be reconsidered and strengthened. This is because coal industry restructuring has an impact on not just former mine workers and their families but also the development of local communities as a whole. Finance and programmes to alleviate problems in the miners' settlements would be more effective if they were managed and implemented by local institutions. Regional bodies should be concentrating on analysis and the elaboration of more effective forms of support for the most vulnerable groups in coal mine communities.

Notes

1 All indicators of employment or unemployment are calculated for the economically active population: people aged 15 to 70.
2 Use of deciles is connected to the absence of a generally accepted poverty line and its correction with regard to regional peculiarities in Ukraine. Such a criterion for defining the groups of different expenditure levels does not allow an estimation of the exact number of poor or non-poor, but allows the tracing of the dynamics of expenditure levels of different social groups.
3 According to the regional experts who participated in our research, mass migration only began when the coal industry restructuring programme commenced. Prior to that time there were no vacant apartments or houses in miners' settlements.
4 For the research conducted in 2001 the group of regional experts included municipal government officials, such as deputy mayors of mining towns responsible for social issues, for economic development and for social assets, and other local experts and

representatives of civil society groups. These included managers of job-creation pro-grammes, local union representatives, leaders of informal groups in the community and the heads of large or growing non-coal enterprises.

References

Kyiv International Institute of Sociology (KIIS) (2000) *Report about Research 'Social Assessment of Coal Industry Restructuring in Ukraine: Mitigating Adverse Social Impacts, November–December 1999'*, Kyiv: KIIS.

State Statistics Committee of Ukraine (1998) *Economic Activity in Ukraine: Statistical Yearbook for 1997*, Kyiv: State Statistics Committee of Ukraine.

State Statistics Committee of Ukraine (2000) *Ukraine in Figures in 1999*, Kyiv: State Statistics Committee of Ukraine.

State Statistics Committee of Ukraine (2002) *Statistical Yearbook of Ukraine for 2001*, Kyiv: State Statistics Committee of Ukraine.

8 Projecting 'transition' in the Ukrainian Donbas: policy transfer and the restructuring of the coal industry

Adam Swain

[O]ften the very revelation of a system is what is needed to undo it or at least to moderate it, particularly a system as extreme as the Ukrainian economic and political system.

(Aslund 2000: 273)

The 'world of projects': the 'projectification' and 'neoliberalisation' of post-Soviet east and central Europe[1]

'Transition' in eastern Europe and the former Soviet Union has been constructed as a *project*, a time-limited process of *realising* capitalism.[2] This mega-project, which Wedel calls the 'Marshall Plan of Advice' (1998: 29), spawned an explosion of technical assistance projects that cascaded downwards, projects within larger projects according to monetary value, disciplinary scope and geographical focus. This 'world of projects' (Sampson 1996: 121) comprises both technical assistance projects, which are the focus of this chapter, and projects undertaken by companies and other organisations. As Dornisch (2002: 308) suggests, 'many activities crucial to transformation [in post-Soviet eastern Europe], such as privatization, business creation, building a marketing unit or legal practice, or creating a local housing policy, all share several of the fundamental traits of project organizations'. Technical assistance programmes and projects varied considerably depending on the priorities of international donors. One of the difficulties in examining such projects is their sheer variety. Some projects operated at the national scale but were confined to a particular sector, such as banking and finance. Others were territorially defined, sometimes including several territories in order to inject an explicit comparative or competitive dimension. Or projects were designed for a narrow specific purpose such as to provide technical assistance to a particular institution. Whilst individual programmes and projects had important effects, for example in changing the function of institutions or providing evidence for an idea or argument, the projectification of 'transition' in east and central Europe (ECE) had broader structural and political implications. Projectification both facilitated and legitimated rapid knowledge transfer from west to east. It connected discursive narratives of reform to specific places, institutions and fields of social action. Projectification also entailed a programmatic way of conceiving and conducting social action. In particular this entailed a reconstitution of the organisational architecture of the state, especially the relationships between different institutions, and the content of public policy. This chapter seeks to trace the transfer of policy related to coal industry restructuring by examining the mechanisms and practices through which knowledge was transferred from the UK to Ukraine.[3] In so doing the chapter examines the articulation of two locales, the Donbas and the UK, through a series of technical assistance projects connected to a World Bank-supported restructuring programme for the Ukrainian coal industry in which in excess of 100 mines were to be closed and 400,000 employees were to leave the industry (Swain 2006).[4] The chapter shows how the process of projectification was a 'trans-local' mechanism that attempted to *redefine* the Donbas, the coal industry and its associated actors as a means to subject them to a new form of governmentality (cf. Smith 2004).

Projectification has been the prime mechanism for the 'neoliberalisation' of post-Soviet ECE (Peck and Tickell 2002). Peck and Tickell distinguish between 'neoliberalism' as an ideology and 'neoliberalisation' as a process. Neoliberalism, they argue, 'combines a commitment to the extension of markets and logics of competitiveness with a profound antipathy to all kinds of Keynesian and/or collective strategies' (2002: 381). In contrast, neoliberalisation is, they argue, 'both an "out there" and "in here" phenomenon whose effects are necessarily variegated and uneven, but the incidence and diffusion of which may present clues to a pervasive "metalogic"' (2002: 383). They go on to say that neoliberalisation 'should be understood as a process, not an end state . . . [I]t is . . . contradictory, it tends to provoke counter-tendencies, and it exists in historically and geographically contingent forms' (2002: 383). Accordingly they argue for analysis that focuses on 'shifts in systems and logics [and] dominant patterns of restructuring' (2002: 383). This chapter argues that the projectification of ECE is a shift in systems, logics and patterns of restructuring that contributes to the neoliberalisation of post-Soviet ECE. Projectification enacted a channel which, in Peck and Tickell's terminology, links the neoliberal 'heartlands' in North America and western Europe to their 'zones of extension' (Peck and Tickell 2002: 381). The neoliberalising project can also be viewed as an example of what Carrier and Miller (1998) call 'virtualism' – the process by which attempts are made to force, in this instance post-Soviet, economies to conform to the premises of textbook economic models.

Projects as an organisational form are central to the post-Soviet neoliberalisation of ECE. Grabher defines projects as 'the *process of realizing an idea or objective*' (Grabher 2002a: 207, emphasis in original) and as 'a temporary organizational arena in which knowledge is combined from a variety of sources to accomplish a specific task' (Grabher 2004: 104). He contrasts 'managed projects' that are designed centrally and involve codified formulas and standard routines of planning, budgeting and management with 'self-organising projects' that involve distributed design and which cut across professional fields and organisational boundaries (Grabher 2002b: 1911–12). Grabher also identifies interdependencies between the process of 'projectification' (the design, management and execution of projects) and the 'project ecology' ('a dense fabric of lasting ties and networks that provide key resources of expertise, reputation and legitimization' – Grabher 2004: 104; see also Grabher 2001, 2002a).

To date much of the literature on projects celebrates corporate projects, especially in new media sectors, as the latest organisational form designed to enhance competitiveness. The technical assistance projects that are the focus of this chapter differ from corporate projects and commercial consulting in three ways. Firstly, in contrast to commercial consulting these projects are initiated and sponsored by government or non-government organisations. Especially in the case of the former, projects have to be seen in their geo-political context and as an instrument of economic diplomacy. Secondly, in most cases technical assistance projects involve three parties: the client or donor that designs and funds the project; the contractor, a consulting company or consortium of companies that implements the project; and the beneficiary of the project, such as a municipality or company. Thirdly, the shortage of institutional, professional and financial resources in post-Soviet ECE meant projects were highly provisional and transitional in nature and were mere phases in a wider development trajectory (Dornisch 2002: 309).

As technical assistance projects explicitly intend to restructure state institutions, regulatory processes and policy formation, there are strong parallels with Peck's work on what he has called the 'welfare/workfare transition' (2002: 342) and the 'workfare project' (2001: 5). In particular Peck emphasises the role of 'policy transfer' in two major ways (Peck and Theodore 2001). Firstly, he argues that the internationalisation of workfare involved 'transnational flows of policy signs and programming technologies' between 'centres of persuasion', 'epicenters of reform' and 'centres of translation' (Peck 2002: 349). Thus:

> [t]he hegemonic power of workfarism is . . . substantially rooted in the capacity not just to *construct* a compelling reform discourse, validated by expert nodes in centers of persuasion like Washington D.C. and London, but to *project and realise* this reform narrative at a distance – across both space and scale.
>
> (Peck 2002: 348, emphasis in original)

Secondly, he argues that 'translocal fast-policy transfer' (Peck 2002: 344) entailing local policy experimentation, orchestrated but uneven policy transfer of disembedded 'successful' methodological models and mutually referential policy validation, all operating at ever increasing speeds, became woven into a 'fast policy regime' structuring policy actors in tangled spatial scales. However, Peck cautions that 'policies are rarely – if ever – transported in toto from one jurisdiction to another, but instead involve path-dependent mutual adjustment' (Peck 2001: 4).

Drawing in part on Peck's analysis of workfarism it is possible to interpret projects as performing three roles in the neoliberalisation of ECE. Firstly, projects were an organisational architecture and site of translation that articulated broad narratives of reform with practical policy problems. The characteristic continuous churning of projects encapsulated the representation of countries in 'transition' travelling along a progressive linear singular historicised process of European modernity. Projects were Trojan horses that sought to embed and download neoliberal 'reform'. Through the definition, redefinition and utilisation of concepts and models, technical assistance projects literally *projected* representations of social life which in turn took on a life of their own (Sampson 1996: 140). This involved policy advisory groups, research organisations, foreign aid communities and consulting companies – a 'transition industry' of project workers that shifted from project to project enacting analyses of post-Soviet economies and societies (Swain 2006). The projects embodied, validated and temporarily institutionalised transnational policy narratives by providing plausible explanations for current circumstances and by offering plausible more-or-less 'off the peg' solutions to perceived problems (cf. Woodruff 2000). They actualised (mis)conceptualisation about the organisation of society and the kinds of interventions required to reconstitute society. For example, Way (2002), in the context of reforming intergovernmental budgetary institutions in Ukraine, argues that the failure to fully comprehend the informal, as opposed to formal, operation of state institutions meant that donor interventions designed to harden budget constraints in reality had the opposite effect.[5]

Secondly, projects were 'transscalar' (Peck 2002: 332) and 'trans-local' in at least three important respects:

1   Projects linked centres of persuasion to centres of translation and linked different centres of translation to one another. Whilst the management of programmes and projects meant that international donor organisations orchestrated policy transfer, the mechanisms of policy transfer were partially privatised. The continuous redesign of projects during their life cycle blurred the distinction between the politicians and public officials who formed policy and the consultants who managed and executed the process of policy implementation. The projects defined ECE governments, institutions, individuals and so on as the objects of restructuring and the project as the agent of restructuring.

2   Projects entangled scales of public governance. Projects were invasive and were not supposed to be bound by existing local regulation but were charged to re-regulate and change the function of institutions (cf. Christopherson 2002). Projects often operated at the boundaries and in the interstices between institutions which, like institutional relationships, were subsequently destabilised by de- and re-centring organisations, which in some cases involved literally hiving off departments, people and resources from one body to another. More often projects destabilised institutions by entangling intra- and inter-institutional hierarchies. In the context of what were, at least formally, centralised states in which territorial bodies were supposed to transmit central edicts, projects were just as likely to be bottom-up, using local project work to unsettle higher authorities, as top-down. However, technical assistance projects inevitably became entangled with existing institutions and rules with the result that in the former Soviet Union by imitating aspects of the Soviet system they '[threatened] the economic and political legitimacy of the

"liberalising project'" (Cooley 2000: 43). Moreover, in countries where large donor programmes operated, such as in Russia, a significant project workforce emerged for whom project work was a post-Soviet survival strategy (Bruno 1998).

3   By rationalising the fast transfer of policies formulated and experimented with elsewhere, projects established equivalence between places with very different histories and in very different circumstances.

Thirdly, projects entailed conducting and disseminating a host of practices involving calculation, tabulation, graphical representation and embodied performance. Sampson argues that projects have their own language and culture, comprising jargon, rituals and ceremonies that produce a kind of 'magic' (Sampson 1996: 142). In the process of formulating, monitoring and evaluating projects, donor organisations engaged in practices such as the logical elaboration of country strategies, project terms of reference, project log-frames and objective verifiable indicators (Dearden and Kowalski 2003). International financial institutions and foreign aid organisations identified transition goals and produced ratings or indicators to act as a benchmark of transition (see, for example, USAID 2002; EBRD 2003). Project contractors elaborated tender documents, identified project methodologies, undertook baseline studies and established benchmarks and other metrics to be used to assess project results. In societies where, despite overbearing bureaucratisation, action was in reality often personalised, non-codified, arbitrary and informal, projects encouraged the programmatisation of organisational behaviour that tended to occlude the political decision-making implicit in project work.

Following Grabher, the remainder of the chapter examines first the projectification and second the project ecology through which knowledge was transferred from the British to the Ukrainian coal industry. The next section examines the clients, the World Bank, the EU and the UK government, which sponsored technical assistance projects connected to the restructuring process. This section of the chapter also includes a discussion of four technical assistance projects. The first two projects were sponsored by the UK government. One involved providing technical assistance to a new state body set up to close coal mines, and the second was designed to provide policy advice to the Ministry for the Coal Industry (MCI) in Kyiv. The second two projects were sponsored by the EU and were intended to mitigate the effects of mass redundancies in the coal industry, first in Luhansk oblast and then in a separate project in Donetsk oblast. The second half of the chapter focuses on the project ecology upon which these projects relied, namely a UK consulting company called IMC Consulting, which was a contractor on all four of the projects, and its consultants.

'Projectification' of the restructuring of the Ukrainian coal industry

International donors 'projectified' the restructuring of the Ukrainian coal industry by sponsoring, incubating and subcontracting projects. A small policy community, initially confined to the World Bank Group's mining division, played the most important role (Swain 2006). Beginning in 1996 the World Bank designed, monitored and evaluated two loan agreements with the Ukrainian government and initiated a third unsuccessful loan to close uneconomic mines and to marketise the sector. This enrolled a wide range of organisations, including other international donors, government ministries, regional associations of coal mines and consulting companies, into the process of restructuring the coal industry. The UK government's Department for International Development (DfID)[6] and the EU, through its TACIS programme, designed, subcontracted, monitored and evaluated a series of related technical assistance projects in coalfield regions.

Projectification involved the formation, transmission and interpretation of policy relating to both coal industry restructuring and the organisation of restructuring. Three claims were particularly important in this instance. Firstly, the IMF and World Bank argued that the world market for coal and the deindustrialisation of 'old industrial regions' in western Europe and subsequently in ECE meant a huge rationalisation of the industry was inevitable. Secondly, project donors and contractors argued that the experience of coal industry restructuring in west European countries was relevant to the Ukrainian situation. After all much

---

Figure 8.1 key:

BDA(L) – Business Development Agency (Luhansk)
C1 – a consortium of contractors including IMCC and CERPAK
C2 – a consortium of contractors led by ABU (Germany) and including IMCC
C3 – a consortium of contractors led by BMB (Netherlands) and including IMCG
CCC – Coal Consulting Centre (Donetsk)
CET – Central European Trust
DCMRI – Donetsk Coal Mining Research Institute
DIs – design institutes
EA – external advice and evaluation
EU TACIS – EU Technical Assistance to the Commonwealth of Independent States
FIGs – Financial Industrial Groups
IMCG – IMC Group
KIIS – Kyiv International Institute of Sociology
MCI/MFE – Ministry for the Coal Industry/Ministry for Fuel and Energy
MoF – Ministry of Finance
MSI (D) – Management Systems International social dialogue project in Donetsk
NBU – National Bank of Ukraine
NEC – National Employment Centre
ODS – oblast divisions
RDs – regional directorates
SACs – social adaptation centres
SC – service contractors
SES – State Employment Service
SIs – scientific institutes
SR – social research provided by universities
TA – technical assistance
TUs – trade unions
UDKR – UkrVuhleRestrukturyzatsiya (Ukrainian State Company for Coal Restructuring Enterprises)
UK DfID – UK Department for International Development
WC (D) – Women to Women Centre in Donetsk

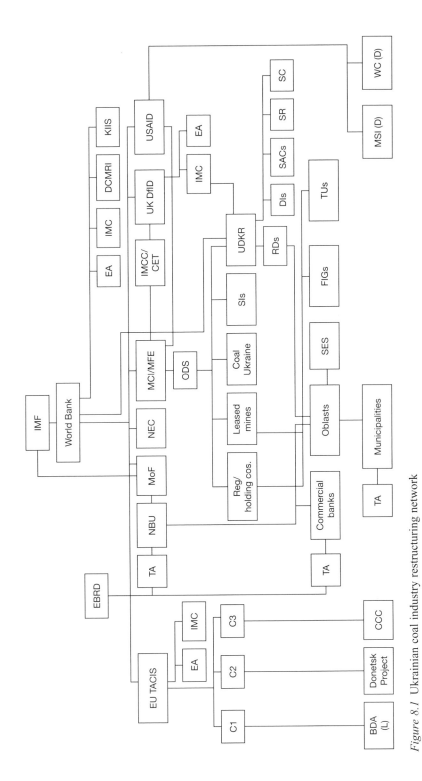

Figure 8.1 Ukrainian coal industry restructuring network

Source: Interviews.

of the west European coal industry had been state owned, and many coalfields had been regarded as 'planned regions' (Hudson 1989; Baeten *et al.* 1999: 250). Consequently Ukrainian policy makers were invited to learn from the experience of western European countries. Initially the World Bank and DfID presented the 'British model', of rapidly and inexpensively closing coal mines compared to France, Belgium and Germany, as the template that Ukraine should follow (World Bank 1996). Thirdly, it was argued that the Western experience was mobile and could be transferred to Ukraine (see Spray 2001[7]). Policy and the mechanisms of policy transfer were represented in project terms of reference, contracts, work programmes and project materials. These textual and graphical artefacts became economic narratives or scripts to be performed by institutions engaged in restructuring (cf. Sampson 1996; Smith 2002). As these immutable material artefacts (Latour 1987) circulated, they enrolled actors into an emergent restructuring network in which the UK was identified as the 'originator region' (Figure 8.1; see also Swain 2006).

   The projects to close coal mines and mitigate the social impacts were embedded in a 'project ecology' (Grabher 2001) comprising complex overlapping networks of organisations and individuals that combined and recombined to form the ephemeral projects. Projectification depended on the existence of a 'community of practice' (Wenger 1998) produced through coal industry restructuring in western Europe in the 1980s and early 1990s. Project clients and contractors literally projected this community into coalfields in ECE such as the Ukrainian Donbas. Specialist consulting companies that employed the individual consultants who managed and implemented projects played a major role in this ecology. One British consulting company, IMC Consulting, which had emerged out of the restructuring and privatisation of the British coal industry, played an important role in exporting this experience to post-Soviet Europe.

The clients

Foreign aid programmes and overseas lending played a key role in 'economic transition' in Ukraine. In 1995, official aid and lending constituted 93 per cent of the total net financial flows into the country (Table 8.1). As net private inflows, including direct foreign investment, increased, the proportion of official aid and lending declined to around 30 per cent by the late 1990s. The IMF and World Bank provided conditional loans that financed either the government's budget or specific activities whilst bilateral and multilateral aid programmes provided grant aid to finance technical assistance projects. In 1998 the IMF agreed a $2.2 billion extended fund facility and between 1992 and the end of 2001 the World Bank lent around $3 billion to Ukraine (European Commission 2001: 14). The largest bilateral donors to Ukraine were the USA and the UK; in 2002, US assistance to Ukraine was $280 million including the $74 million USAID programme (http://www.state. gov, accessed 6 August 2004) and UK bilateral aid to Ukraine was £8 million in 1999. Including its contributions to the EU TACIS programme, the UK provided up to 11 per cent of annual grant aid to Ukraine in the late 1990s. The largest

Table 8.1 Financial flows to Ukraine

	1995 £m	1996 £m	1997 £m	1998 £m	1999 £m
Official aid (grants)	202	255	110	231	297
Of which:					
Bilateral	100	239	102	165	248
Multilateral	103	16	8	66	49
UK total aid	22	11	12	22	16
Of which:					
Bilateral	7	9	11	9	8
Through multilateral institutions	16	2	1	13	8
UK aid as a percentage	11%	4%	11%	10%	5%
Net other financial flows (non-concessional)	206	415	230	272	292
Of which:					
Bilateral	3	119	6	1	2
Multilateral institutions	202	296	223	273	290
Net private capital flows	30	363	866	1,260	–
Of which:					
FDI	163	337	355	451	302
Total	438	1,033	1,206	1,763	–
Of which:					
Official aid and lending	408	670	340	503	–
As a percentage	93%	65%	28%	29%	–

Source: DFID 2001: 8; author's calculations.

multilateral donors were the European Bank for Reconstruction and Development (EBRD) and the EU TACIS programme. By the end of 2001 the EBRD had allocated EUR1.2 billion to Ukraine, and between 1991 and 2001 the TACIS programme allocated EUR1 billion (European Commission 2001: 13, 10).

In late 1994 the IMF identified state subsidies to the Ukrainian coal industry as a source of macroeconomic instability within the country. To address this the IMF invited the Ukrainian government and the World Bank to collaborate on a restructuring plan for the industry. In 1995 the World Bank formed two missions to prepare loan agreements with the government. One mission was established to design a $300 million coal sector adjustment loan (or coal SECAL) to close uneconomic mines and commercialise the sector. The second mission was to design a $15.8 million coal pilot loan to fund the technical closure of three mines and the cost of mitigating the social and environmental impacts of the closures. Although the pilot loan was to elaborate the procedures to be followed in the closure of mines, to be published in the form of a manual that was to be adopted nation-wide under the terms of the SECAL, the two missions were composed of entirely different people. Each mission was led by an official from the World Bank Group's mining division, and comprised a number of World Bank specialists in, for example, statistics or employment, and a number of external private consultants.

Both missions included officials and consultants who had knowledge and experience of the restructuring and privatisation of the British coal industry. The SECAL mission included an external consultant who had been a mining engineer at the UK's National Coal Board (later renamed British Coal – BC). Once BC had been compelled to be market orientated, he specialised in modelling the economic viability of investment projects. In 1992 he was appointed to the Privatisation Group at BC where he was one of a very few executives involved in preparing the company for privatisation. After BC was privatised in late 1994 he joined a small consulting company in London called Hillary Wharf that specialised in undertaking 'design projects' that involved elaborating restructuring plans in the coal sector for donors such as the World Bank. The SECAL mission visited Ukraine twice to oversee an analysis of the sector by Ukrainian civil servants and academics that was subsequently published by the World Bank and which formed the basis for the confidential loan agreement between the Bank and the Ukrainian government in December 1996 (World Bank 1996; Swain 2006). The pilot loan mission, meanwhile, included a consultant who had been a mining engineer at BC who was an expert in the technical aspects of mine closure.[8] Another member of the pilot loan mission was an external adviser who drew up the terms of reference for technical assistance projects in Ukraine for what was then called the UK government's 'Know How Fund' (KHF).

The selection of people with experience in the UK reflected the way the World Bank Group's mining division regarded the UK as a model that Ukraine should follow. Beginning with Poland in the early 1990s the mining division drew parallels between post-Soviet coal industry restructuring and the restructuring that was then taking place in the UK (see Beatty and Fothergill 1996; Waddington *et al.* 2001). Led by a British mining engineer, the division commissioned a number of studies on the restructuring and privatisation of the UK coal industry. The way the UK had rapidly removed subsidies, reduced output and closed coal mines – including the closure of entire coalfields – apparently more cheaply than elsewhere and then privatised the industry appealed to the Bank. Internal and external advisers elaborated a basic strategy that involved rapid closure of uneconomic mines, marketisation and privatisation. As the division and its advisers shifted its focus from country to country, the basic strategy was replicated across ECE.

In Ukraine the British experience influenced the restructuring programme in several ways. Firstly, the programme involved the almost immediate closure of 54 mines in 1996–1997 and the closure of a further 93 mines by 2004. This entailed a 300,000 reduction in employment in coal extraction. Secondly, the plan promoted the marketisation of the remainder of the sector to include the cessation of production subsidies, the transfer of social assets belonging to coal enterprises to local government,[9] de-monopolisation and corporatisation leading to privatisation. Thirdly, the plan established a new state-owned company – UkrVuhleRestrukturyzatsiya (UDKR) – to manage the closure programme and the environmental and social mitigation measures.

The World Bank's missions judged that provision of technical assistance in procuring services for the physical closure of mines and the elaboration of measures to alleviate the social and economic impacts of mine closures would be required. The KHF in turn agreed to fund and design a project to support the newly established UDKR and another to provide policy advice to the MCI in Kyiv.[10] The terms of reference for the contract to design the project to assist UDKR, devised by the KHF in early 1996, indicated that the new organisation was modelled on British Coal Enterprise (BCE) even though, unlike BCE, UDKR was responsible for both social mitigation and the physical closure of mines (Spray 2001). BCE had been established by Ian MacGregor, the then CEO of the state-owned BC, in the winter of 1984–1985 during a major strike, to find jobs for redundant mine workers (Pickering 1995: 104). MacGregor imported the idea of BCE from the USA and had previously established a similar body, British Steel Industries (BS(I)) when he was at the state-owned British Steel Corporation. BCE imitated BS(I) by providing credits to businesses that created new jobs in coalfield areas and by establishing managed workspace or business incubators. BCE's major innovation was its Job and Career Change Scheme (JACCS), which combined the existing concept of 'job shops' with a new concept of providing employment counselling and training to match redundant miners with local job vacancies. 'Outplacement', as it became known, had been introduced into the UK in 1987 when the US company Sikorski acquired Westland Helicopters and employed US consultants to set up an on-site office to counsel and provide local labour market advice to redundant workers. JACCS involved tele-marketers contacting local employers to find out about vacancies before they were notified to job centres, and on-site counsellors at closing mines to deliver interview training and CV preparation. Regional training centres were also established to develop literacy and numeracy skills and to tailor miners' existing skills to non-mining careers.

The KHF project to deliver policy advice to the MCI was designed and put out to tender at the same time as the UDKR project. The MCI project was designed to improve rational policy making through the provision of policy advice and organisational assistance to the MCI during the World Bank-supported restructuring programme. These two technical assistance projects meant the UK government played a considerable role in the restructuring of the Ukrainian coal industry. Subsequently the EU TACIS programme developed four related projects. One project was intended to undertake an audit of one mine and to provide management training. In 1997 TACIS began to design a three-year project to use 'bottom-up' approaches to mitigate the social impact of coal industry restructuring in Donetsk oblast, in part by drawing on experience from countries other than the UK. However, during the design phase TACIS officials formed the opinion that the oblast administration was not committed to the aims of the project or the TACIS programme more generally and transferred the project to Luhansk oblast. Perceiving a changed attitude in Donetsk, in 1998 TACIS officials once again initiated and this time put out to tender a social mitigation project in Donetsk. In the same year TACIS designed a project intended to establish an organisation in Donetsk to provide consulting services to the mining industry.

Once the execution of projects commenced, the role of project clients changed from design and contracting to one of monitoring and evaluation. For example, the World Bank mining division produced an implementation completion report for each of the two loans in 2001. Subsequently the Operations and Evaluation Department produced an evaluation summary and a project performance assessment report that systematically rated both loans (World Bank 2002). Moreover, these documents were reinterpreted by World Bank officials who conducted research on the loans and the broader issues that surrounded them in part to inform any subsequent loans (see, for example, World Bank 2003 and Fretwell 2004).

The projects

In addition to the two World Bank loans, 10 implementation technical assistance projects related to the restructuring of the coal mining industry were established in Donetsk or Luhansk between 1996 and 2004 (see Table 8.2). (Over a similar time scale a further nine technical assistance projects were set up in the field of economic development in the Donbas – see Table 8.3.) The lead contractor in three of the coal sector projects, and a major subcontractor in a further project, was a British consulting company, IMC Consulting (IMCC).[11] I now examine, first, the two UK-sponsored projects to assist in the closure of coal mines and to provide policy advice in Kyiv and, second, two EU-sponsored projects designed to mitigate the effects of mass redundancies in the coal sector in, first, Luhansk oblast and, second, Donetsk oblast.

Technical assistance to UkrVuhleRestrukturyzatsiya (UDKR) and policy advice to the Ukrainian Ministry of the Coal Industry: transplanting British Coal Enterprise to Ukraine

BCE and five other companies submitted bids to win the contract to assist UDKR. One of those companies was IMCC. Its bid envisaged a project team comprising former senior BCE employees and the transplantation of the BCE model to Ukraine. The KHF awarded the design contract and subsequently the implementation contract to IMCC. The project began in September 1996 and was extended twice until September 2002. The project contract manager, a former finance director of BCE and official of the EU-funded European Resource Centre on Industrial Restructuring and Re-conversion (CERRM), divided his time between the UK and Donetsk to ensure the project team complied with the terms of the contract. The project manager, also formerly of BCE, and a small number of long-term IMCC consultants were initially based in an office in the UDKR headquarters in Donetsk. A succession of consultants made short visits to provide specialist training, and local specialists were recruited. After a year the project manager left to manage a new project in neighbouring Luhansk oblast (see page 176) and was succeeded by another former BCE manager. The British consultants deployed a variety of methods including training, coaching and mentoring of key staff, twinning organisations and study tours to the UK.

Table 8.2 Technical assistance projects related to the restructuring of the Ukrainian coal sector

Donor	Project	Location	Value	Contractor(s)	Date
DfID	Technical assistance to UDKR	Donetsk	£1.4m (Phase 1)	IMCC (UK)	1996–2002
DfID	Technical assistance to the Ministry for the Coal Industry	Kyiv	–	IMCC and Central European Trust	1996–1998
TACIS	Coal mine management	Donetsk	–	IMC	1997
TACIS	Support to address the social impact of the restructuring of the coal industry in Luhansk	Luhansk	ECU3m	IMCC, Charbonnages de France, the Guidance Centre for the Limburg Mining Area, the International Federation of Mine Workers	1997–1999
TACIS	Technical assistance to Coal Consulting Centre	Donetsk	–	IMC and BMB (Hol)	1998–2002
TACIS	Support to address the social consequences of coal restructuring through local economic development in Donetsk	Donetsk	Euro 1.5m	ABU-Consult (lead contractor), IMCC, BMB	1999–2001
USAID	Technical assistance to the Ministry of Fuel and Energy	Kyiv	–	no data	1999–2002
USAID	BIZPRO	Donetsk, Luhansk	$4.75m	Development Alternatives Inc. (US)	2000–2005
Polish Know How Foundation	Reform of the coal mining industry, Polish experience from 1990 to 2002	Donetsk, Luhansk	–	Polish Know How Foundation, Eastern Studies Institute	2002
SIDA (Swe)	Social mitigation of coal mine closures	Donetsk, Luhansk	–	The Swedish Cooperative Centre	2004–2006

Table 8.3 Technical assistance projects related to economic development in the Donbas

Donor	Project	Location	Contractor(s)	Date
USAID	'Partnership for Integrity' anti-corruption programme	Donetsk	Management Systems International (US)	1998–2000
USAID	Ukraine Micro Lending Programme	Donetsk	EBRD	1998–2004
USAID	Women's economic empowerment	Donetsk	Winrock International (US)	1999–2004
USAID	BIZPRO	Donetsk, Luhansk	Development Alternatives Inc. (US)	2000–2005
DfID	Social sphere assets transfer and maintenance in Donetsk	Donetsk	IN-CO, Enterplan, British Power International	2000–2003
DfID	Community development in Donetsk oblast	Donetsk	Birks Sinclair (UK), the Back to Work Company (UK)	2000–2002
DfID	Enterprise education in vocational schools	Donetsk	University of Durham (UK)	2003–2005
DfID	Improving the business environment in three oblasts in Ukraine	Donetsk, Luhansk	Enterplan (UK)	2002–2004
DfID	Economic regeneration and social mitigation in the Donbas	Luhansk, Donetsk	IMCC (lead contractor) plus 13-member consortium	2002–2007

The project attempted to influence the organisation and operation of UDKR to ensure it remained in existence, was adequately financed and operated according to the World Bank's manual for closing mines. Consultants provided generic organisational and management training for UDKR's senior managers at its head office. To minimise the costs of physically closing mines, consultants advised management on the establishment and operation of a competitive tendering system to contract out the work. Consultants also introduced managers to strategies to reduce the recurrent costs of closure, such as the use of submersible pumps, and to offset closure costs, for example through the re-use of mine sites. The project established a public relations department within UDKR, trained its personnel and devised a public information strategy designed to draw maximum media and political attention to the measures designed to ameliorate the impact of job losses. The consultants also sought to focus UDKR management on cost-effective job creation by analysing 'cost per job' data and by setting targets.

The project also demonstrated the social mitigation measures that had been used by BCE. The project, largely independent from UDKR, established 'social adaptation centres' in settlements where mines were being closed. The centres were modelled on 'job shops' but also provided counselling to redundant mine workers. A job subsidy scheme for employers that recruited redundant mine workers was established, as well as a micro-finance facility and business incubator to encourage the formation of small firms. However, these activities largely ceased once the project finished in 2002. Towards the end of the project, and in part reflecting DfID's new poverty-focused country strategy (DfID 2001), the team concentrated on community development and instilling the 'self-help' idea in coalfield communities. Training programmes for unemployed women from coal mining settlements that covered the establishment and operation of NGOs and credit unions and job search and business planning skills were organised (Chambers 2003). The project provided financial support for trainees to set up NGOs to provide community services as well as credit unions. This aspect of the project was perceived to have been so successful that in 2000 DfID designed a 'spin-off' community development project covering a wider territory. IMCC submitted a bid for this contract but it was awarded to a consortium led by another UK consulting company, Birks Sinclair.

IMCC considered it was unlikely it would be awarded the contract to provide policy advice to the MCI in Kyiv and decided to submit a joint bid with Central European Trust (CET), a consulting firm based in London, as the lead contractor. The project contract was awarded to CET in 1996 and, whilst CET managed the contract, IMCC provided the two consultants who established an office within the ministry. The consultants attempted to advise the minister and deputy minister by producing papers on policy issues, such as privatisation and corporate governance, related to the restructuring programme. The consultants also attempted to facilitate MCI's negotiations with the World Bank and other government ministries. However, the rapid turnover of ministers and senior officials and the inability to deploy diplomatic pressure to ensure co-operation meant the two-year project had only a modest impact.

The social mitigation of coal industry restructuring: the multiple identities of Actiondonbass

IMCC responded to the tender for the TACIS project to mitigate the social impacts of mine closures in Luhansk by building a consortium under its leadership. Considering its role in UDKR and the MCI and its association with the 'British model' of coal industry restructuring, IMCC sought to compile a consortium designed to project a European identity. IMCC's consortium included the French coal mining company Group Charbonnages, Begeleidingsdienst Limburgs Mijngebied (BLM) (Guidance Centre for the Limburg Mining Area) and the International Federation of Chemical Energy Mining and General Workers' Unions (ICEM). The consortium also included the Coalfield Communities Campaign that represented UK local authorities affected by coal industry restructuring. IMCC used a brand name, Actiondonbass, considering that the name could be seen equally as French or as English, to identify the consortium.

Actiondonbass won the contract in 1998, and the project manager of the UDKR project moved to the Luhansk project. The project team included a long-term consultant from ICEM, ten local consultants and 20 short-term foreign consultants. The project subcontracted activities to local organisations such as the Luhansk Investor Support Agency which was established by the Soros-funded International Renaissance Foundation. The project, which ended in September 2000, comprised three components. Firstly, it sought to implement local economic development measures including the establishment of a business development agency to deliver training and consulting services, a micro-credit scheme to encourage SME formation and the introduction of place marketing. Secondly, consultants from Belgium organised round tables in Kyiv, Luhansk and mining settlements to encourage social dialogue relating to coal industry restructuring. Regional round tables were organised to encourage the formation and articulation of a new post-coal regional identity. In coal mine settlements the closure of mines was discussed by representatives from UDKR, municipalities and where possible trade unions. Thirdly, the project published local newsletters designed to encourage local people to organise community projects for women and young people.

When the TACIS project in Donetsk was put out to tender, IMCC once again considered it was unlikely it would win the second tender alone and began to form a new consortium, but once again under the Actiondonbass brand. To downplay the role of IMCC, the consortium was led by a small German consulting company, ABU-Consult, and also included BMB, a Dutch consulting company. ABU-Consult managed the contract, contracted subcontractors and oversaw the logistical require-ments of the project team. However, the project team leader was an IMCC associate who had previously worked on the UDKR project and was a former manager at BCE. The project, which ran from September 1998 until September 2001, was broadly similar to the Luhansk project. It encouraged local economic regeneration through retraining ex-miners, administration or an investment fund, and by estab-lishing community projects. To ameliorate the impact of coal industry restructuring the project provided counselling to redundant miners and developed a public information strategy. The project also tried to use social dialogue and international twinning agreements to build a new vision for the region.[12]

The project ecology: contractors, consultants and careers

These projects depended on a project ecology comprising institutions, networks and discourses. The restructuring of the coal industry in western Europe produced a community of policy makers, institutions and practitioners that accumulated, interpreted and transmitted specialist knowledge on coalfield re-conversion (cf. Lagendijk and Cornford 2000). Whilst there were important differences in the ways countries managed the decline of their coal industries, three broad models emerged. The 'continental model' adopted a long-term consensual approach to strategically planning for the decline of employment in the coal industry and the creation of alternative employment. In contrast the 'British model' involved fragmented initiatives designed to minimise the number of ex-miners who registered as unemployed. The 'Belgian model' contained elements of both the continental and the British models. These models were interpreted and circulated in a number of ways. Coal sector organisations in ECE became members of the European association of employer associations representing coal and lignite industries (EURACOAL) and the European Association of Mining Communities (EUR-ACOM). Also research on the lessons of the experience of coal industry restructuring in western Europe for ECE was undertaken by, for example, the International Energy Agency's Clean Coal Research Centre (Walker 2001). Moreover, as the 1990s progressed, an interpretative community dedicated to coal industry restructuring in ECE emerged. Within this the World Energy Council undertook comparative research (Brendow 2000) and the UNECE's Ad Hoc Group of Experts on Coal in Sustainable Development regularly analysed 'restructuring indicators' for 11 post-Soviet coal industries and sought to assist restructuring and marketisation through providing training activities.

The contractor: IMC Consulting

IMCC was an important node in the network of institutions and individuals that constituted the project ecology that underpinned the projectification of the restructuring of the coal industry in Ukraine. IMCC combined very few permanent employees with a large network of specialists (economists, accountants, marketing experts and so on) who could be flexibly employed to form teams tailored to meet donors' terms of reference. In 2002, IMCC employed 17 full-time permanent consultants at its headquarters in Huthwaite near Mansfield, Nottinghamshire, UK, to oversee the company's strategy and to write tenders, compile teams and manage contracts.[13] The company marketed itself as a 'management consulting and economic development advisory group strengthening the strategies, tools and skills needed to create sustainable economic and social development' (IMCC n.d.: 2). IMCC claimed to capture strategic and methodological experience to augment its own organisation, and that of its clients and their beneficiaries, through compiling interdisciplinary teams of 'consultants, advisors and trainers . . . [to act as] catalysts, bringing additional experience and expertise to clients who are already in the processes of change' (IMCC n.d.: 2, 16). To staff projects, the company drew on a pool of associate consultants who were either contracted to work on a specific project or projects or were retained and guaranteed a minimum number of project days per year. At any one time up to 400 consultants, formally employed by IMC Associates Ltd. to minimise non-wage costs, worked on projects around the world. In 1995, IMCC's turnover had been around £5 million, whereas by 2001 it accounted for £23 million of the £33 million revenue for its holding company, IMC Group (IMCG), whose managing director was also chairman of the British Consultants and Construction Bureaux.[14]

Until June 2004 IMCC was a subsidiary of IMCG, which was in turn majority-owned by Rio Tinto, one of the largest mining companies in the world (see Figure

8.2). IMCG, formerly called British Mining Consultants (BMC), was established in 1947 to provide technical consulting funded by the British government's aid programme to mining industries in the British Empire and Commonwealth.[15] BMC had close connections to BC, whose engineers were regularly seconded to BMC to work on specific overseas projects. In 1990, BMC saw the potential to provide economic consulting to coal mine industries in ECE. To tap into this emerging consulting market, BMC formed a strategic alliance with BC's Operational Research Executive (ORE), which performed a role analogous to that of an internal management consulting company. BMC provided technical mining consulting expertise and ORE provided basic economic and commercial expertise. After the privatisation of ORE in April 1992,[16] three senior employees left to join BMC to establish International Economic and Energy Consultants (IEEC) to export the British experience of coal industry restructuring to ECE. IEEC marketed itself as a 'joint venture' with BC's research and development department, the Coal Research Establishment (CRE), and BCE. Though not legally a joint venture these alliances permitted IEEC to draw on experts working for CRE and BCE to fulfil contracts to provide technical assistance to the mining industries in Hungary and the Czech Republic in the early 1990s. This informal arrangement meant that BMC and BCE were both collaborating and competing with one another in the market for coal sector technical assistance projects in ECE.

Having initially confined its activities to responding to requests from international donors, BCE established an international division in 1993 to compete for profit-bearing contracts to deliver services in ECE. The division marketed the 'BCE experience' in bidding documents and called on experts from BCE's other divisions as well as a pool of external consultants to compile project teams. Whilst BCE managers performed project manager roles, project teams consisted of external consultants but, once it became apparent that BCE would be broken up as part of the privatisation of the coal industry, managers began to volunteer to join project teams. Alone or with the British Council, BCE won a series of contracts that included the establishment of a business incubator in Ostrava in the Czech Republic, and the retraining of former mine workers and the establishment of micro-credit schemes in coalfields in eastern Poland, Hungary, Romania and Russia.

These contracts and the EU RECHAR programme to assist coalfield areas Europeanised the coalfield re-conversion 'industry'. BCE established a formal exchange programme with its counterpart in Belgium, BLM, and at least one senior BCE official worked at CERRM based in France. Both these organisations became involved in transferring knowledge from west to east. BLM had been established in 1989 following the so-called 'Gheyselinck Plan' in 1986 that outlined the strategy for the closure of the Limburg coalfield. The author of the plan, Thyl Gheyselinck, advised the Czech and Polish governments on coal industry restructuring between 1991 and 1993. In 1992 Gheyselinck, who had been appointed by the Czech government to chair the newly created department for the restructuring and privatisation of the coal mining industry, published a plan to liberalise prices, eliminate subsidies and restructure the sector leading to privatisation whilst minimising social impacts and expenditure (Pavlinek 1997: 201ff.). In 1993 he became an external consultant

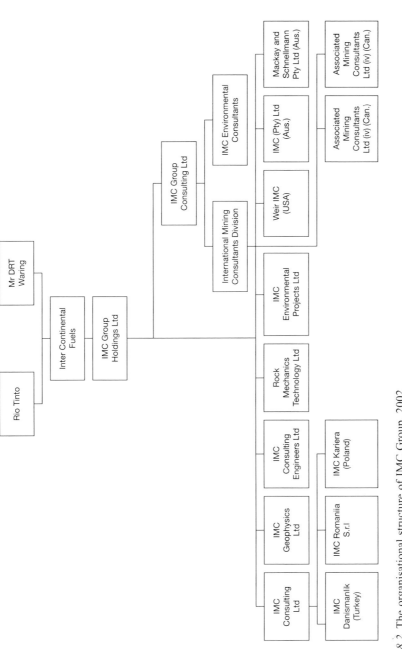

Figure 8.2 The organisational structure of IMC Group, 2002

Source: IMC Annual Review 2002; interviews; industry sources.

for a newly formed consulting company that provided consulting services to the energy industry, regulators and international development projects in the Czech Republic. In the late 1990s CERRM, which had been established by the EU to research, develop and disseminate methods of industrial restructuring and social re-conversion, managed an EU-funded project designed to transfer experience of the restructuring of the Ruhr to declining coalfields in Upper Silesia and Ostrava.

Shortly before the privatisation of BCE, which was to entail the closure of the international division, a senior manager left to become a full-time consultant for IEEC based at BMC's headquarters.[17] At the same time half a dozen other senior BCE managers, including its financial director, joined BMC as associate consultants. As the market for technical consulting declined and the market for economic consulting increased, IEEC became increasingly central to BMC's corporate strategy and, in response to donors combining technical and economic consulting within single projects, BMC reorganised its corporate structure. BMC was renamed International Mining Consultants and became one of several wholly and jointly owned subsidiaries providing different types of consulting owned by a new holding company, IMCG. IEEC became a wholly owned subsidiary within the group called IMC Consulting. This structure diversified the expertise of the company and established an internal market in which the subsidiaries could subcontract consulting activities to one another.

IMCC initially competed and won contracts, funded by the World Bank, EU and DfID, to deliver technical assistance projects connected to the coal industry. These included contracts in Poland to establish, deliver and promote training programmes for workers leaving the coal industry and to advise on the privatisation of mining enterprises. In Romania, IMCC won contracts to support SME development, social mitigation and local partnerships in coal mining areas. Other subsidiaries in IMCG provided technical services, such as consulting services, surveys and appraisals, mine development and restructuring plans, mine closures audits and competent persons' reports, as part of the privatisation of mines primarily as subcontractors to IMCC. IMCC also won a series of contracts in Russia in the context of the World Bank's coal industry restructuring programme. These included projects to assist the privatisation of coal mining enterprises and the establishing of Coal Consulting Centres, modelled on IMCG, to provide technical and management/economic consulting to the coal industry.[18] One of the company's largest projects, funded by the TACIS programme,[19] aimed to diversify the economies of five mining settlements that belonged to the Association of Mining Towns. The project team developed strategies, and created strategy teams for municipalities, and developed local economic and social programmes that included business centres, investment funds and the delivery of business advice and training. A website was constructed to disseminate the project's findings to all 80 towns belonging to the association.

Whilst IMCC concentrated on the larger and more profitable implementation projects it also undertook analytical projects. In 1993, IMCC, with CERRM, won an EU PHARE contract to review the experience of coalfield re-conversion in Belgium, France, Germany and the UK for the Hungarian Ministry of Industry to identify the most successful re-conversion strategies to be deployed in ECE (IMCC 1998). A 'balance sheet' that compared job losses, the destination of redundant miners (alternative employment, retirement or unemployment) and the cost per job for a range of employment creation measures was produced for each country. The analysis concluded that whilst a lower proportion of former miners in the UK found alternative employment the cost of creating new jobs was the lowest (Spray 2001). The analysis was repeated by IMCC under contracts from the EU and DfID for beneficiaries in Poland, Romania, Russia and Ukraine.

As the priorities of international donors changed, IMCC diversified its knowledge base through recruiting new permanent consultants and extending its pool of associates to broaden expertise into new sectors and new regions and countries. Equally, as projects became larger and increasingly multidisciplinary the company focused on project management, involving the compilation and management of consortia of consulting companies from the UK and across Europe. As expertise became obsolete (for example, as mines were closed) the company competed for and won contracts to restructure and privatise large state-owned enterprises in a variety of different sectors. In turn, as privatisation was accomplished and donors' priorities changed to, for example, poverty reduction, IMCC diversified in to the delivery of projects to support small and medium-sized enterprises, vocational training programmes, government economic and social reform programmes, regional development and partnership initiatives. Also as the donors' geographical focus changed, IMCC extended its coverage to include, for example, China, Turkey and Egypt. The company also sought to localise the management and operation of projects to reduce costs and create a permanent project workforce to break into the commercial consulting market. IMCC established subsidiaries in Poland, where it employed 120 permanent staff, Romania and Turkey. As the company established a track record of delivering projects in new sectors and countries and in commercial consulting, IMCC's coal sector heritage became less and less prominent.

Conclusions

This chapter has tried to reveal the mechanisms and practices through which policy is transferred from one country to another and to trace the projection of, in this instance, the 'British model' of coal industry restructuring in the Ukrainian Donbas. This involved the projectification of the restructuring of the Ukrainian coal industry by a tight-knit policy community (Marsh and Rhodes 1992) initially confined to the World Bank but subsequently extended to include DfID to *project* the 'British model' of coal industry restructuring. Moreover, the practices associated with projectification served to reinforce the cohesion of the policy community and the exclusion of outsiders. That said, as the EU TACIS programme became involved, elements of other models, such as social dialogue, began to play a minor role. The 'British model' emerged as the preferred template for several reasons. Firstly, the 'British model' of rapid mine closures, marketisation and fragmented social programmes fitted the hegemonic logic of post-Soviet economic transition. Moreover, the UK was perceived as a neoliberal heartland that validated the 'transition' narrative. Secondly, officials with experience of the British coal mining industry and its restructuring and privatisation occupied prominent positions in the World Bank mining division. Thirdly, a community of practice, or to use Grabher's terminology a 'project ecology', existed in the UK which could provide the resources, expertise and validation needed to enact projectification. The projects were episodes that temporarily crystallised a complicated ecology of colliding institutional and personal biographies that constantly dissolved and recombined as projects came and went. It was an ecology of biographies that spanned a host of organisations including various parts of the British coal industry. This included various different organisations within British Coal, such as the Operations Research Executive, the Coal Research Establishment, the Privatisation Group and British Coal Enterprise, as well as project clients, such as the DfID and the World Bank, and project contractors, such as IMC Consulting.

Projects combined features associated with both 'managed projects' and 'self-organised projects' (Grabher 2002b: 1911). These projects were centrally designed, and the relationship between the client and lead contractor was highly managed, but the relationship between the contractor and subcontractors and between the contract manager and project team members was self-organised. The life cycle of the projects involved a design phase led by the donor, but usually involving external consultants, either before the project itself had commenced (i.e. during a pre-project phase) or early in the life of the project to identify the objectives. This was followed by a competitive tendering phase, involving the compilation of consortia and project teams and the writing of bidding documents, which culminated in face-to-face interviews. Once a contractor had been selected the donor and contractor negotiated a contractual agreement covering the work programme and project finance. Thereafter, for the client, the evolution of the project was predictable even though contracts could permit the opportunity to renegotiate the work programme at specified points during the life of the project. Contractual agreement between the client and the lead contractor triggered the reopening of negotiation between the contractor and subcontractors over the distribution of activities and finance. A feature of these negotiations was the blurring of the boundaries between contractors as consultants were sometimes loaned by one contractor to another to portray a different project identity or to finesse financial transactions between contractors. Thus while project objectives were always final, the work programme and its allocation to subcontractors was only ever provisional.

The projects tended to be highly bureaucratic and codified. The design, contracting, monitoring and evaluation of projects involved bureaucratic systems of reporting and little face-to-face interaction. That said, contractors were dependent on a limited number of clients and required informal inside knowledge as well as the formal information gathered from tender documents. A key feature was the way individuals shifted from organisation to organisation and undertook a variety of different roles in the projectification process (cf. Wedel 1998). Bureaucratisation was in part due to the 'transscalar' (Peck 2002: 332) qualities of projects in which clients and contractors were not co-located and because they were also just phases in wider foreign aid programmes (Dornisch 2002). Projects were scientifically represented through logical frameworks that linked aims, interventions and outputs and a tendering process in which arguments about which methodologies would realise an idea were presented and evaluated. The emphasis on methodologies and practices such as peer review highlighted the parallels with the academic research process. Many projects were reduced to standardised activities (micro-credits, business incubators and so on) that had been replicated throughout the region since 1990. Projects primarily transferred cognitive knowledge, models and concepts represented through text, illustration and performance. The representation of projects in textual artefacts (decision-making manuals, role-play scenarios and websites, etc.) was in part a response to the tension that existed between the temporary nature of the project and the donors' desire for sustainable outcomes.

The practices and discourses associated with projectification and the project ecology encouraged programmatic policy formulation, selection and execution that opened a channel for fast policy transfer relating not only to coal sector restructuring but also to public policy in general. Projectification and associated fast policy transfer became structural components in Ukraine's policy regime. Whereas centralised top-down reform had been frustrated, the cacophony of projects that entailed not only local policy implementation but also local policy formation produced a nascent 'learning system' that served macroeconomic and political objectives (Peck and Theodore 2001: 457). The projects were rooted in precepts that undermined what has been described by two influential economic advisers to the Ukrainian government as the 'absurd Ukrainian economic model' (Aslund and de Ménil 2000: 25). The de facto decentralisation of the Ukrainian state – which was encouraged by projects – in which regional and local state institutions in the Donbas enjoyed considerable autonomy provided opportunities for the bottom-up reconstitution of the state and economy. Whilst to date policy elites in Ukraine have not been particularly receptive towards the holy trinity of stabilisation, deregulation and privatisation rooted in neoliberalism, interlocal and international policy transfers have been gradually neoliberalising the state.

Notes

1 Sampson 1996: 121; Midler 1995; Peck and Tickell 2002: 382.
2 Earlier versions of this chapter were presented at 'The Miners' Strike 20 Years On: Challenges and Changes' conference at the University of Northumbria at Newcastle, July 2004, and at the workshop on 'Old Industrial Knowledges' at the University of Newcastle in February 2005. Thanks to participants at each event for their useful comments and to Andrew Leyshon for comments on an earlier draft of this chapter. The usual disclaimers apply.
3 This chapter draws on semi-structured interviews with permanent and temporary officials of international financial institutions and other donor organisations, permanent and temporary employees of consulting companies, beneficiary organisations and individual consultants in the UK and in Ukraine between 1997 and 2004. The chapter also draws in part on my position as a member of the 'transition industry' involving formal participation at conferences and meetings as well as informal socialising. Undertaking research on projects poses particular methodological problems. The diversity of projects and the fact that respondents have worked on many projects (often simultaneously) for

different donors and consulting companies and are probably self-employed make tradi-tional key informant interviewing problematic.

4 The World Bank supported a similar programme to restructure the Russian coal industry (see Robertson 1997).

5 Way argues that donor pressure on states to decentralise their budgeting systems reduced central oversight of revenues and expenditures, encouraging local informal decision making (2002: 583).

6 Originally the UK government's aid programme to ECE was called the Know How Fund and administrated by the Overseas Development Administration that was part of the Foreign and Commonwealth Office.

7 Bob Spray was a contract manager for a DfID-funded project from 1996 to 2002.

8 He subsequently worked on a project to close coal mines in Romania as part of the World Bank's coal industry restructuring programme there.

9 British Coal had sold its housing in the early 1980s.

10 The Ministry of the Coal Industry was subsequently subsumed within the Ministry of Fuel and Energy.

11 In addition, a mine engineering consulting company, International Mining Consultants, that belonged to the same group as IMCC was the lead contractor for two projects in Donetsk oblast.

12 Actiondonbass was re-formed for a third time in 2002 when it won the contract to imple-ment a five-year DfID project entitled 'Economic regeneration and social mitigation in the Donbass' (see Chambers 2004).

13 They were supported by a similar number of support staff who performed a treasury function for individual projects.

14 This was the British association of consulting companies.

15 In June 2004 IMCC was acquired by White Young Green Plc, a British construction and environmental consulting company. (At the same time IMC Group reorganised the IMC Environmental Consultants Division and IMC Consultant Engineers Ltd to form a new subsidiary, IMC Europe, which was also sold to White Young Green.) The combined cost of the acquisition was £10 million. IMCC became a wholly owned international management service company with its own board of directors and head-quarters.

16 ORE was acquired by Hoskins, a subsidiary of the Cap Gemini Group.

17 The privatisation of BCE involved the cessation of some activities whilst on-going activities were sold to private investors.

18 A Coal Consulting Centre was also established in Donetsk under a TACIS project contracted to IMC (see Table 8.2).

19 The UK's KHF took over the project after EU funding ended. The project finished in 2001.

References

Aslund, A. (2000) 'Why has Ukraine failed to achieve economic growth?', in A. Aslund and G. de Ménil (eds), *Economic Reform in Ukraine: The Unfinished Agenda*, Armonk, NY: M. E. Sharpe, pp. 255–77.

Aslund, A. and G. de Ménil (2000) 'The dilemmas of Ukrainian economic reforms', in A. Aslund and G. de Ménil (eds), *Economic Reform in Ukraine: The Unfinished Agenda*, Armonk, NY: M. E. Sharpe, pp. 3–26.

Baeten, G., E. Swyngedouw and L. Albrechts (1999) 'Politics, institutions and regional restructuring processes: from managed growth to planned fragmentation in the recon-version of Belgium's last coal mining region', *Regional Studies*, 33: 247–58.

Beatty, C. and S. Fothergill (1996) 'Labour market adjustment in areas of chronic industrial decline: the case of the UK coalfields', *Regional Studies*, 30: 627–40.

Brendow, K. (2000) *Restructuring and Privatising the Coal Industries in Central and Eastern Europe and the CIS*, London: World Energy Council.

Bruno, M. (1998) 'Playing the co-operation game: strategies around international aid in the Russian Federation', in S. Bridger and F. Pine (eds), *Surviving Post-Socialism: Local Strategies and Regional Responses in Eastern Europe and the Former Soviet Union*, London: Routledge, pp. 170–87.

Carrier, J. G. and D. Miller (eds) (1998) *Virtualism: A New Political Economy*, Oxford: Berg.

Chambers, M. (2003) 'Community development in mono-industrial coal regions', Paper presented to conference on 'Old Industrial Regions of Western and Eastern Europe in Conditions of Integration', Donetsk, November.

Chambers, M. (2004) 'Economic regeneration and social mitigation in the Donbass', Paper presented to conference on 'The Problems of Foreign Economic Relations Development and Attraction of Foreign Investment: Regional Aspect', Donetsk, January.

Christopherson, S. (2002) 'Project work in context: regulatory change and the new geography of media', *Environment and Planning A*, **34**(11): 2003–15.

Cooley, A. (2000) 'International aid to the former Soviet states', *Problems of Post-Communism*, **47**(4): 34–44.

Dearden, P. N. and B. Kowalski (2003) 'Programme and project cycle management (PPCM): lessons from South and North', *Development in Practice*, **13**(5) (online version).

DfID (2001) *Ukraine: Country Strategy Paper 2001–2005*, London: DfID.

Dornisch, D. (2002) 'The evolution of post-socialist projects: trajectory shift and transitional capacity in a Polish region', *Regional Studies*, **36**(3): 307–21.

EBRD (2003) *Transition Report 2003*, London: EBRD.

European Commission (2001) *Country Strategy Paper 2002–2006, National Indicative Programme 2002–2003, Ukraine*, Brussels: European Commission, http://europa.eu.int/comm/external_relations/ukraine/csp/02_06en.pdf (accessed 30 July 2004).

Fretwell, D. H. (2004) *Mitigating the Social Impact of Privatization and Enterprise Restructuring*, Washington, DC: World Bank.

Grabher, G. (2001) 'Ecologies of creativity: the Village, the Group, and the heterarchic organisation of the British advertising industry', *Environment and Planning A*, 33: 351–74.

Grabher, G. (2002a) 'Cool projects, boring institutions: temporary collaboration in social context', *Regional Studies*, **36**(3): 205–14.

Grabher, G. (2002b) 'The project ecology of advertising: tasks, talent and teams', *Regional Studies*, **36**(3): 245–62.

Grabher, G. (2004) 'Learning in projects, remembering in networks? Communicality, sociality, and connectivity in project ecologies', *European Urban and Regional Studies*, **11**(2): 103–23.

Hudson, R. (1989) *Wrecking a Region*, London: Pion.

IMCC (n.d.) *A Catalyst for Change*, Nottingham: IMCC.

IMCC (1998) *Experience in Reconversion of Coalfield Regions in Europe*, Huthwaite, Nottingham: IMCL.

Lagendijk, A. and J. Cornford (2000) 'Regional institutions and knowledge: tracking new forms of regional development policy', *Geoforum*, 31: 209–18.

Latour, B. (1987) *Science in Action: How to Follow Engineers and Scientists around Society*, Cambridge, MA: Harvard University Press.

Marsh, D. and R. A. W. Rhodes (eds) (1992) *Policy Networks in British Government*, Oxford: Oxford University Press.

Midler, C. (1995) '"Projectification" of the firm: the Renault case', *Scandinavian Journal of Management*, **11**(4): 363–75.

Pavlinek, P. (1997) *Economic Restructuring and Local Environmental Management in the Czech Republic*, Lewiston, NY: Edwin Mellen Press.

Peck, J. (2001) *Workfare States*, New York: Guilford Press.

Peck, J. (2002) 'Political economics of scale: fast policy, interscalar relations, and neoliberal workfare', *Economic Geography*, 78: 331–60.

Peck, J. and N. Theodore (2001) 'Exporting workfare/importing welfare-to-work: exploring the politics of Third Way policy transfer', *Political Geography*, 20: 427–60.

Peck, J. and A. Tickell (2002) 'Neoliberalizing space', *Antipode*, 34: 380–404.

Pickering, D. (1995) 'British Coal Enterprise', in C. Critcher, K. Schubert and D. Waddington (eds), *Regeneration of Coalfield Areas: Anglo-German Perspectives*, London: Pinter, pp. 104–10.

Robertson, A. (1997) 'The experience of change in the coal industry: Russia and the World Bank', University of Warwick mimeo, http://www.warwick.ac.uk/fac/soc/complabstuds/russia/docs/employ1.doc (accessed 27 April 2005).

Sampson, S. (1996) 'The social life of projects: importing civil society to Albania', in C. Hann and E. Dunn (eds), *Civil Society: Challenging Western Models*, London: Routledge, pp. 121–42.

Smith, A. (2002) 'Imagining geographies of the "new Europe": geo-economic power and the new European architecture of integration', *Political Geography*, 21: 647–70.

Smith, A. (2004) 'Regions, spaces of economic practice and diverse economies in the "new Europe"', *European Urban and Regional Studies*, **11**(1): 9–25.

Spray, B. (2001) 'The do's and don't's of coal industry restructuring: the transfer of experience between western and eastern Europe with emphasis on the UK and Ukraine', Paper presented to conference on 'Confronting Change: North East England and Eastern European Coalfields', Institution of Mining and Metallurgy, Newcastle, November.

Swain, A. (2006) 'Soft capitalism and a hard industry: virtualism, the "transition industry" and the restructuring of the Ukrainian coal industry', *Transactions of the Institute of British Geographers*, 31: 208–33.

USAID (2002) *Monitoring Country Progress in Central and Eastern Europe and Eurasia*, Washington, DC: USAID, http://www.usaid.gov/locations/europe_eurasia/country_progress/eighth/mcp-october-2002.pdf (accessed 6 August 2004).

Waddington, D., C. Critcher, B. Dicks and D. Parry (eds) (2001) *Out of the Ashes? The Social Impact of Industrial Contraction and Regeneration on Britain's Mining Communities*, London: Stationery Office.

Walker, S. (2001) *Experience from Coal Industry Restructuring*, London: IEA Coal Research.

Way, L. A. (2002) 'The dilemmas of reform in weak states: the case of post-Soviet fiscal decentralization', *Politics and Society*, 30: 579–98.

Wedel, J. R. (1998) *Collision and Collusion: The Strange Case of Western Aid to Eastern Europe*, Houndmills: Macmillan.

Wenger, E. (1998) *Communities of Practice: Learning, Meaning and Identity*, Cambridge: Cambridge University Press.

Woodruff, D. M. (2000) 'Rules for followers: institutional theory and the new politics of economic backwardness in Russia', *Politics and Society*, **28**(4): 437–82.

World Bank (1996) *Ukraine Coal Industry Restructuring Sector Report*, Washington, DC: World Bank.

World Bank (2002) *Project Performance Assessment Report: Ukraine Coal Pilot Project and Coal Sector Adjustment Loan (Loans 4016 and 4118)*, Report 24298, Washington, DC: World Bank.

World Bank (2003) 'Mine closure and its impact on the community: five years after mine closure in Romania, Russia and Ukraine', *Social Development Papers*, 42, Washington, DC: World Bank.

Index